MW00447390

Karen & Mike gave
this book from their
— 11-6-'07
Trip

From the library of:

Glenn Marsh
RR 2 Box 34
Marshall, MO 65340

LEGENDARY
DEERSLAYERS

ROBERT WEGNER

©2004 Robert Wegner

Published by

An F+W Publications Company

700 East State Street • Iola, WI 54990-0001
715-445-2214 • 888-457-2873
www.krause.com

Our toll-free number to place an order or obtain
a free catalog is (800) 258-0929.

Library of Congress Catalog Number: 2004100819

ISBN: 0-87349-667-1

Designed by: Gary Carle

Edited by: Joel Marvin

Printed in China

For Serena Christina Wegner
of Deer Valley

In *The Disputed Shot* by John Mix Stanley, three buckskinned-clad deerslayers debate whose ball made the hit and ponder the disposition to be made of this magnificent 11-pointer on Christmas Eve in 1858.

"The first American is not really a Puritan, Thanksgiving

notwithstanding. He's not really a Christian with starched

collar and blunderbuss. And he's not a Thomas Jefferson,

the Fourth of July notwithstanding, with his intellect and his

words. He's a (deer) hunter with a Kentucky long rifle and

a long knife, and he's gone more or less native. And he first

comes to us fighting with a judge over the carcass

of a Christmas deer."

–Charles Bergman,
*Orion's Legacy: A Cultural History
of Man as Hunter*, 1996, p. 257.

ACKNOWLEDGMENTS

The author is greatly indebted to the following individuals, institutions, historical museums, archives and private art collections:

Joel Marvin, Editor, Krause Publications

Don Gulbrandsen, Senior Acquisitions Editor, Krause Publications

Historian Jim Casada, Ph. D.

James A. Swan, Ph. D.

Carol Lueder, Fair Chase Inc.

The Library of Congress, Washington D. C.

Wisconsin State Historical Society

The Remington Art Collection

Arthur Wheaton, Remington Arms Company

The Corcoran Gallery of Art/CORBIS

The State Museum of Pennsylvania

The Fenimore Art Museum, Cooperstown, NY

The Toledo Museum of Art

The Adirondack Museum, Blue Mountain Lake, NY

The Museum of the City of New York/Harry T. Peters Collection

The Sterling and Francine Clark Art Institute, Williamstown, MA

The Smithsonian / National Museum of American History, Washington D. C.

The White House Historical Association, Washington D. C.

The Museum of the City of New York / J. Clarence Davies Collection

Artist Jack Paluh

Christie's Images Incorporated

Gerstaecker Museum, Braunschweig, Germany

The Denver Art Museum

Historical Society of the Town of Warwick, NY

National Portrait Gallery, NY

Wayne Hyde and Lord Nelson's Gallery, Gettysburg, PA

Artist Lee Teter

Publisher Ivan Rowe

Wildlife Photographer Leonard Lee Rue III

The Historic Beaufort Foundation

The National Geographic Society

Bentley Historical Library, University of Michigan

Chicago Historical Society

San Diego Historical Society

John Stein

William N. Headrick

Bob Kuhn

Chris Thiesing

Gary Ziegler

Judge Irvine H. Rutledge

Thomas A. Heberlein, Ph.D.

Valerius Geist, Ph.D.

CONTENTS

FOREWORD

At a recent conference I met an Eskimo, or Inuit, from Greenland. Hunting, he told me, was essential to Inuit culture. Not just a way to keep food on the table, but rather a driving force whose spirit pervaded all areas of the culture, religion, art, dance, song, social customs and especially story-telling.

"A good hunting story," he said, "passes along the accumulated wisdom of our people and conveys the spirit of the hunt. It brings a sense of meaning and purpose into our lives and ties the present to the past to keep the human spirit vital, as well as us well-fed."

Anthropologist Franz Boas once observed, "There can be no doubt that in the main the mental characteristics of man are the same all over the world."[1] Even today, when most people do not have to hunt for food, the power of the hunting story remains a root of human nature. The hunting story is one of the most basic elements of culture, as basic as the love story, and perhaps even older.

A good story of the hunter's quest captivates the listener, engages mind and emotions, engraves lessons in the mind, and kindles the campfires of the soul, because the hunter is a hero, symbolically and mythically, as well as in real life. And heroes are very important.

"The hero," writes Joseph Campbell, "is the man or woman who has been able to battle past his personal and local historical limitations," and ventures forth into the wilderness, as well as the wild places of the psyche, seeking success, and often drawing upon wisdom that is as old as life itself.[2]

Heroes become heroic, not just by performing brave acts, but when their actions are recognized by the culture of a time and place as being exemplary. In *Legendary Deerslayers* Rob Wegner has assembled a stellar cast of hunter-heroes. As North America is the home of the white-tailed deer, tales of heroic deerslayers John James Audubon, Natty Bumppo, John Dean Caton, Theodore Van Dyke, Archibald Rutledge, etc.—are a cornerstone of American culture. Heroes become heroes because they dare to tackle the nuts and bolts of life. In these times when many people fly about like mourning doves from one politically-correct branch to another, grasping this or that fad as if it was truth and stability, they forget that only by sinking to the earthly realities of life can one find the truths of the heart-mind that are eternal and healing. The blood on a hunter's hands reminds us of the basic tenet of life that "flesh eats flesh" is what drives the food chain. Such a principle, one might say, is an "instinctual truth;" something that is basic to survival and ingrained in the soul.

If hunting is instinctual, as the great minds of psychology of the 20th century maintain,[3] it must be one of the most basic driving forces of human nature. Primal instincts of the human soul that deal with the forces of life and death call out for rules of proper conduct. Setting such standards through example is the work of heroes. One cannot help but wonder if the decline in the telling of tales of the hunt among the general public is not a contributing factor in the confusion among young people about what is heroic,

---

[1] Boas, Franz, *The Mind of Primitive Man*, NY: MacMillan Co., 1911, p. 104.

[2] Campbell, Joseph, *The Hero With A Thousand Faces*, Princeton, NJ: Princeton University Press, second edition 1968, p. 19.

[3] Fromm, Erich, *The Anatomy of Human Destructiveness*, NY, NY: Fawcett, 1973.

8   Legendary Deerslayers

and subsequent forays into delinquency and drug experimentation.

The most pervasive storytellers of our times are TV and feature films, but heroic hunting tales recounted on these mediums exist, such as *Jeremiah Johnson*, or *Dances With Wolves*. They are, however, outnumbered by those casting hunters as outlaws. In two of the best-known modern popular deer hunting tales, *Bambi* and *The Deer Hunter*, hunters are villains. A closer examination of these films shows that these tales are really not about deer hunting at all, but use hunting as a metaphor for war.

The 1942 Disney animated feature *Bambi* targets audiences of women and children. The hunter kills the daddy of Bambi, the hero. Taken literally, it makes daddy's recreational deer hunting trip seem cruel and it turns daddy into a bad guy. Released in 1942, in the midst of World War II, in the metaphoric minds of young children, daddy and the enemy become confused in the story of *Bambi*, because daddy has been taken away to war and is being hunted by an evil man with a gun. Movie critic Roger Ebert has wisely observed that *Bambi* is ultimately "a parable of sexism, nihilism, and despair, portraying absentee fathers and passive mothers in a world of violence," more than a hunting tale.[4] The initial popularity of the film may have had little to do with anti-hunting feelings. Today, in a culture where increasingly few people have first-hand experience with hunting, the real hunter ends up with a bum rap because of the confusion associated with the symbolism of the hunter as an armed person. The deer, incidentally, is a common symbol for our inner animal nature. People who are far from nature tend to want to protect animals because they symbolize what they have not treated well within themselves, which in turn colors their feelings about hunting.

Such confusion also is seen in the 1978 classic, *The Deer Hunter*, where soldiers returning home from the Viet Nam War find that shooting deer brings up troubling guilt feelings and flashbacks. The title suggests that the movie is about deer hunting, but the actual story is about post-traumatic stress syndrome.

The motivations of the hunter and the warrior or soldier are quite different, though both carry lethal weapons into the field. The soldier defends his culture against evil and kills people. He or she is fighting against fear. The hunter extracts both food and spirit from nature to nourish his culture. The motivations of the hunter are positive, pleasurable, and cultivate respect for nature that is the root of a true conservationist.

This beautiful book by Rob Wegner will remind many of the potent power of the story of the hunt, especially the deer hunt, and its importance in America's heritage. Maybe if the right person in Hollywood reads it, it will inspire that modern storyteller to spin a good deerslayer's yarn or two on the big or little screen that will have as much positive influence on hunting as Robert Redford's telling of Norman MacLean's memorable *A River Runs Through It* has had on fly fishing.

–James A. Swan, Ph.D.
author of *In Defense of Hunting*
and *The Sacred Art of Hunting*

---

[4] Ebert, Roger, *Roger Ebert's Movie Home Companion* (1990 edition) NY, NY: Andrew and McMeel, 1989, p. 53.

INTRODUCTION

Legendary Deerslayers (2004), a complimentary volume to *Legendary Deer Camps* (2001) was written to serve as a preliminary script for a documentary film and a national museum. I have gathered the material – the images, poems, diaries, prints, postcards and miscellaneous artifacts over the past 25 years – as I traveled throughout white-tailed deer country with the dream of a documentary film and a national, white-tailed deer museum in mind.

Our whitetail heritage is in great jeopardy. As deer hunters we are currently an endangered minority fast fading into the dustbins of history. We now constitute less than nine percent of the population and our actual numbers continue to shrink. With increasing deer numbers nationwide and decreasing hunter numbers, we are reaching the upper limits of deer management via deer hunting. Worse, the paradigm of managing a public resource on private property is broke.

Today, most deer hunting organizations are talking about promoting and perpetuating our white-tailed deer hunting heritage, but, unfortunately, they are not doing anything in a concrete way. If we are to preserve our heritage and survive as deer hunters in the 21st century, a cultural history of our deer-hunting heritage in documentary films, books and a world-class museum is a necessity.

During the 19th century, deer hunting was part of American culture – a major part of mainstream society – as evidenced by the publication of articles on deer and deer hunting in general monthly magazines and weekly newspapers, appearing next to and interspersed with articles on music, drama, literature and the arts. Today, deer hunting is a minority activity played out in cow culture and hyped in highly specialized magazines.

We need to look back on our heroic, distant past so that we can make claims to the future. We need to present our story in cultural terms – in art, literature, anthropology, Native American culture, music, and poetry – and then transfer the story to TV and the movies and popularize it in a national museum. In his classic essay, "*Wildlife in American Culture*," Aldo Leopold reminds us that as deer hunters we must reenact our cultural past, create cultural values from our deer-hunting heritage, be aware of them and create a pattern for their continued growth. This book represents a contribution in that regard.

Historically, the deer hunter has been a cultural hero throughout most of human history.

In this book, you will find the great heroes of our white-tailed deer hunting culture: the buckskin-clad Natty Bumppo, as he shoots deer along the shores of Lake Otsego with his long rifle named "Killdeer;" John James Audubon driving deer through Gum Thicket at "Liberty Hall," South Carolina; Friederich Gerstaecker and his deerhound "Beargrease" fighting wounded bucks in the swamps of the Ozarks and Deer Lick Hollow; and Philip Tome jack lighting deer in Pennsylvania's magnificent Pine Creek Gorge.

In this volume, you will also meet the delightful "Frank Forester" as he courses whitetails near the Dutchman's Tavern in the Catskill Mountains with "Smoker," his Scottish, wire-haired deer hound; Meshach Browning and his deerhound "Gunner" as they wrestle with bucks in the Yough River in western Maryland; William Elliott, who chases white-tailed bucks in the Chee-Ha area of South Carolina with the enthusiastic gusto of starry-eyed generals engaged in sylvan warfare; and Judge Caton hunting whitetails on horseback on the Grand Prairie of Illinois.

You will experience T. S. Van Dyke still-hunting whitetails in the pinelands of the Midwest; Paulina Brandreth pursuing them in the Adirondacks; Larry Koller shooting whitetails from Patterson's Rock, the Twin-Oak Stand and Skunk Gully; and you will confront the great hunt master himself, Archibald Rutledge, known as "Flintlock," chasing the eternal Black-horn Buck through the pinelands of the Hampton Plantation in the South Carolina Low Country with his deerhound "Old Hickory."

This book focuses on the basic components of the whitetail experience: deer camp (known as "Holy Week" in some parts of the country); buck fever, that vicious malady that affects all deer hunters; venison loin seasoned with gunpowder when necessary; the exquisite beauty and alluring aroma of buckskin; legendary deer rifles like the Winchester '73; whiskey and lies around the pot belly stove at the deer shack; unbeliev-able deer-shooting tales; classic whitetail art; blue-chip deer books; poems and diaries.

These cultural components of our whitetail-heritage need Ken Burns' type of documentary film and a North American White-Tailed Deer Museum—a national Mecca, a distinct, national monument with a world-class library built in concrete by an internationally-known architect that will mesmerize the hunting and non-hunting public alike. Man has taken more from this unique animal than he has given to it. We need to manage this animal, and stop mismanaging it. We must pay homage to this magnificent animal, *Odocoileus virginianus*, and its historic relationship with man. In failing to do so, our whitetail cultural heritage will continue to decline.

Robert Wegner, Ph.D.
Deer Valley
January 1, 2004

ABOUT THE AUTHOR

In 1979, Robert Wegner received his Ph.D. from the University of Wisconsin-Madison where he was trained as a cultural historian. After a short-term teaching career at the university, he became the editor and, later, a co-owner of *Deer & Deer Hunting* magazine. After the magazine was sold to Krause Publications in 1992, he became a freelance writer specializing in the cultural history of white-tailed deer and deer hunting.

His award-winning work has appeared in such magazines as *Hunt Club Digest, Wisconsin Sportsman, Pennsylvania Game News, Michigan Sportsman, Fur-Fish-Game, Quality Whitetails, Whitetail Hunting Strategies, Wisconsin Outdoor Journal* and many others. His landmark book trilogy, *Deer & Deer Hunting*, has sold more than 100,000 copies. Fred Bear referred to this three-volume work as "a classic in American hunting literature."

Wegner resides in Deer Valley, a secluded land filled with whitetails and wild turkeys in the heart of "The Uplands" in southwestern Wisconsin with his wife, Maren, and daughter, Serena. Wegner has studied, observed and hunted whitetails for more than 40 years.

If you want to share your deer camp stories and whitetail experiences, Wegner can be reached at: Deer Valley, 6008K, Blue Mounds, WI 53517. Or call (608) 795-2721, FAX (608) 795-4720, or email him at robert_wegner@angelfire.com.

ALSO BY THE AUTHOR

Deer & Deer Hunting, Book 1
Deer & Deer Hunting, Book 2
Deer & Deer Hunting, Book 3
Wegner's Bibliography on Deer
  & Deer Hunting
Legendary Deer Camps

EDITED BY THE AUTHOR

Trails of Enchantment, Paul Brandreth
Whitetail, George Mattis
The Still-Hunter, T.S. Van Dyke

DEERSLAYER

By JAMES FENIMORE COOPER
PICTURES BY
N.C. WYETH

N.C. Wyeth's *The Deerslayer*, an oil on canvas, is etched into the collective consciousness of generations of American readers of James Fenimore Cooper's classic novel. During the 1920s—the Christmas season of 1926 for example—Scribners turned out tens of thousands of copies of *The Deerslayer* with this classic image of Natty Bumppo on the cover, which made N.C. Wyeth one of America's greatest illustrators. The illustration gave life to Cooper's mythic hero in a way no other modern media ever touched. Cooper was acutely aware of the physical exposure and spiritual loneliness of man's experiences in the deer woods during the frontier era of our history.

In looking at it, one can smell the pine needles, the white-tailed buckskin and the odor of the deer from which it came as well as the smell of the gunpowder that brought the whitetail down with the Kentucky rifle called "Killdeer."

Chapter One

NATTY BUMPPO

O n a cold, clear, Christmas Eve in 1793, a green-colored sleigh drawn by two noble horses covered with hoar frost approached a small clearing near Cooperstown, New York. Suddenly, the passengers of the sleigh heard the howling cry of deer hounds in pursuit of whitetails. The owner of the sleigh and the land it was on, Judge Temple, ordered the driver to halt. The Judge knew that the deer hounds belonged to Leatherstocking, vicariously called Natty Bumppo, Hawkeye, The Trapper, Long Rifle, Pathfinder, and perhaps most famously, The Deerslayer.

As the sleigh stopped, Judge Temple grabbed his "double-barrelled fowling piece" in anticipation of acquiring a saddle of venison for his Christmas dinner. While examining his priming, a ten-pointer started to cross the clearing just ahead of the sleigh. In his classic historical novel, *The Pioneers* (1823), James Fenimore Cooper (1789-1851) describes the incident:

"The appearance of the animal was sudden, and his flight inconceivably rapid; but the traveller appeared to be too keen a sportsman to be disconcerted by either. As it came first into view, he raised the fowling piece to his shoulder, and with a practiced eye and steady hand, drew a trigger. Without

© Fenimore Art Museum, Cooperstown, NY. Photo by Richard Walker.

James Fenimore Cooper's Otsego Hall, which burned to the ground in 1853, two years after Cooper's death.

Inset: A ca. 1822 portrait by John Wesley Jarvis of James Fenimore Cooper, creator of the legendary deerslayer, Natty Bumppo.

lowering his piece, the traveller turned its muzzle towards the buck and fired again. Neither discharge, however, seemed to have taken effect."

As the magnificent buck continued his escape across the clearing, two more reports came from Kentucky long rifles; one fired by Natty Bumppo and the other by his companion, Oliver Edwards. The buck sprang high off the ground, and dropped immediately in his tracks. When the three deer hunters converged on the buck, Natty Bumppo chided the Judge for wasting more gunpowder than filling stomachs:

"You burnt your powder, only to warm your nose this cold evening. Did ye think to stop a full grown buck ...with that popgun in your hand?"

The long-standing, historic controversy over using shotguns versus rifles for deer hunting begins with this remark. As the three hunters studied the carcass, they soon began to argue over who shot the Christmas buck, who owns it, and who has rights to shoot deer. As Charles Bergman notes in his cultural history of man as hunter, *Orion's Legacy* (1996), "If the first act in the first American novel is the killing of the deer, the real drama is over *possession* of the deer."

In their lively dispute over the shot, we learn that Natty Bumppo hit the deer with his shot in the neck and his partner Oliver hit the buck in the heart. The Judge's buckshot clearly went astray. But because the Judge owns the land, he claims the right of ownership to the deer and wins the dispute, even though Natty claims the right of best shot. As the frontier gradually became private property and as game laws emerged, we see the deerslayer, Natty Bumppo, losing his struggle to defend his fiercely cherished freedom to hunt deer when and where he likes.

The earliest law regulating white-tailed deer in New York was enacted in 1705. The law prohibited killing deer except between August 1 and January 1 in several counties.

Village Tavern, an oil on canvas by John Lewis Krimmel, 1813-1814. The village tavern served as the social centerpiece of the deerslayer tradition. One can imagine Natty Bumppo joining the boys for "lobskous," a cracker hash consisting of salted deer meat, baked or stewed with preserved vegetables and hardtack. One can still hear the boys singing in a most vivacious manner:

*"Come, let us be jolly,
And cast away folly,
For grief turns a black head to gray."*

New York passed the first statewide deer law on March 15, 1788, which established a closed season for deer hunting from January to July. This law made the possession of green deerskins and fresh venison during the closed season prima facie evidence of guilt. This early deer law already expressed an increasing concern for perpetuating the species. But law enforcement was lax and deer hunting went on at will during all seasons of the year, particularly in the frontier districts.

In the Introduction to the second edition of *The Pioneers* (1832), Cooper himself laments the disappearance of whitetails: "Though forests still crown the mountains of Otsego, the bear, the wolf, and the panther are nearly strangers to them. Even the ...deer is rarely seen bounding beneath their arches; for the rifle, and the activity of the settlers, have driven them to other haunts." Several years later his daughter Susan Fenimore Cooper also pointed out that white-tailed deer had already become rare in her *Rural Hours* (1840), the first significant piece of nature writing by an American woman.

After shooting that white-tailed buck on Christmas Eve in 1793, with his Kentucky long rifle named "Killdeer,"—a rifle historian Richard Slotkin refers to as "of simple perfection in design with a mythlike reputation for accuracy"—in the deer woods along the shores of Lake Otsego, the buckskin-clad Natty Bumppo, deerslayer par excellence, steps forward from a pine plantation, so vividly portrayed in N. C. Wyeth's 1925 illustration, and assumes mythic proportions in the American consciousness.

In his classic essay on Cooper's Leatherstocking novels (1923), D. H. Lawrence notes that Natty Bumppo "seems to have been born under a hemlock tree out of a pine cone ...He is silent, simple, philosophic, moralistic and an unerring shot." Indeed, he got his deepest sense of gratification when he placed a bullet through the heart of a Catskill Mountain, white-tailed buck. Lawrence said Cooper's description of the pristine wilderness in which Bumppo tramped and chased whitetails was "lovelier than any place created in language."

Historically, American literature begins with this Christmas white-tailed deer hunt, which is faithfully recorded in America's first national bestseller: *The Pioneers*. Within hours of its publication, Cooper's historical novel sold more than 3500 copies in New York City, making it not only America's first bestseller, but America's first conservationist novel. In this classic novel, the blue-eyed, buckskinned deer-hunter hero introduces America to the world as a deer-hunting culture.

Indeed, Natty Bumppo, the spiritual father of all deer hunters, gives us our symbolic origins, our very foundation as a deer-hunting culture. This noble woodsman embodies our conscience; from him we learn to articulate ourselves to ourselves, as well as to non-hunters. Through this famous, folklore hero, this quintessential frontiersman, we define our character and trace our historic roots. From this romantic huntsman, we learn about correct conduct in nature and see the deer hunt as a proper form of ecological thinking. This mythical character instills in us a profound, spiritual communion with nature. Leatherstocking emerges as a great steward of natural resources, who respects nature, who uses but does not abuse the bounties of nature.

Natty Bumppo, the hero of Cooper's Leatherstocking saga, kills deer only out of necessity, not for plunder. The deerslayer's chief virtue resides in the fact that he does not view the presence of whitetails as an insult to his powers and skills. He hunts deer both for food and for what historian Richard Slotkin calls "the spiritual satisfaction of participating in the ennobling rite of the kill." Like Audubon, upon whom Cooper modeled his hero, Natty Bumppo loves the exquisite smell of deer meat roasting on a spit and eats the savory venison with great delight while telling stories at the fire pit. When you eat the venison, Natty Bumppo tells us in *The Deerslayer* (1841), you become the deer. He assumes a homeopathic view of eating deer meat:

"I crave no cloth better than the skin of a deer, nor any meat richer than his flesh. Well may you call it strong! Strong it is, and strong it makes him who eats it!"

"They call me Deerslayer. I'll own; and perhaps I deserve the name, in the way of understanding the creature's habits, as well as for the certainty in the aim; but they can't accuse me of killing an animal when there is no occasion for the meat or the skin. I may be a slayer, it's true, but I'm no slaughterer... I never yet pulled a trigger on buck or doe, unless when food or clothes was wanting."

Natty Bumppo lived by eating venison. Each day's hunt ended in the local village tavern with venison tenderloins cooked over oak coals. As D. H. Lawrence noted, "he breakfasted on deer meat, or nothing, lunched the same and supped the same."

The village tavern served as the social centerpiece of the deerslayer tradition. One can imagine Natty Bumppo joining the boys at Krimmel's *Village Tavern* for "lobskous," a cracker hash consisting of salted deer meat, baked or stewed with preserved vegetables and hardtack. One can still hear Bumppo and the boys singing in a most vivacious manner:

"Come, let us be jolly,
And cast away folly,
For grief turns a black head to gray."

Going Out: Deer Hunting in the Adirondacks by A.F. Tait, 1862. The figure with the rifle is A.F. Tait with his companion and guide, Captain Calvin Parker. In the other canoe, we see James B. Blossom and Seth Warner, the former a friend of the artist and the latter, in the stern, a guide. In 1863, Currier and Ives reproduced this image under the title *American Hunting Scenes—An Early Start.*

The Pioneer's Home: On the Western Frontier, Currier & Ives, 1867. Unlike deerslayer Nat Foster, Cooper's Natty Bumppo was a sustenance hunter. In this lithograph, the buckskin-clad deer hunters return with wild turkeys and a white-tailed buck astride the meat pole.

This great character with his tremendous dignity, simplicity, rough honesty and rare skill in whitetail woodcraft represents a living portrait of the American frontiersman. *Books In Print* (2003), lists 10 different editions of *The Deerslayer*. While Natty Bumppo is certainly a literary creation, different individuals known to Cooper at the time all presented themselves in addition to Audubon as models. One thinks of such prototypes as Daniel Boone for example. It's hard to miss the deliberate echo and similar configuration in their names: Daniel Boone and Nathaniel Bumppo.

Two New York regional folk heroes also present themselves as possible models for Natty Bumppo: David Shipman, an aged deer hunter living in the woods near Cooperstown, and Nathaniel Foster (1767-1840), who reportedly killed more deer collectively than any other individual in New York during the same period of time—having killed no less than 76 deer in one season.

As a young boy, Cooper hunted whitetails with bow and arrow and rifle and listened for untold hours to David Shipman's wondrous tales of deer stalking at Otsego Lake and his hairbreadth escapes from the dangers of frontier life. Shipman not only inspired Cooper's passion for deer hunting but also supplied Otsego Hall, the great manor at the Cooper estate known as "the noblest mansion west of Albany," with fresh venison.

Several historic sources, however, suggest that Cooper based the deerslaying character on the life and adventures of Nat Foster, who once killed two wolves, five panthers and a deer in one hour. We know that as a young boy Cooper knew Nat Foster. In studying the life of Foster, historian A. L. Byron-Curtiss reaches the conclusion that Foster is the hero of Cooper's Leatherstocking tales—Natty Bumppo.

On July 4, 1937, *The New York Times* reported that Nat Foster was the real hero of the Leatherstocking tales. On July 3 of that year in Rome, New York, a dedication ceremony was held at Foster's gravesite. J. P. Edgerton of Solsville, a great-grandson of Nat Foster, said at the dedication that, "Natty Bumppo is buried here on the knoll. Our family has always known that Nat Foster was Cooper's hero." Foster was also called "The Leatherstocking" in real life. In 1787, Foster, clad in buckskins, announced in a St. Johnsville tavern that his name was Leatherstocking.

Like Natty Bumppo, Foster dressed in a buckskin hunting shirt laced with thongs of deerskin. He supported his buckskin breeches with a wide belt of deerskin. A pair of leggings and moccasins made of buckskin neatly beaded with porcupine quills covered his feet and legs. A fox-skin cap rested on his long, sandy hair.

Foster carried a rifle called a "double shooter" made after a pattern designed by a gunsmith named Willis Avery of Salisbury, who, expressly for Foster, made the rifle light at the muzzle and heavy at the breech for shooting deer on the move. The octagon barrel was 28 inches long and the brass inlay handsomely designed. Local tradition explains that the small curve in the butt of the Avery rifle made possible firing it from the crook of the elbow instead of the shoulder. Foster paid 70 dollars for the Avery. As an expert in loading and firing this rifle, Foster could begin with the gun unloaded and shoot it off six times in one minute—an incredible feat for this type of rifle.

Joseph Benchley, a prominent musician, who deer hunted with Foster in the famous John Brown Tract in the Adirondacks said that Foster conversed but little. But his eyes were always roaming to discover deer "worthy of his never erring aim." On one of their hunts, Foster discovered a deer feeding on a grassy beach nearly a mile away while

A Good Time Coming by A.F. Tait, 1862. During the 1850s, Raquette Lake, New York, was a favorite spot for deer hunters year around. Here the guide cooks venison tenderloin while fresh fish arrives at the camp on Constable Point. These lean-tos at the time were called deer shanties. Hunters frequently roofed them with great slabs of living hemlock bark. Their provisions and attire clearly reflect the American hunter's new interest in European traditions of elegance in all matters pertaining to the chase.

canoeing across a lake. He told Benchley to put him on shore so that he could get some venison for the evening meal. Benchley agreed and then rowed out into the lake far enough to see the deer. In his deer hunting journal, Benchley describes the scene:

"I soon saw Foster step suddenly from the bushes upon the beach, some distance from the deer. Almost the very instant the deer raised its head from feeding, I saw the flash of his rifle and the deer fall. Well Nat, said I, have you killed him? He straightened up like a soldier, with his head erect, and eyes glistening; and grasping his Avery rifle in his right hand and holding it above his head, he said, 'Benchley, he (the Avery) never told a lie. When you hear him speak, he always tells the truth.' I stepped on shore and found he had put his ball precisely in the centre of the deer's forehead. He must have been a full 25 rods from the animal, and fired the instant it

raised its head. In a very few minutes he had a fine piece of venison roasting before a good fire, and ere long we had a sweet morsel to dine upon."

One day while still-hunting whitetails at sunset with his brother Shubael in St. Lawrence County, New York, Foster suddenly encountered two white-tailed bucks engaged in rutting combat, two noble bucks "trying titles to the soil," as Foster's biographer Jeptha Simms reports. To end the confrontation, Foster fired his Avery rifle; one buck dropped to the soil and the other bounded off for several yards and then halted to witness an even more novel engagement than it had just experienced. For the downed buck was only badly stunned after being hit by the ball near its backbone. As Foster ran up to it to cut its throat, the twelve-pointer sprang up and

An October Day by Winslow Homer, 1889. In this watercolor, Homer clearly had the adventures of Natty Bumppo in mind.

struck furiously at Leatherstocking with its massive antlers. In his celebrated history of hunting in upstate New York during the latter part of the 18th century and early part of the 19th century, *Trappers of New York; or, a Biography of Nicholas Stoner and Nathaniel Foster* (1850), historian Jeptha Simms documents the event:

"Quick as thought, this modern Leatherstocking placed the knife between his teeth, and grabbed the weapons of his unexpected foe. The struggle for mastery was long and fierce, the hunter not daring to let go; but, as good luck would have it, he got the head of the deer between two trees, against one of which a horn was broken, and the animal thrown down. Before it could recover, the hunter dealt it a blow upon the head with a club fortune had placed at his command, and then succeeded in cutting its throat. The tussle lasted more than 30 minutes with the grass and bushes trampled down for several rods and the strength of the hunter nearly exhausted in the engagement."

Nevertheless, after wiping the blood and dirt from his face, the six-foot, huge-framed Foster exclaimed to his brother: "Let's track down that other buck!" A short while later he sighted a white patch of the fleeing deer among the leaves of the forest. Once more his Avery rifle belched fire; the bullet whizzed through the air from its muzzle hitting the buck in the back of its neck and dropping him immediately.

In his biography of Foster, Simms recalls that even at the age of 60, Leatherstocking could still carry a deer on his shoulders for three miles. Unlike Natty Bumppo, who was primarily a subsistence hunter, Nat Foster not only shot for the pot, but for the markets as well. As a market hunter, he shot in excess of 1000 animals, selling the saddles of venison and the deerskins for the eastern markets. He also sold deerskins to museums in New York and Pennsylvania. Two of his contemporaries also downed their share of white-tailed deer in their lifetimes: Alisha Risdon (1782-1851) killed 579 deer during a 28-year period near the Town of Hopkinton, New York, and Thomas Meacham of St. Lawrence County, who died in 1850, killed 2550 deer.

These incredible deer-kill statistics by market hunters and subsistence hunters occurred long before the Adirondack white-tailed deer herd ever reached its peak. Cooper's plea for restraint and conservation was still a faint cry in the wilderness. Several decades would have to pass before America would experience the end of market hunting and the advent of the hunter-naturalists, who hunted for sport and endorsed a deer-hunting ethic that Cooper would have greatly admired.

To this day, the ghost of the buckskin-clad Foster still stalks the deer woods of the Adirondacks. Several years ago, the people of Dolgeville decided to salute this famous Leatherstocking of their pioneering period by scheduling a Nat Foster Day to collect hunting memorabilia from this legendary deerslayer. Eleanor Franz, a folklorist and co-chairperson for that Nat Foster Day, recalls how one white-tailed buck reacted to Nat Foster Day:

"Early in the summer morning of Nat Foster Day, a buck sprang from the dew-fresh woods and loped across the lawns of the village street. It was as though the ghost of Nat Foster had driven it from cover to salute his day."

During Foster's day, white-tailed deer hunters employed a large variety of methods to hunt deer: still-hunting; stalking; coursing deer with horses, hounds, and bugles; shooting from platforms elevated over salt licks; "crusting" with snow shoes on icy snow; jacklighting at night in canoes; floating down streams at dawn and sunrise; and finally, the most common and perhaps most controversial practice, hounding deer to water, where hunters wait in canoes—commonly referred to as "withing whitetails." In withing whitetails, the hunter would cut down a birch sapling. And then strip off all but the two most upper branches. These branches the hunter twisted into a loop or noose. As he approached the deer in water, the hunter would drop the noose over the deer's head and pull it up to the canoe.

A fierce debate raged throughout the 19th century between advocates and opponents of these various modes of deer hunting. In his *Wild Scenes in the Forest and Prairie* (1839), writer and editor Charles Fenno Hoffman labeled the feuds between these different types of deer hunters "interminable bickerings." These bickerings filled the sportsman's journals of the period.

In one of the closing scenes of Cooper's novel, *The Prairie*, we find Natty Bumppo in hot pursuit of a noble whitetailed buck in his birch bark canoe with his hunting companions, old John Mohegan and young Oliver Edwards in his hunting skiff. After Natty's deer hounds drive the buck into the lake, Leatherstocking cries out:

"Tis a noble creater! What a pair of horns! A man might hang up all his garments on the branches."

Leatherstocking's birch bark canoe traveled over the water like a meteor as it approached the swimming buck. Oliver's bateau also arrived near the buck, nobly swimming against the odds. Cooper describes the scene:

"The buck was now within 50 yards of his pursuers, cutting the water gallantly, and snorting at each breath with terror and his exertions, while the canoe seemed to dance over the waves, as it rose and fell with the undulations made by its own motion. Leatherstocking raised his rifle and freshened the priming, but stood in suspense whether to slay his victim or not."

He decided not to use his rifle but rather to engage in what Cooper calls "lake play."

While Mohegan manipulated the canoe, Natty raised his spear and threw it like an arrow. But the buck turned and the spear buried itself in the lake after glancing off the buck's shining antlers. Mohegan whirled the canoe around and renewed the chase. In his classic novel, Cooper documents the mind of the American deerslayer:

"The dark eye of the old warrior was dancing in his head, with a wild animation, and the sluggish repose in which his aged frame had been resting in the canoe was now changed to all the rapid inflections of practised agility. The canoe whirled with each cunning evolution of the chase, like a bubble floating in a whirlpool; and when the direction of the pursuit admitted of a straight course, the little bark skimmed the lake with a velocity that urged the deer to seek its safety in some new turn. It was the frequency of these circuitous movements, that, by confining the action to so small a compass, enabled the youth to keep near his companions. More than 20 times both the pursued and the pursuers glided by him, just without the reach of his oars . . ."

But suddenly the buck came directly towards Edwards and the young hunter managed to slip the noose of his birch withe around the antlers of the buck. For an instant, the buck dragged the skiff through the water.

" ...but in the next, the canoe glided before it, and Natty, bending low, passed his knife across the throat of the animal, whose blood followed the wound, dying the waters. The short time that was passed in the last struggles of the animal was spent by the hunters in bringing their boats together, and securing them in that position, when Leatherstocking drew the deer from the water, and laid its lifeless form in the bottom of the canoe.

" ...'This warms a body's blood, old John; I haven't killed a buck in the lake afore this, sin' many a year. I call that good venison, lad; and I know them that will relish the

Life in the Woods: Returning to Camp, Currier & Ives, 1860. During the 19th century, Natty Bumppo and his clan used canoes and bateaus in their pursuit of white-tailed deer.

creater's steaks, for all the betterments in the land.'"

This lover of good venison, this deerslayer clad in white-tailed buckskins, loved to roam the deer forest in pursuit of the white-tailed deer with his cherished deer hounds. Cooper's hero entered the deer woods around Otsego Lake (known as the "Glimmer-Glass") and American folklore as the classic archetype of frontier deer hunters.

This man dressed in deerskins and lived alone in the wilderness. He avoided human entanglements, estrangement and intrigue. He despised decadent, modern civilization and cherished the whitetails he hunted.

Theodore Roosevelt emulated him and labeled his buckskin deer-hunting outfit, "the most picturesque and distinctively national dress ever worn in America."

This image of the buckskin-clad backwoodsman reoccurs in the subsequent legendary deerslayers of the next two centuries: Audubon, Friedrich Gerstaecker, Philip Tome, "Frank Forester," Meshach Browning, William Elliott, Judge Caton, T. S. Van Dyke, Paulina Brandreth, Larry Koller and Archibald Rutledge. Instinctually gifted in deer hunting, respectful of the ways of the deer forest and cool under fire, this mythical character in deerskin sets the stage for all who follow in his footsteps.

White-tailed Deer, an imperial folio plate from Audubon's *The Quadrupeds of North America*, 1848.

"No species of wild animal inhabiting

North America deserves to be regarded with more interest

than the Common or Virginian Deer; its symmetrical form,

graceful curving leap or bound, and its rushing speed,

when flying before its pursuers, it passes like a meteor

by the startled traveler in the forest, exciting admiration,

though he be ever so dull an observer."

—Audubon/Bachman,
The Quadrapeds of North America, 1848.

Chapter Two

JOHN J. AUDUBON

I n 1831, John James Audubon (1785-1851) published the first significant essay on "Deer Hunting" in America in his *Ornithological Biography*. This landmark essay, frequently reprinted and widely distributed during its time, first appeared as a reprint in the September 1838 issue of the *American Turf Register and Sporting Magazine*, the leading sportsman's journal of the day.

Several years later in 1846, Peter Hawker (1786-1853) published it in his popular guide *Instructions to Young Sportsmen, in All that Relates to Guns and Shooting*. In 1869, Audubon's widow reprinted it in her edited edition of *The Life of J. J. Audubon*. In 1897, it became part of *Audubon and His Journals*. And again in 1926, it was reprinted in *Audubon's Delineation of American Scenery and Character*. As a standard chronicle of American deer hunting lore, it still remains in print 172 years after the original date of its publication.

The essay is remarkable in several ways. First of all, it represents the first serious attempt to systematically describe the three modes of deer hunting prevalent at the time:

"Minnie's Land," was the Audubon house on the Hudson River, a 30-acre estate where Audubon kept deer in special enclosures for painting and research (now West 156th Street in Manhattan). This sketch is by William R. Miller, 1852. It appeared in *Valentine's Manual* in 1865.

Inset: A portrait of John James Audubon by Scottish artist John Syme, 1826." … the deer runs free, and the Hunter as free forever … America will always be my land."—Audubon, November 25, 1827

Still Hunting on the Susquehanna by Currier & Ives. Audubon deplored the method of hunting deer by fire-lighting, which is shown in this Currier & Ives scene.

the terror of the herd, but now containing a pound of the best gunpowder; his butcher knife is scabbarded in the same strap; and behind is a tomahawk, the handle of which has been thrust through his girdle. He walks with so rapid a step that probably few men ...could follow him ...He stops, looks to the flint of his gun, its priming, and the leather cover of the lock, then glances his eye towards the sky, to judge of the course most likely to lead him to the game."

The literary quality of Audubon's description of the still-hunter as a monumental figure in the deer woods reads like a novel:

"As he proceeds he looks to the dead foliage under his feet, in search of the well-known traces of a buck's hoof. Now he bends towards the ground, on which something has attracted his attention. See! he alters his course, increases his speed, and will soon reach the opposite hill. Now he moves with caution, stops at almost every tree and peeps forward, as if already within shooting distance of the game.

"He advances again, but how very slowly! He has reached the declivity, upon which the sun shines in all its growing splendor; but mark him! he takes the gun from his shoulder, has already thrown aside the leather cover of the lock, and is wiping the edge of the flint with his tongue. Now he stands like a monumental figure, perhaps measuring the distance that lies between him and the game which he has in view. His rifle is slowly raised, the report follows, and he runs.

" ...There lies the buck, its tongue out, its eye dim, its breath exhausted; it is dead."

still-hunting, firelight hunting and driving. Secondly, it induced many deer hunters nationwide, James Fenimore Cooper included, to take up the chase of whitetails as a pleasurable form of recreation, as early as 1831.

In this classic essay, Audubon observes that still-hunting was the standard trade of the American frontiersmen. It required great skill with the rifle, a thorough knowledge of the woods and a detailed, intimate acquaintance with deer behavior—all of which Audubon possessed to a unique degree. Like James Fenimore Cooper's Natty Bumppo, Audubon believed that the still-hunter should wear buckskin shirts, trousers and moccasins. In early pencil sketches drawn by him as early as 1826, we see the young deer-slayer dressed in white-tailed deerskins from head to toe. Audubon's description of "the true hunter," as he calls the buckskin-clad still-hunter, reads like a passage from one of Cooper's Leatherstocking tales:

"He wears a belt round his waist; his heavy rifle is resting on the brawny shoulder; on one side hangs his ball pouch, surmounted by the horn of an ancient Buffalo, once

In Audubon's account of the still-hunter, we find the first mention of buck rubs and scrapes in the American literature on deer and deer hunting. We also learn that Audubon grunted and decoyed deer to within reach of his rifle as early as the 1830s. He loved to decoy deer and antelope and did so until shortly before his death in 1851.

In his essay on deer hunting, Audubon, like his contemporary "Frank Forester," who hung out at the Dutchman's Tavern in Orange County, New York, deplores the mode of "destroying" deer by fire-lighting, a method of deer hunting originally prohibited in Mississippi and Alabama as early as 1803, but not in New York until 1897. Although he admits, like Forester, that "there is something in it which at times appears *awfully grand:*"

"The blaze illuminates the near objects, but the distant parts seem involved in deepest obscurity. The hunter who bears the gun keeps immediately in front, and after a while discovers before him two feeble lights, which are produced by the reflection of the pine-fire from the eyes of an animal of the deer ...The animal stands quite still. To one unacquainted with this strange mode of hunting, the glare from its eyes might bring to his imagination some lost hobgoblin that had strayed from its usual haunts. The hunter, however, nowise intimidated, approaches the object, sometimes so near as to discern its form when raising the rifle to his shoulder, he fires and kills it on the spot."

This kind of hunting, Audubon insists, can prove fatal not only to deer, but to wolves, and now and then to cows and horses as well.

Deer Hunting by Torchlight by Currier & Ives shows another fire-lighting scene. Catlin, the original artist, writes, "I was on the water all night with my Colt's Revolving Rifle, and in the morning soon looked up seven of my victims, several others were wounded, but made their escape."

Of these modes of deer hunting, Audubon clearly preferred driving or coursing deer in the European tradition with horses, hounds and buckshot. Indeed, Audubon found great excitement in this mode of deer hunting and considered it a very agreeable form of outdoor recreation. His cherished, deeply engraved, long, double-barreled shotguns spoke often to the sight of fleeing whitetails in punctuation to the clamor of baying hounds, hunting horns, and galloping horses.

While driving deer, Audubon noticed that whitetails frequently retreat from their home range but soon return to their original haunts after the drive has ended. In Audubon's day, as in ours, hunters designated the drives with names such as Crane Pond, Gum Thicket, The Pasture, The Oak Swamp and so on. To his great mortification, his colleagues named one bay after him, a bay where Audubon missed several deer. In his essay on deer hunting, Audubon gives us one of the most dramatic descriptions of the deer drive ever penned:

"Now, kind reader, prepare to mount a generous, full-blood Virginian horse. See that your gun is in complete order, for hark to the sound of the bugle and horn, and the mingled clamor of a pack of harriers! Your friends are waiting for you, under the shade of the wood, and we must together go driving the light-footed deer. The distance over which one has to travel is seldom felt when pleasure is anticipated as the result; so galloping we go pell-mell through the woods, to some well-known place where many a fine buck has dropped its antlers under the ball of the hunter's rifle. The servants, who are called the drivers, have already begun their search. Their voices are heard exciting the hounds, and unless we put spurs to our steeds, we may be too late at our stand, and thus lose the first opportunity of shooting the fleeting game as it passes by. Hark again! The dogs are in chase, the horn sounds louder and more clearly. Hurry, hurry on, or we shall be sadly behind!

"Here we are at last! Dismount, fasten your horse to this tree, place yourself by the side of that large yellow poplar, and mind you do not shoot me! The deer is fast approaching; I will go to my stand, and he who shoots him dead wins the prize.

"The deer is heard coming. It has inadvertently cracked a dead stick with its hoof, and the dogs are now so near that it will pass in a moment. There it comes! How beautifully it bounds over the ground! What a splendid head of horns! How easy its attitudes, depending, as it seems to do, on its own swiftness for safety! All is in vain, however; a gun is fired, the animal plunges and doubles with incomparable speed. There he goes! He passes another stand, from which a second shot, better directed than the first, brings him to the ground. The dogs, the servants, the sportsmen are now rushing forward to the spot. The hunter who has shot it is congratulated on his skill or good luck, and the chase begins again in some other part of the woods.

"I hope that this account will be sufficient to induce you, kind reader, to driving the light-footed deer in our western and southern woods . . ."

Audubon's spirited and enthusiastic account of this mode of deer hunting induced many deerslayers nationwide to chase whitetails across hills, ravines and morasses. One thinks, in particular, of William Elliott (1788-1863), that Harvard-educated deerslayer, who drove deer with the enthusiastic gusto of starry-eyed generals engaged in sylvan warfare. "This sport is extremely agreeable," Audubon writes, "and proves successful on almost every occasion."

In dress and appearance, Audubon was the personification of Natty Bumppo. In fact, we might say that Audubon *was* Natty Bumppo. As contemporaries, both Cooper and Audubon knew and admired one another; they both died in the same year. Audubon read the Leatherstocking tales with great delight, and Cooper modeled his hero after the man who self-styled himself as the "American Woodsman," the Rousseau of the West.

Audubon certainly loved the image of the frontiersman, the self-reliant hunter, trapper, fisherman and man of nature. He became the prime exemplar of this breed, the symbol of the mountain man, the patron saint of hunting. Close study reveals Audubon as a sportsman and hunter/naturalist, who studied deer to hunt them and hunted them to study them.

In reading his journals, we see a self-constructed celebrity in buckskins, traveling long distances, watching, observing, taking notes, hunting, shooting, fishing, drawing and exploring. He played the role of the frontier deerslayer with flair and drama throughout his entire life. His favorite potraits of himself depict Cooper's Leatherstocking hero dressed in buckskins with long, flowing locks of curly hair down to his shoulders. He was, as one of his biographers writes, literally "infatuated with the carefully nurtured image of himself as the exotic woodsman."

In all of his self-portraits, we see the beloved shotgun and in many of them the essential deerskin clothing. In his *Quadrupeds of North America* (1848), he notes that deerskin "is of the greatest service to the wild man." In a letter to his wife Lucy, dated Thursday, June 1, 1843, Audubon writes that he had not pulled off his buckskin breeches at night to sleep since he left St. Louis on April 4.

Europeans regarded him as the eccentric, legendary American woodsman, the fearless frontiersman, who hunted white-tailed deer in unexplored territory; as a man addicted to blood sports and lavishly dressed in exquisite leather frontier clothing.

During his life, he sought the wilderness and its charms; its freedom to roam unrestricted by the mores of civilization. He hunted deer with Indians in unexplored territory. In one episode, Audubon recalls how he celebrated one Christmas day by joining an Indian deer hunting party as they floated down streams in canoes in pursuit of deer:

"I seated myself on my haunches in the canoe, well provisioned with ammunition, a bottle of whiskey, and in a few minutes the paddles were at work . . ."

One observer, who met and interviewed Audubon in St. Louis as Audubon started up the Missouri River in April of 1843, later reported in the *Buffalo Courier* on August 22, 1843, that Audubon was a man of robust

This portrait of America's premier deerslayer dressed in deerskin and with his beloved shotgun was done by his son, John Woodhouse Audubon.

constitution who could walk 35 miles a day with ease. He loved to role up in a buffalo robe and sleep in the snow. He enjoyed returning to civilization with a beard down to his chest and his knees full of mud. He lived for the drama and excitement of living off the land.

As an expert marksman, Audubon shot deer for the table and for purposes of scientific and artistic observations. He was a man of his time, a time when marksmanship with animal targets was common sport. He loved the exquisite taste of venison. "The tender, juicy, savory, and above all, digestible quali-

Hunting by canoe, as shown in this Currier & Ives piece entitled *The Life of a Sportsman: Coming Into Camp*, was common in Audubon's day.

our guns by our sides, we were soon fast asleep."

In a letter dated November 3, 1843, Audubon reports that he "brought home alive a Deer which he thought would prove new." Like such premier deerslayers as Wisconsin's David W. Cartwright (1814-1892) Pennsylvania's Philip Tome (1782-1855), and Maryland's Meshach Browning (1781-1859), Audubon already caught deer alive at this time for some of America's earliest experiences in deer parks and deer study.

ties of ...venison are held in highest esteem from the camp of the backwoodsman to the luxurious tables of the opulent ...A fat haunch with jelly and chafing dishes is almost as much relished as a hunter's steak cooked in the open air on a frosty evening far away in the West."

Many of his deer hunts ended with him and his companions sitting before the cheerful, blazing fire, drinking ample portions of Claret wine and eating roasted venison. When he lacked salt, Audubon seasoned his venison steak with gunpowder. He once remarked that after having a steady diet of venison, beef was tasteless by comparison.

In his journal, *Up the Missouri With Audubon* (1843), Edward Harris (1799-1863), Audubon's deer hunting friend and fellow naturalist, reported on May 26, 1843, that most hunting days ended in a similar way:

"It was not long before some of the choice morceaux were roasting before the fire impaled upon sharp sticks stuck in the ground. We all agreed it was the best venison we ever tasted and none failed to do ample justice to the repast. Our beds were soon blown up and wrapped in our blankets with

In his journals, Audubon describes one episode in which old Daniel Boone himself relates his deer hunting adventures to the young Audubon and teaches him how to "bark" squirrels by shooting beneath them, so that the impact of the bullet on the bark actually kills the squirrel, thus avoiding serious damage to the meat.

Audubon claims he spent a night with Boone in a log cabin. Like Boone, Audubon greatly prided himself for his marksmanship and wrote with great admiration about frolics with the rifle, such as snuffing out a candle by shooting off the wick. Apparently, Audubon saw such marksmanship by Daniel Boone at a Frankfort, Kentucky tavern in 1810.

Like Daniel Boone and other frontiersmen, Audubon maintained a profound passion for fine firearms. Audubon used the gun not only to provide venison for the table, but as a specimen collector for scientific and artistic purposes. He loved the long, double-barreled shotgun. In 1835, Audubon ordered a shotgun from a Manchester gunsmith named Conway. In his biography of Audubon, Stanley C. Arthur describes the gun and Audubon's admiration for it:

"Audubon was spending all his spare time in the woods and fields with the new gun he brought back from London. It was a handsome expensive weapon, with mountings of gold and silver. The fowling-piece was double-barreled, of 18-gauge bore, and was fired by means of a percussion cap, a remarkable advance over the old flintlock. The length was extraordinary, measuring 63 inches, and it weighed 12 pounds. Deeply engraved between the barrels was the inscription, John J. Audubon, Citizen of the United States, E. L. S. L., the initials evidence of his fellowship in the Linnean Society of London. The gun carried a concealed trap door in the butt-plate, greatly exciting the curiosity of Doctor Pope and Augustin Bourgeat when they fondled and fired the beautiful weapon."

This gun, which appears in many of the portraits of Audubon, now reposes in Princeton University's Library. Indeed, Audubon infused a great deal of passion and intensity in the very act of loading his weapon. He describes it in a loving manner, step by step:

"He blows through his rifle, to ascertain that it is clear, examines his flint, and thrusts a feather into the touch-hole. To a leather bag swung at his side is attached a powder horn; his sheathed knife is there also; below hangs a narrow strip of home-spun linen. He takes from his bag a bullet, pulls with his teeth the wooden stopper from his powder horn, lays the ball on one hand, and with the other pours the powder upon it until it is just over-topped. Raising the horn to his mouth, he again closes it with the topper, and restores it to its place. He introduces the powder into the tube; springs the box of his gun, greases the patch over with some melted tallow, or damps it; then places it on the honeycombed muzzle of his piece. The bullet is placed on the patch over the bore, and pressed with the handle of the knife, which now trims the edges of the linen. The elastic hickory rod, held with both hands smoothly pushes the ball to its bed: once, twice, thrice has it rebounded. The rifle leaps as it were into the hunter's arms, the feather is drawn from the touch-hole, the powder fills the pan, which is closed. 'Now I'm ready,' cries the woodsman."

In 1848, Audubon presented to the American public his detailed scientific account of the white-tailed deer and the hunting of them in *The Quadrupeds of North America*, published jointly with Dr. John Bachman. It remained the standard reference on the subject of white-tailed deer and deer hunting until 1877, when John Dean Caton published his scientific treatise *The Antelope and Deer of America*.

The account contains everything from detailed anatomical measurements to hunting methodology, and discussions on such topics as food habits and preferences, movement patterns, bedding habits, rutting behavior, antler development, fawning, and a unique observation of three pairs of interlocked antlers. It ends with a colorful description of one of Audubon's annual deer hunts in South Carolina at a plantation called "Liberty Hall," owned by a planter named Dr. Desel, who served as the hunt master incarnate.

On this particular hunt, Audubon was joined by one of his sons and his friend Edward Harris. After a substantial breakfast, the party loaded their double-barreled shotguns and saddled their horses. As the horn sounded, the impatient deerhounds started the chase. After a lengthy trailing session, the hounds started two majestic bucks.

At the report of Harris' shotgun, one noble buck hit the forest floor. Since this was Harris' first deer and his introduction to what Audubon called "the mysteries of deer

Camping Out, Currier & Ives, 1856. Many of Audubon's deer hunts ended with him and his companions sitting before the cheerful, blazing fire, drinking ample portions of Claret wine and eating roasted venison.

hunting," he had to submit, according to Audubon, "to the ordeal of all who have fleshed their maiden sword, and killed their first Deer ...So his forehead and cheeks were crossed with the red blood of the buck, and the tail was stuck in his cap."

The next buck the hounds started headed toward Audubon, who recalls the event: "One barrel snapped—then came a sharp report from the other."

Audubon's loud whoop indicated to the entire entourage that another noble buck had fallen. By the end of the day, five white-tails hung from the old pecan tree in view of Dr. Desel's festive hall. That evening Audubon reports "passed off in pleasant conversation—some of those present displayed their wit and poetical talents by giving the details of the hunt in an amusing ballad, which however has not yet found its way into print. Thus ended a Carolina Deer hunt."

The cry of the deerhounds, the sight of galloping horses and the sound of hunting horns at this famous deer club inflamed Audubon's imagination. As a voracious reader of the sporting literature of his day,

Audubon read the highly popular South Carolina deer-hunting epistles in great anticipation for his annual deer hunt at Dr. Desel's deer club. He fondly quoted historian David Ramsay (1749-1815) on the immortality of the southern deer hunting clubs and deer hunting as war in miniature:

"The members will die, but the clubs are immortal; so far that a constant succession is kept up, and has been so for near half a century and bids fair to continue.

"Impediments apparently insurmountable are readily got over. Dangers that seem to threaten life and limb—to tear riders from their horses, or horses from them, are escaped without injury. Hunting in some respects is war in miniature.

"Hunters discharge their weapons when the shooter and the stricken deer are both in motion."

Audubon also read with great delight the colorful anecdotes and accounts of the early American deerslayer in *The Cabinet of Natural History and American Rural Sports* (1830-1833), founded by John and Thomas

Doughty in Philadelphia on November 2, 1830:

"Sound the horn—sound the horn,
O gaily the hunters meet,
Each on his prancing courser borne,
For the chase—for the chase they greet;
Come, for the morning is on the mountain,
Come, for the deer is at the fountain,
The mists are melting away in the air,
There's not a moment of day to spare.
On—on—the stag must yet be slain,
Strike the spur and slacken the rein,
Slacken the courser's rein—
The notes of the bugle unceasingly play,
To the chase—to the chase away."

Audubon loved the daily meetings at the clubhouse with horses, hounds and guns. Boys not more than ten years old could show with great pride the white-tailed bucks they shot. Deer hunting was a social diversion as carried out by the clubs. Members of the clubs rode the deer forests in official uniform—scarlet coats—and adhered to rules and regulations of a strict code of ethics:

"Any member who shall fire at a deer less than forty yards distant and not **hit** or **kill**, when the **opportunity is fair**, shall be fined. No deer shall be considered hit unless killed, or unless **blood is seen**."

The neighboring deer clubs often vied with each other, the losers paying the costs of elaborate venison dinners with exquisite wines, brandy and whiskey in the grandiose traditions of European gusto. At these sacred venison feasts at "Liberty Hall," Audubon would read aloud to all assembled passages from David Ramsay's two-volume

Oregon White-tailed Deer, an imperial folio plate from Audubon's *The Quadrupeds of North America*, 1848.

History of Carolina:

"The cravings for food and drink, highly excited by the chase, are not always satisfied without subsequent irregularities; but such occurrences are rare."

Audubon subscribed to and wrote material for both the *Spirit of the Times* (1831-1861), edited by William T. Porter (1809-1858), a country journalist and graduate of Dartmouth, and the *American Turf Register and Sporting Magazine* (1829-1844), founded and edited by John Stuart Skinner, a young lawyer from Baltimore. The deer hunting epistles written by the deerslayers themselves in this early sporting journal best epitomize the romance, adventure and early interest in the natural history of deer during Audubon's time:

> "Hark! the leafy woods
> resounding
> Echo in the bugle-horn,
> Swift the stag with vigor
> bounding,
> Leaps the brake and clears
> the thorn."

In one of the earliest published articles on South Carolina deer hunting, published in the December 1829 issue of the *American Turf Register and Sporting Magazine*, the author, writing under the pen name of "Ringwood," refers to the deer hunt as a fine and manly amusement but also reports that he knew people who preferred to partake in the savory dish of sacred venison over the exhilaration of the chase itself. He noted that after sending his neighbor a fine haunch of venison, he received the following message:

> "Thanks, good sir, for your venison,
> for finer or fatter,
> Ne'er ranged in a forest,
> or smoked in a platter."

He ended his epistle with *The Horn of Chase*:

> "To join the chase at break of day,
> The hunter fearless leaves his dwelling;
> O'er hill, through vale, he speeds his way,
> His cheering horn on echo swelling.
>
> Attentive mark the eager hounds,
> With list'ning ears, and watchful eyes,
> The thicket beat, now swiftly bounds
> The stag, and from the covert flies.
>
> Thro' brakes he shuns the hunter's sight,
> But o'er the plain or upland bounding;
> The rifle ball arrests his flight,
> The horn of chase his knell resounding.
>
> At close of day, the sport now o'er'
> T'wards home the hunter's steps are bending,
> The bugle sounds to chase no more,
> But notes of glad return is sending.
>
> His anxious fair one hails the sound,
> Her heart no longer throbs alarms;
> He gains the door with one swift bound,
> And clasps her in his longing arms.
>
> The festive board displays its store,
> Good cheer with social joys abounding;
> A welcome call to friends once more,
> The horn of chase is gaily sounding."

Not only did the hunting horns resound throughout the day as Audubon hunted deer at Dr. Desel's southern plantation, but as the festive board appeared with steaming venison each night, the horns again sounded loud and clear throughout the walls of "Liberty Hall" as musicians performed Haydn's *Hunt Symphony*, W. A. Mozart's *Hunt Quartet*, Leopold Mozart's *Hunt Symphony* for four horns and the spectacular hunting horn fanfare of Vivaldi's *Hunt Concerto*.

Deer hunting during Audubon's day remained part of mainstream American culture. As he listened to the hunting music of the day, he read deeply into the pages of the *Spirit of the Times*, one of the most influential popular weeklies of its day, which eventually reached a circulation of 40,000 subscribers by 1856.

Editor William T. Porter clearly catered to the well-to-do classes of the deer hunting fraternity: "We are addressing ourselves," he wrote in the *Spirit*, "to gentlemen of standing, wealth and intelligence—the very Corinthian columns of the community." Interspersed between deer hunting narratives one found commentary and analysis of classical literature, drama and music. But its highbrow prose, however, was also read by the whiskey-guzzling, tobacco-spitting,

buckskin-clad backwoodsmen of the day. The stories, filled with backwoods humor and briar-patch philosophizing were unusual, lively, factual and picturesque; the colorful and pungent language came from earth-drawn material. In these high-spirited sporting tales, the dead, noble buck was often referred to as "the dead body of Caesar." Groups of hunters were referred to as "grand divisions."

These deer hunting epistles (165 in number between 1831 and 1861) were written by journalists, travelers, visiting sportsmen from the North and Europe as well as landowners and planters. These vivid descriptions of the deer hunting adventures of the time are masterpieces of their kind. They not only entertained Audubon, but they give us a splendid portrait of the early 19th-century deerslayer that needs to be preserved.

In one of them entitled "The Death of the Buck," published on August 15, 1840, Audubon read a great tribute to the memory of a noble old buck killed near McPhersonville, South Carolina, on the deer hunting grounds of Captain William Heyward. The anonymous author of the article reported that the pack put up the gallant old fellow immediately into the drive, which went through a large rice field. After being severely shot, he made a desperate effort to reach Hemlock Swamp, but the hounds eventually pulled him down at the end of a two-mile race. The author, with high-powered verbiage, paid homage to the noble buck and characterized the course he ran:

Courtesy of The Adirondack Museum.

Morning on the Loon Lake by A.F. Tait was a classic deer print of Audubon's time.

*"'Twas early morn—for scarce the sun
An hour his onward course had run—
When the deep tones of busy hound,
That wake the echoes all around,
And ring so loud, so shrill and clear,
So welcome to the sportsman's ear,
Had roused a stag from dewy lair,
And told his deadliest foe was near.*

*"The pack burst out with eager haste,
And through the old field's
glittering waste
The noble stag runs headlong on,
'Till loud is heard McPherson's gun:
His tow'ring antlers downwards fall—
The dogs obedient to the huntsman's call,
Stand still; and wait the hunters all,
As quick they rally to the call.*

*"They meet, consult and quick pursue
The wounded stag, who, just in view
In tangled copse wood bleeding lay,
His life-blood ebbing fast away.
One dying effort now he makes,
And from the thicket bounding breaks,
Throws from his sides the gory flakes,
And flies for Cooachatchie's cooling lakes.*

*"But ah! that effort proves in vain,
The dogs upon his haunches gain,
While bold Pizarro* leads the pack,
Now followed close by babbling Track.
Poor bleeding stag! thy race is run;
And little deemed thou, when the sun
This morn his glorious course begun,
Thy race on earth today was run."*

---

*The names of two dogs—Pizarro, remarkable for speed,
and Track for babbling.

Audubon and his fellow deer hunters at "Liberty Hall" took great delight in these high-spirited tales and clearly believed that deer hunting should be dramatic, fun and exciting, as revealed in the stanzas above, with a metaphysical level of mystery and merriment; an activity emphasizing romance, adventure and natural history.

These three elements of the deer hunt also clearly reveal themselves in Audubon's deer hunting adventures while journeying up the Missouri in 1843, from St. Louis to Fort Union on the Wyoming/North Dakota border. On this eight-month hunting expedition, Edward Harris, a patron of science, John Bell, a taxidermist, Isaac Sprague, artist and illustrator, Lewis Squires, Audubon's secretary and aide-de-camp and Captain Mayne Reid, a popular novelist, accompanied Audubon among others. They all assisted Audubon in gathering skins, specimens and detailed information on animal behavior for his classic book, *The Quadrupeds of North America.*

Audubon's entourage traveled on a large steamboat called the "Omega." The expedition also included, in addition to those already mentioned, 100 French and Canadian trappers. The entire party hunted deer on a daily basis and consumed vast quantities of fresh venison.

On Saturday, May 27, 1843, at a deer camp Audubon called "Six Trees," he recorded in his journal that, "the best portions of the Deer, i. e., the liver, kidneys and tongue, were cooked for breakfast, which all enjoyed." At the campfire each night they chewed "chunks" of venison and their plugs of real "James River Tobacco." In the dim light of the roaring fire they read Washington Irving's deer shooting adventures in *A Tour on the Prairies* (1835) and James Fenimore Cooper's *The Deerslayer* (1841). At night they slept to the howls of the wolves.

"When Daniel Boone goes by at night
The phantom deer arise
And all lost, wild America
Is burning in their eyes."

– Stephen Vincent Benét, *Daniel Boone* (1942)

Jacking Deer by A.F. Tait.

In his book, *The Hunters' Feast; or, Conversations Around the Camp-Fire* (1855), Captain Reid, who accompanied Audubon on this trip, recorded that they frequently left the steamboat "Omega" in birch tree "dug-outs," used as canoes, to fire-hunt deer on the streams and adjoining lakes of the Missouri River. The drama and excitement of these wild deer hunting excursions left an indelible picture in Audubon's mind:

"I shall never forget the romantic effect which was produced upon my mind during those wild excursions. The scenery of the river upon which we had launched our craft was at all times of a picturesque character: under the blaze of pine-wood—its trees and rocks tinted with a reddish hue, while the rippling flood below ran like molten gold—the effect was heightened to a degree of sublimity which could not have failed to impress the dullest imagination. It was autumn season, too, and the foliage, which had not yet commenced falling, had assumed those rich varied tints so characteristic of the American sylva—various hues of green and gold, and yellow and deep red were exhibited upon the luxuriant frontage that lined the banks of the stream, and here and there drooped like embroidered curtains down to the water's edge. It was a scene of that wild beauty, that picturesque sublimity, which carries one to the contemplation of its Creator."

Blue Dick, a French voyageur, who served as Audubon's guide, muttered a sound that roused Audubon from his reverie. In the dark shadows of the dug-out, birch-bark canoe, Audubon could see Blue Dick's arm pointing to the right bank. His eyes soon saw the eyes of a deer reflecting the light of their torch. Blue Dick whispered, "It's a buck!" Audubon sighted his rifle between the luminous spots. His rifle cracked like a whip. Both hunters heard the plunge of a body falling into the water as Dick paddled the dug-out toward the bank.

"The torch, blazing brightly, lit up the scene ahead of us, and our eyes were gratified by the sight of a fine buck, that had fallen dead into the river."

The Frontiersman by N.C. Wyeth, 1912, which appeared as the cover of the March 15, 1912, cover of *The Popular Magazine.*

"I stalk through life like a deer."

–A German deerslayer called "Miller" in an
unpublished letter, October 16, 1838.

Chapter Three

"MILLER" AND "BEARGREASE"

On May 16, 1837, a young, 21-year-old, German deer hunter well versed in the deer hunting tales of James Fenimore Cooper's Natty Bumppo and Audubon's writings on deer and deer hunting, set sail from the Port of Bremmerhaven on a ship called the "Constitution" bound for New York and arrived in America on July 25.

Inspired by the deer hunting tales of James Fenimore Cooper and Audubon, this German Natty Bumppo saw the new land as a "golden paradise" for deer hunting. It is not surprising that the American deer forests would prove very attractive to this young adventurer, a man steeped in the European aristocratic tradition of deer hunting dating back to the Middle Ages, when Gaston Phoebus roamed the deer forests of Europe during the 14th century.

On October 24, 1837, this highly-spirited world traveler, who introduced himself simply as "Miller" because most Americans mispronounced his German name, Friedrich Gerstaecker (1816-1872), embarked upon a six-year, deer-hunting adventure through seven states and one Canadian Province in pursuit of white-tailed deer.

He traveled to Albany by steamboat and to Utica by train; he then took a barge on the Erie Canal to Lockport and went on foot to

"Home is wherever I happen to be … " said Miller, who, like the hunter in this photo, used hollow logs as his sleeping quarters from time to time.

Inset: A portrait of Friedrich Gerstaecker, better known as "Miller."

Wegner's Photo Collection.

In *Bringing Home Game: Winter Shanty at Ragged Lake* by A.F. Tait, 1856, the hunters bear the spoils in triumph to the deer shanty.

the Falls of Niagara. Still dressed in his German deer-hunting costume—leather trousers; short, green, shooting jacket; green cap and carrying a beautiful German double-barreled shotgun—and looking very different from the buckskin-clad American frontiersmen with their Kentucky long rifles, he hiked through southern Ontario in search of deer. Filled with wanderlust and thrilled by what he found, he reported that deer hunting was still the great romantic adventure as described so well in Cooper's best-selling novel, *The Pioneers* (1823), which he read in German translation before coming to America.

He soon discarded his German hunting clothes and dressed himself completely in white-tailed deerskins like Natty Bumppo and Audubon. As he wandered through the deer forest, he lived off the land, eating venison, whortle berries, acorns, sassafras leaves, tender stems and wild honey, which he drank out of a deer's leg—out of a laced-up, tanned buckskin case made from the end of a deer's leg. Most settlers at this time did not conceive of the deer forest as "belonging" to anyone save the person who made use of it.

One of Gerstaecker's descriptions of the American deer hunters he encountered in his travels is taken from his book *Wie ist es denn nun eigentlich in Amerika?* (1849) and reads and sounds like a passage from Cooper's *The Deerslayer* and/or Audubon's essay "Deer Hunting:"

"He is a muscular, manly figure dressed in the customary deerskin clothes of the backwoodsman with leather shirt and leggins of the same material. He wears deerskin moccasins. On the left side of a broad leather belt a long hunting knife could be seen. His hair was curly, his eyes blue, the expression of his face definitely honest and straightforward."

Miller traveled from backwoods cabin to backwoods cabin, like those portrayed in A. F. Tait's classic deer and deer hunting prints, taking jobs of a menial sort to support himself, frequently paying fifty cents for an overnight stay with breakfast. At other times, he merely stretched himself out in his woolen blanket in the "untrodden forest, wet, hungry, alone and a prey to mosquitoes, longing in vain for the society of men," as he wrote in his deer hunting journal.

The woods and streams were his home; they sustained and sheltered him. After shooting one of his first bucks, he wrote in his hunting journal: "I walked home. But where was my home? Wherever I happened to be—where I had erected a bark shed, or spread my blanket, or lighted a fire, or where the hospitable roof of a farmer or back-woodsman received me; though the next morning might find me with all my goods on my back—no heavy burden—seeking a new

This hunter's ingenuity has earned him a splendid sleeping place in the hollow of a log, which, while a bit cramped, will keep out the wind and rain and make a most satisfactory sleeping place.

deer shooting ground, and a new home."

Deep in the deer woods, he often slept in hollow logs, caves and panther and bear dens. Before magnificent campfires at his backwoods retreats, he shared his deer hunting tales over a jug of whiskey with the wild and legendary deerslayers of yesteryear. "He shared easily in their ways," writes one of his biographers. "He could drink raw whiskey out of a tumbler with time-hardened drinkers, though he never allowed himself to lapse from the perpendicular." When day-break came each day, he took to the track of the white-tailed deer with great delight.

"I sallied joyfully forth, making the Canadian woods resound with German hunting songs," he wrote in his deer-hunting journal, published as *Streif-und Jagdzuege* in 1844. This classic journal of wild deer-hunting adventures remains a critical document in the history of American deer hunting, since so few deerslayers of the 1830s and 1840s left first-hand accounts of their deer hunting exploits. It represents one of the best portraits of the total freedom of the early deerslayer—the drifting, wander-lust, roving disposition of the great deer hunting hobos of yesteryear—whose great passion for the deer hunt Cooper inspired and intensified with his best-selling novels, which Miller read as he tramped the deer forests. After going through 15 different printings, this popular travel book of the Ohio and Mississippi Valley, *Wild Sport in the Far West: The Narrative of a German Wanderer Beyond the Mississippi, 1837-1843*, remains out of print as of 2003.

Much as this free-spirited backwoodsman liked the deer hunting terrain of Canada, he traveled south by steamboat on Lake Erie to Cleveland, Ohio, where he might have crossed paths with such legendary Ohio deerslayers as Oliver Hazard Perry and "Big" Sam Edwards.

Remaining unimpressed with city life, he moved westward toward Cincinnati on steamboats, railroad cars, canal boats and on foot, arriving there on November 26, 1837. But since city life never attracted him, this self-reliant, rambling vagabond again set out on foot in search of the deer hunting adventures of the backwoods that always occupied his fantasy and walked down through eastern Missouri until he reached the Arkansas-Missouri boundary. On January 22, 1838, he crossed the Current River and entered the newly-created state of Arkansas with the soles of his hunting boots frayed to ribbons and 12 cents in his pocket.

For the next six years, with the exception of a few short forays into Texas, Louisiana, Missouri, Illinois and Indiana, Arkansas became the center of his constantly-shifting movements in pursuit of whitetails in the river swamps and Ozark and Ouashita Mountains, regions that still produce trophy bucks because of their steep, rugged mountains that allow bucks to reach that magical 4.5-year-old age group. He also hunted whitetails in earnest on the so-called "Congress Lands" on the Fourche La Fave, near Nimrod Dam, as well as the Old Hurricane-Mulberry deer hunting grounds in the remote White River Valley section of northwestern Arkansas.

Miller was a deer hunter by training and instinct and fully indulged that passion with a rare sense of sportsmanship for his day. Although his daily existence depended upon venison, he was first and foremost a buck hunter; he dreamed of big Ozark bucks with giant "horns." Bucks with "12-branches" greatly impressed him. He sought out Ozark bucks like the legendary 12-pointer shot in Natural Dam by Tom Sparks in the fall of 1975 that reigns supreme as Arkansas' state record typical—189 0/8 Boone and Crockett points—and that inspired Ken Carlson's classic deer print, "An Ozark Legend."

When he shot a trophy buck, he nailed the rack to his favorite backwoods lean-to,

where it gradually weathered away in time. In his journal, he described one backwoods cabin that had 60 sets of massive, white-tailed deer antlers piled on top of the roof to keep the bark shingles in place. These white-tailed deer antlers of the past clearly served more practical functions than the famous Tom Sparks buck of today, which continuously appears at deer classics and buck-a-ramas and even graced the program cover of the 22nd Annual Meeting of the South East Deer Study Group, the nation's most distinguished deer group meeting, held in Fayetteville, Arkansas, in February of 1999.

FRIEDRICH GERSTÄCKER
Wild Sports in the Far West

The narrative of a German Wanderer beyond the Mississippi, 1837-1843. *Reprinted from the English translation of 1854, with Introduction and Notes by* EDNA L. STEEVES *and* HARRISON R. STEEVES.

Duke University's 1968 edition of Gerstaecker's classic *Wild Sports in the Far West.*

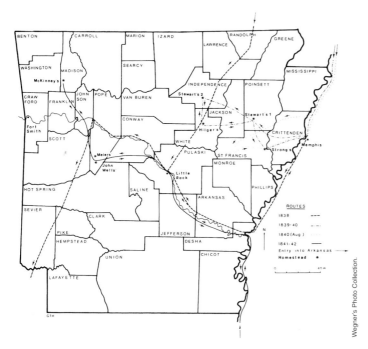

Gerstaecker's travels from 1838-1842 in the newly-created state of Arkansas, which became Miller's favorite place to chase white-tailed deer.

On one of his first still-hunts in Arkansas in early 1838, in Buck Point Hollow near the Little Red River, he encountered an 11-pointer not more than ten paces off. "My ball pierced his heart, and he fell dead in his tracks without a sound." He dined on venison loin that night; lacking salt, he seasoned the deer meat with gunpowder in the tradition of Audubon. When the last remains of venison were discreetly devoured, he found a hollow tree, crept in and placed his German double barrel on one side of him and his Bowie knife, made by an Arkansan blacksmith named James Black and originally designed for deer hunting by Rezin P. Bowie, a wealthy planter who lived at Walnut Hills in Lafayette County, on his other side.

"There I passed one of the most uncomfortable nights of my life. I heard the howling of wolves near by and the roar of a panther in the distance; but nothing came to disturb me, and the bright morning sun saw me early on the march for deer."

He frequently took moonlit walks for five to ten miles at a time and often roamed over 30 miles a day in search of deer. His deer hunting rambles would end each day in front of a magnificent roaring campfire—eating smoked deer tongue, venison loin, and corn bread while sipping whiskey. His nocturnal entertainment consisted of singing hunting songs, playing his zither to the sounds of owls, fighting mosquitoes and keeping wolves and panthers at bay with a blazing fire, while staring into the starry night. When the howling wolves approached within sight, he would shoot at them, driving them back into the impenetrable sassafras bushes and the darkness of the night.

In early January of 1840, Miller, the most authentic observer of the cultural characteristics of the early American deerslayers, arrived in Batesville, located on the White River in Independence County. His insatiable appetite to understand the local people lead him to the Green Tree Tavern, where he drank half-pints and ate "Varmint Mash" with one of the most colorful and bazaar characters of all of the whiskey guzzling, tobacco-spitting, buckskin-clan backwoodsmen of the Ozarks: Pete Whetstone, a true-blue southern redneck, who reportedly once killed five white-tailed bucks in 25 minutes with his old Ozark Mountain Arms Muskrat Rifle in 50 caliber—getting three bucks with one shot. Yes, Whetstone burned the barrel hot.

According to one biographical account, Pete Whetstone was "powerful in stature, course in manner, and yet honest and loyal as ever man was . . ." He lived on the Devil's Fork of the Little Red River, where Miller spent much of his time chasing deer. Whetstone regaled Miller with his deer

Nocturnal Entertainment, from a lithograph in the original 1854 edition of *Wild Sports in the Far West*, shows Miller sharing the campfire with howling wolves.

hunting yarns, for he lived with several packs of deerhounds and spent most of his life in long, involved deer hunts to such sacred places as Oil Trough Bottom, War Eagle Creek and Devil's Fork. Pete Whetstone was, of course, the alter ego of Arkansas' first outdoor writer, Charles Fenton Mercer Noland (1812-1858), who portrayed Whetstone and his buddies in the pages of New York's *Spirit Of The Times* as a roguish bunch of "tavern roisterers."

The backwoods tavern served as the social centerpiece for such early Ozark deerslayers as Pete Whetstone, and writer Nolan rightly placed the early Ozark deer hunt as a cultural institution in the context of hard-drinking, hard-fighting, "cavorting and bantering." Miller himself would later portray the mid-19th century deerslayer as "the wild man of the woods." In his description of the small town of Francisville on the banks of the St. Francis River in northeastern Arkansas in his book *Western Lands and Western Waters* (1864), he wrote, "the neighborhood was composed of wild, careless and independent deer hunters, who rarely had a cent of ready money, but often brought in the produce of the forest, such as bear's fat, honey, smoked deer-hams, and deerskins, which they exchanged for powder and shot, whiskey and the other luxuries of forest life."

According to the books of one Arkansas factory, shaved deerskins sold for 40 cents a pound as early as 1806—30 cents a pound for deerskins in the hair. By 1840, in the absence or scarcity of money, deerskins became for a time an article of currency in both Arkansas and Missouri. Indeed, in St. Louis at this time, white-tailed deerskins became the basis of trade. The earliest settlers in the Ozarks were essentially deer hunters, who sought

Miller and Whetstone loved to fire-hunt deer along the banks of the Fourche La Fave as shown in this engraving from an 1858 edition of *Harper's New Monthly Magazine*.

Wegner's Photo Collection.

In this 1840 painting by Alfred Jacob Miller, *Portrait of Antoine*, the artist used the legendary Canadian deerslayer Antoine Clement as his subject.

the deer to such an extent that it shrouded the hunters in total obscurity. After five nights of fire-hunting at this lick, they shot 22 deer. In the *Spirit of the Times*, Fent Nolan ("T"), recalled the scene:

"We took our seats, remaining perfectly quiet, with the exception of occasionally replenishing our fire, it glared brightly like a spark in the surrounding gloom, causing the most total darkness, immediately out of this range of light to the occupier of the scaffold. I suppose it was near ten o'clock ...when in steps a tremendous buck, with his velvet horns showing distinctly, his eyes having the appearance of two stars, evincing more caution than I ever since have known one, owing to his being old and cautious. At the crack of my gun, he falls, rises and falls again—we are at his side, we seize his hind legs and drag him to the scaffold—he all the while offering no resistance ...My *Couteau de Chasse* penetrates his neck, and in less time than it takes to narrate it, to our utter astonishment he is up and away, scattering the blood in every direction, in an instant we are after him with, not exactly fire and sword, but torch and knife, expecting him to drop every instant, but in that I was mistaken."

Whetstone and his German companion had to wait for the following morning to retreive the old monarch of the woods.

In 1837, Miller reported meeting an extraordinary deer hunter named John Wells, who lived on the banks of the Fourche La Fave, a clear stream flowing west through Arkansas. According to Gerstaecker, people in the area just called him "the hunter."

"This was quite a distinction in a land where every settler hunted deer and a third of the population did almost nothing other than wander around the forest with a rifle on their shoulders. But if anyone deserved such a designation, it was Wells."

When Gerstaecker set out to immortalize this backwoods, buckskin-clad deerslayer, a

deer, honey and bear meat for their livelihood, raising only small crops of corn to supplement their diet.

In the spring of 1841, Miller and Whetstone fire-hunted deer at a salt lick 20 miles south of Little Rock. They erected a scaffold within 15 feet of a well-used lick. They drove four posts into the ground forming a square of five feet making it high enough to sit under. They covered the top with sticks, bark and enough ground to prevent the fire from burning the sticks. They then surrounded three of the four sides with bushes. With pine knots burning on top, the brightness of the fire dazzled the eyes of man of supreme deer-hunting abilities and shooting skills, in print, his description read like a passage from James Fenimore Cooper's *The Deerslayer*:

"In his very appearance he bore some resemblance to the Indians, although he denied any kinship with those sons of the forest. He preferred to go bare-head, his long, black, straight hair bound by a light clothe. His neck he kept free, and his hunting shirt, leggins, and moccasins were of deerskin he tanned himself, an art he had mastered completely.

"It was extraordinary how fast and artfully he could skin a deer, scrape the skin with his small knife and tie up the various openings to make an excellent sack for carrying bear grease, honey or whatever else.

"With his long rifle, which shot 50 balls to a pound of lead, over his left shoulder and his left hand casually thrown over the stock, he glided rapidly through the woods like a shadow, accompanied by a gray, short-hair dog who was just as cautious. The man's gait seemed half to suspend him in air, as if he had no limbs, and more by instinct than conscious thought he avoided even the slightest, most unimportant noise. His eyes were generally focused on the ground, although they moved constantly from side to side, quickly but carefully taking account of every bush turned red by the fall frost, every twig moving in the wind. Not a leaf out of place escaped his attention.

"His figure was lean, one could say slight, but also lithe and agile. In running, jumping and climbing, he knew no equal."

The image of John Wells, this deer hunter extraordinaire, was probably based on Alfred Jacob Miller's oil on canvas and illustration of Antoine Clement, who stalked deer in the area around St. Louis. It seems conceivable that Gerstaecker may even have met Antoine, the great deerstalker, in St. Louis during the late 1830s.

As this German Hawkeye traveled through the Ozarks dressed in buckskin and a wind-battered coonskin cap, he indeed took on the appearance of Alfred Jacob Miller's classic illustration of "Antoine" (1837). Miller exemplified the lone, powerful, manly figure dressed in deerskins and buckskin moccasins. This muscular man with blue eyes, rough and deeply tanned complexion and ruddy cheeks carried a long Bowie knife and tomahawk in his deerskin belt and a long rifle.

He was accompanied by an old backwoodsman named "Slowtrap"—one of the most picturesque and colorful characters living on the Arkansas frontier—and the ever-present deerhound—"Beargrease."

This humorous, tough, courageous, genuine, lovable character, this inveterate adventurer, woodsman and explorer not only dressed in deerskins but often slept in raw deerskins to keep warm. He dreamed of stretched deerskins and of Beargrease chasing bucks of mythic proportions.

Everyday he collected dry firewood for the evening blaze and deerskins to sell and make into buckskin clothing to wear. He used the brain tanning method of the American Indians for dressing and preparing his buckskin and spent many days mending and stitching his buckskin shirts, leggings and moccasins in which he took great pride. After weeks of industrious tailoring, he mastered the art of creating his own personal buckskin attire.

Miller still-hunted, tracked and jogged along well-beaten deer runways, from deer kill to deer kill, relying on the keen nose of his faithful Beargrease to lead him to deer. At other times, he fire-hunted over salt licks. He frequently shot as many as five to six deer before breakfast. One day in 1841, while jogging runways in Buck Point Hollow, he had three bucks hanging in the trees by 10

AM and had stalked a fourth one for a half mile. One of Arkansas' famed deerslayers of the time, Frank Lane, whom Miller met at the Green Tree Tavern in Batesville, claimed Miller killed 300 deer a season and sold them for two dollars each.

Due to the primitive nature of the weapons, most deer kills ended in hand-to-hand conflict with knife-wielding artistry, so that the hunter lessened the chance of accidentally shooting his cherished deerhound while chasing the wounded animal. Miller always followed the wise advice of that southern aristocratic deerslayer Wade Hampton III: "Whatever you do, save the dogs."

While conducting deer hunting expeditions in the Ozarks on December 21 of 1841, with a hunting partner named Curly, the backwoodsmen tried their luck in fire-hunting deer along the banks of the Mulberry River during the evening hunts but to no avail. Several days later they arose at daybreak and started to jog deer trails behind Beargrease in Deer Lick Hollow near Ozark. Their luck suddenly changed:

"At length Beargrease found a fresh trail, and followed it up, often looking round to see if I was near him; so I kept as close as possible. Suddenly he stood still and pointed, and an old noble buck got up about fifty yards from us, and made a half circle round us. When I gave a hail, he stood still as if to ask what I wanted. It happened that I was too windward of him; and snuffing the air he gave a bound, which caused my ball to strike too far backwards under his spine bringing him on his haunches.

"Beargrease had been observing it all with remarkable patience, only turning his head from one to the other; but now giving vent to his eagerness he darted on the deer, seized him by the jaw, and springing over his back, brought him to the ground. I had now a good opportunity of cutting the deer's throat, but wished to give the dog a little practice, and

I watched the struggle with the greatest interest.

"The buck was one of twelve branches and had the full use of the forepart of his body. He strove to hit the dog with his sharp hoof, and to run his horns into him; but the dog cleverly eluded all his attempts, and at last seizing him by the throat, held him fast, while I ended his torments with my knife.

"I skinned the deer, packed the haunches and loins in the skin, fed the dog and trudged away heavily laden up and down hill to Curly's shack."

In early February of 1842, Miller hunted deer along the banks of Bayou de View, a little river running between and parallel to the Cache and l'Anguille in eastern Arkansas. A bough breaking with the weight of snow one morning roused him out of his sleep. Having no breakfast to cook, he was soon on the march for deer.

While following Beargrease, he devoured acorns and chewed tender stems and leaves of *sassafras albidum*, the whitetail's preferred choice of food, in response to his own raging hunger. Not far from his bivouac, he came upon the fresh trail of an "old noble buck." After trailing the buck for three hours through thickly tangled thorn-brush, the buck suddenly stood before the German deerslayer with inquiring eyes, but quickly vanished while jumping over an eight-foot-high thorn-bush clearing 20 feet in one bound, as Miller steadfastly recorded the details in his hunting journal. After another hour of intimate tracking, he again encountered the buck a second time standing in a thicket about a hundred paces off. As the smoke cleared from the old muzzleloader, the buck fled in wild haste into the thick brush. He soon found the buck lying dead on the snow on the other side of the Bayou de View.

"Had I not been half starved, I should not have thought of venturing into the cold

This deer hunter's camp, an evergreen shanty in the Northwest, circa 1845, resembles the primitive hemlock brush shanties Miller improvised while hunting deer in Arkansas between 1837 and 1842.

Wegner's Photo Collection.

water; but necessity would admit of no hesitation. I bound together some logs of decayed wood, as floating lightest, laid on the raft my rifle, zither, blanket, hunting-shirt, powder-horn, game-bag and stepped into the icy, cold water. I kept on my lower garments, as they were already wet through from the small streams I had waded in the course of the chase. I dipped my head as soon as I could, and then swam across pushing my raft before me.

"Shivering with cold, I had some difficulty in making a fire, on account of the deep snow which covered everything; — but I managed it at last with the help of my tomahawk; dried myself, and having laid some steaks on the fire, I devoured them ere they were well warmed through.

"The exertion of the chase and the cold bath were too much for my weakened frame. I threw myself down by the fire and soon felt an attack of ague. The shivering fit lasted for two hours, and seemed the worst I had ever experienced: it was succeeded by a hot fit, which made me forget ice and snow. Toward evening I was somewhat better, but not in condition to continue my hunt; so I cleared away the snow, piled it up like a wall to keep off the wind, collected a good store of wood and slept calmly and sweetly through the night. Next day the ague had left me, but I felt very weak and remained all day extended before my warm fire, reading and enjoying my venison."

Like Audubon, this German Hawkeye enjoyed reading deer hunting tales while in the woods. Before the campfire that day, he read the deer hunting stories about famed Adirondack guide and deerslayer John Cheney (1800-1877), as recorded in Charles Fenno Hoffman's *Wild Scenes in the Forest and Prairie* (1839), a popular book which Gerstaecker later translated into German when he returned to his native country. Miller admired Cheney's prowess and mild demeanor as he chased whitetails in Essex County in the heart of the Adirondacks. Cheney reportedly shot more than 600 deer during a 13-year period of time.

Like Miller, Cheney had one cherished deerhound named "Buck," which by the time he was four years old had helped his master bag several hundred deer. "The only manly way to kill deer," Cheney insisted, "is by driving them, as I do, with a couple of hounds." Miller agreed. Like Miller, Cheney conducted most of his deer hunts for the sole purpose of venison acquisition, but like Miller, he too remained sensitive to matters of sportsmanship. It seems highly likely that both men in their quest for intimate knowledge of deer and deer hunting read Audubon's classic essay, "Deer Hunting," published in 1831 and widely disseminated during the late 1830s and early 1840s.

Like Oliver Hazard Perry on the Cass River in Michigan, Miller confronted violent storms with little more than a woolen blanket. As the sky grew cloudy and threatening one day, while deer hunting along the banks of the Fourche La Fave near Little Rock, he made a tent with his woolen blanket and collected enough dry fire wood to defy any quantity of rain:

"About midnight I was awakened by a formidable thunderstorm. Beargrease began to howl dreadfully, and close behind me an oak burst into flames. Flash followed flash, while the thunder was incessant; the whole forest seemed to swim in a lake of fiery brimstone, the rain poured in torrents, and the Fourche La Fave swelled into a foaming sea. When the storm ceased, silence and darkness took its place, only disturbed by the rustling of the rain falling perpendicularly on the leaves. My blanket protected me well; I was perfectly dry, and soon fast asleep again."

It seems incredible that he survived at all, sleeping in the wild during violent lightning storms, bunking in bear dens, dealing with malaria-infested swamps, attending a lynching, drinking whiskey with wild backwoods desperadoes, fighting with wounded bucks and bears, while relying only on a Bowie knife and a deerhound named "Beargrease."

This rough-cut, German deerslayer admitted himself that he did not shy away from a fight when his blood "was on the boil." Living in the high temper of backwoods society brought him into contact with some of the wildest barbarians imaginable. According to one of his biographers, "he was quick-tempered, ready with a blow when a blow seemed called for, and perhaps on the whole not adverse to a shindy."

On one of his last recorded deer hunts in the spring of 1842, along the Fourche La Fave, we find this great deer-hunting hobo "shooting deer again to my heart's content," as he writes in his hunting journal. For two days he lived exclusively "on whortle-berries, a fruit which by no means suited my stomach." After gaining access to the Arkansas River, he erected his fire-hunting equipment in his canoe and awaited the approaching night.

"As soon as it was dark I lighted my fire, then leant back, giving the reins to my fancy and gazing on the beautiful starry sky. After a time, raising myself silently and looking towards the place where I expected the deer, I saw a glowing eye just above the water, and another reflected from its surface; it was a deer, which had descended without the least noise, and was eagerly drinking the brackish water, about twenty paces from the canoe. I raised the rifle slowly, took a careful aim and fired; loud sounded the report over the water's surface, returning in repeated echoes from the hills, and then all was as quiet and silent as the grave. Taking a brand from the fire, I found a yearling buck lying dead at a short distance from the spot where he had been drinking."

After field dressing the buck, he roasted no small portion of deer meat to quell his painful hunger. He then placed the buck in his canoe, covered himself in raw deerskins and floated softly downstream in the stillness of the night, while lying next to the dead buck and Beargrease.

As he drifted along, he listened to the whippoorwills and the monotonous hooting of the owls and battled the infernal mosquitoes; sleep finally came and he arrived at Little Rock the next morning in good condition.

In many ways this vagabond spirit *became* the deer. He killed the deer and ate the deer meat seasoned with gunpowder. He stalked and aimlessly wandered through life like the white-tailed deer. He slept in raw deerskins next to dead bucks and dressed in buckskin that he himself tanned and made. He drank wild honey from a deer's leg and ate *Sassafras albidum* leaves and stems—the whitetail's preferred choice of food in the Ozarks.

A Good Chance, Currier & Ives, 1863, from an original painting from A.F. Tait. Between 1838 and 1842, Miller traveled the water-ways of the Ozarks in pursuit of white-tailed bucks with Slowtrap and his deerhound "Beargrease."

In his intimate attachment with the white-tail, this legendary Ozark deerslayer, this German Hawkeye, not only became the deer, but Natty Bumppo re-incarnated! This chronicler of American deer hunting considered himself a disciple of Cooper. Cooper inspired him to come to America and hunt deer. Like Cooper, he romanticized the deer-slayer and chastised arrogant man for his wasteful ways in managing nature, but unlike Cooper, he actually lived the life of Natty Bumppo.

After his six-and-a-half-year deer-hunting hiatus in America ended, Gerstaecker returned to Germany and wrote: "Of all I had seen in America, Arkansas was the place that pleased me most; I may never see it again, but I shall never forget the happy days I spent there hunting deer, where many a true heart beats under a deerskin leather hunting shirt."

Deer Driving on the Lakes, Northern New York, A.F. Tait, 1857.

"When we came within sight of the deer, the canoe

was allowed to float down with the current, and the steersman

laid it in a position the most advantageous for those who

were in the bow with guns. The deer would generally raise

their heads and stand looking … until the canoe came

within a few yards of them."

–Philip Tome

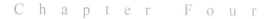

Chapter Four

THE PINE CREEK
DEERSLAYER

Throughout the pioneer stage of American history, deer hunters followed the track of the white-tailed deer not merely as a pleasure, but as a business and often a very important business. Many of these deer hunters, as frontier farmers, depended as much upon venison for their existence as on their cultivated crops and livestock.

Historically, every pioneer farmer became a deer hunter; they had to, for the whitetail supplied them with deerskins and venison, which they used to barter for the supplies they so direfully needed. But some of these pioneer farmers so enjoyed the deer hunt they became professional deer hunters, ultimately saying, "farewell to the plough."

Perhaps the most famous of these backwoods, pioneer deerslayers was Philip Tome (1782-1855), the Pine Creek Deerslayer of the Alleghenies, who wrote that classic hunting autobiography, *Pioneer Life, Or Thirty Years A Hunter* (1854). "This indomitable, Indian-looking Nimrod," as Pennsylvania historian Henry W. Shoemaker called him, whose prowess in the deer forest will never be forgotten, seemingly had but one ambition: to challenge the wiles of the whitetail in such a way that every hazard favored his adversary. In his *Extinct Pennsylvania Animals* (1917), Col.

The Hunter's Shanty, Currier & Ives, 1861. Tome lived in improvised hemlock deer shanties as he traveled Pennsylvania's Pine Creek Valley in pursuit of whitetails.

Inset: A portrait of Philip Tome, the "Pine Creek Deerslayer."

Courtesy of The Adirondack Museum.

Shoemaker called Tome, "the greatest of all Pennsylvania hunters of big game. He was a sportsman as well as a hunter, never killing recklessly."

Like his predecessors, this pioneer farmer turned deerslayer viewed white-tailed deer hunts as arduous, military campaigns to be waged, campaigns that often entailed blazing trails through dense, virgin underbrush for 10 to 12 miles at a time only to be interrupted by short catnaps in hollow trees or in the skins of freshly-killed, black bears. These Homeric deer hunts in the "Grand Canyon" of the Alleghenies literally lasted for months at a time, frequently terminating only when the snow melted and the deer tracks could no longer be followed. Through the mountainous terrain of the Alleghenies, he traveled by canoe, horse and sleigh, frequently hiring porters, cooks and camp-keepers to assist in the everyday activities of pioneer life.

From his earliest boyhood days in the Pine Creek Valley of Pennsylvania's Lycoming County, Philip Tome accustomed himself to the rugged life of the frontiersman. He shot deer with his father, Jacob Tome (1758-1814), with an old Jaeger Flintlock smooth bore musket loaded with buckshot at the early age of 12 and quickly learned the secrets of hunting them as well as the language of the Seneca Indians. He rattled antlers to attract bucks, snorted to stop them in their tracks and grunted to lure them into the vicinity of his shooting platforms.

He built fences around cornfields to entice and entrap does, which he then used as decoys for killing bucks during the rut; his deer hunting strategies were at a par with America's modern-day deer hunters. Like his Indian comrades, he loved living in quickly improvised hemlock shanties and regaled himself at the campfire eating trout and venison steak. But above all, he took great pride in the moment when he nailed a trophy

Greatly inspired by Tome's *Pioneer Life, or Thirty Years a Hunter*, modern-day Pennsylvania artist Jack Paluh illustrates the Seneca Indian deer hunting methods and traditions in which Tome participated and greatly cherished.

skull to the top of his hemlock lean-to.

Like most deer hunters, Tome served an apprenticeship with his father, but he also learned his first lessons in deer hunting from an old Pennsylvania buck hunter named John Mills, a pioneer farmer, who became so enamored with deer hunting that he quit farming and left for the Canadian wilderness. Before doing so, he offered to sell Tome one of his cherished deerhounds and to teach the young lad all he knew about white-tailed deer and deer hunting for 15 dollars; Tome accepted.

By the second decade of the 19th century, Tome established his deer hunting grounds near the headwaters of the Kettle, Pine, Sinnemahoning and Allegheny Rivers. In this area, especially the area near Pine Creek and Stump Creek, he killed a large number of white-tailed deer with his new 45-caliber, Kentucky-style Flintlock rifle made by E. Remington II, known as "Lite" around 1818, that he called "Sure Kill." He used part of the meat for his own purposes, but most of it he salted, cured and rafted downstream to be sold in the settlements along the river.

Tome loved outdoor adventure and "Big Woods" excitement; he was a good-natured man, rugged, muscular, active, and not easily frightened by anything. One pioneer settler, J. M. English of Jersey Shore, Pennsylvania, observed Tome at Irving Stephenson's Tavern at the mouth of Pine Creek pick up a barrel of whiskey and take a drink out of the bunghole. As Tome himself admitted, he "was never conquered by any man or animal."

By the age of 18, Tome was clearly more conversant with the howl of the wolves and the snort of white-tails than with the tones of civilized oratory. While hunting deer in October of 1800 along the banks of Pine Creek in Lycoming County, wolves flocked around him in droves. "Their unearthly howling," Tome recalls in his autobiography, "mingled with the dismal screeching of the owls overhead made a concert of sounds that banished sleep from my eyes the greater part of the night. I sat in my shanty, with my gun in one hand, a tomahawk in the other, and a knife by my side. When the wolves became unusually uproarious, I would send the dog out to drive them away, and if they drove him back in, I would fire in among them. At length, toward morning, I fell asleep from sheer exhaustion and slept until daylight, when I arose, ate my breakfast and started again on the deer track."

Indeed, while hunting and tracking deer, Tome actually used the wolves as his allies to his advantage, for they followed him for the entrails of the deer. "We could hear the wolves and foxes howling and barking in our rear, guided by our fires," Tome records. "We encouraged them in pursuing the deer ...The wolves and our dogs hunted together, sometimes one and sometimes the other obtained the deer and if it fell into our hands we always left the wolves their portion to keep them near, for we considered them of great assistance to us in deer hunting."

Tome employed various modes of deer hunting: fire-hunting, stalking, hounding and stand-hunting in elevated platforms over salt licks. Fire-hunting, however, remained his most successful mode of killing deer from the first of June to mid-January. Although fire-hunting deer was banned in Mississippi and Alabama as early as 1803, and prohibited in Florida in 1828, it wasn't banned in various counties in Pennsylvania until 1848. In his autobiography he describes this mode of deer hunting:

"The deer would come to the river after dark to eat the moss which grew on the bottom and collect together about the ripples in groups of from three to ten. The hunters would build a fire of yellow pitch pine in the middle of a canoe and station a man in the stern to steer and one or two more in front to fire at the deer. When there were no deer in sight they could push and paddle the canoe along. When they came within sight of the deer, the canoe was allowed to float down with the current, and the steersman laid it in a position the most advantageous for those who were in the bow with guns. The deer would generally raise their heads and stand looking at the fire until the canoe came within a few yards of them.

"The hunters could judge by their movements whether they would make a break or stand still until they came near them, and fired or not according to the movements of the deer. When the deer attempted to run out of the water where the bank was bluff and steep, they would see their own shadows and thinking it was a dog or a wolf, would utter a snort and spring back into the water, sometimes coming near enough to the canoe to give the hunter two or three more shots at them."

In this manner, Tome sometimes killed four deer in one place. After field dressing the deer, he laid the venison on shore and proceeded down the river in search of another group. Some nights he obtained as many as ten whitetails following this spectacular procedure. On his return, he would fish for salmon and pick up the venison as he came along. His canoes could carry up to 4000 pounds safely; when he returned to his log cabin in the morning, he had enough salmon and venison for two months for an ordinary family. On one occasion while fire-

Yukon Trouble by Lynn Bogue Hunt. Tome was clearly more conversant with the howl of wolves and the snort of whitetails than civilized oratory.

hunting deer along the banks of Pine Creek with a Nimrod named Clark from Vermont, Tome got one deer without even firing old "Sure Kill:"

"Pushing up the stream about seven miles, we turned and commenced floating down at nine o'clock. After proceeding about a mile, Clark, who sat forward, saw a large buck, a short distance ahead. He fired and wounded the animal, when it wheeled and attempted to plunge over the canoe. Clark held up his hand to protect himself, which frightened the buck still more; he sprang across the canoe giving Clark a blow between the eyes with its hind feet, knocking him prostrate. I asked him if he was hurt, and he replied that he was nearly killed. I pushed ashore as soon as possible, and took him out of the canoe. His face was bathed in blood and presented a ghastly appearance. Upon washing away the blood I discovered that he was not as badly injured as I had feared. There was a severe contusion in the spot where he was struck, but the skin was not broken; the blood had dropped from the wounded deer.

"I then went after the deer which I found lying down badly wounded but not dead. I finished it with a ball through the head and dragged it to the canoe. We floated down a mile, when we saw a buck and doe eating moss. Clark fired, killing the buck and the doe ran ashore, when, becoming frightened at her shadow, she leaped back toward the canoe. As she raised to spring over, I hit her on the nose with a paddle, and she fell back into the canoe, when I cut her throat. We then floated down, picked up our buck, and proceeded homeward with three deer, one of which had not cost us even a shot."

On another occasion, it seemed that even an infinite supply of gunpowder and lead from "Sure Kill" could not down the deer. In his autobiography, Tome recalls what happened:

"About the middle of July in 1805, Morrison, Francis and myself were out on a hunt. Going up the creek about five miles, we commenced floating down, and soon shot a deer, which we stowed away in our canoe. When we had gone a short distance farther,

Life in the Woods: Starting Out, a hand-colored lithograph by Currier & Ives, based on a painting by Louis Maurer (1880), shows a group of deer hunters preparing for a night's hunt on the river.

Let Him Go, circa 1851, shows a typical float-hunting scene from Tome's time.

© Christie's Images, Inc.

flour, potatoes, sugar, chocolate, corn and a good quantity of salt with which to cure the venison. They also equipped themselves with six empty barrels for the meat, an iron pot holding about six gal-lons, a camp kettle, four axes, a broadax, a chalk line, a canoe howel (an instrument for scooping water out of canoes), a drawing knife, two augers, six tomahawks and three to four pounds of gunpowder and lead. Each hunter took a rifle and a musket, two knives, a quart cup, four shirts, two blankets and a good supply of soap. Thus equipped and accompanied by four deer hounds, Tome and his comrades pushed upstream with their hewed-out canoe; two hunters in the canoe while the other two hunted along the shore.

The augers Tome carried with him were used to bore holes in black oak logs into which he poured three pints of salt and a small quantity of saltpeter. He would then insert a plug in each hole. He found that when the wood became saturated with salt, the deer would gnaw at it. When the deer responded to his salt lick, he proceeded immediately to build a scaffold within three to four rods of the salt so that the deer became accustomed to the sight of it before he attempted to hunt from it. While in pursuit of venison and buckskin, he traveled from deer lick to deer lick—from Stony Lick to Mud Lick to Rock Lick—for all of these deer licks were eventually named and placed on the hunting maps of his time. His travels frequently ended at Irving Stephenson's Tavern at the mouth of Pine Creek where in the company of other deerslayers and pioneer farmers he ate venison jerky, drank

two of us saw a deer in the stream and both fired at the same time but neither appeared to hit it. We re-loaded and directed the man who was steering to run the canoe to the shore. We then stood on the shore, about thirty rods from the deer and each fired eight shots at it, as rapidly as we could load, when our guns became so hot that we were compelled to stop. The steersman had been holding up the torch for us to see by, yet the position of the animal was the same as when first observed. At each shot it seemed to spring up, each time higher and higher, then dropping into the same spot. We then threw sticks at it, to drive it away, when it gave two or three leaps and suddenly disappeared. This affair may appear somewhat strange to the reader, as it did to me, but the facts are as I have stated, and always appeared to me unaccountable."

Most of us would probably attribute this unaccountable affair to that vicious malady—buck fever. Southern deer hunting gentlemen today would characterize the incident as "burning the barrel hot!"

Expecting his deer hunting campaigns to last about six weeks at a time, Tome always took along an abundant supply of provisions. For four hunters they consisted of wine "pretty freely," as he acknowledged, and talked about deer and expanded upon the deer hunting tales of his time.

Tome also enjoyed hunting deer with hounds. Hounding deer was not prohibited in Pennsylvania until 1897. He kept two large deerhounds for this purpose and believed that the best dog for deer hunting was "half bloodhound, a quarter cur and the other quarter greyhound." He took great pride in his deerhounds. In his *Pioneer Life*, he proudly boasted "when they were once in chase of a deer, they would not lose one in ten. So famous did they become for their prowess, that if any of the neighbors saw them running, they would exclaim, 'There are Tome's dogs; the deer cannot be far off.' The deer could never baffle them by any of their usual stratagems, and they would often run them down before they reached the water. Those wishing to deer hunt successfully should always procure, at any cost, the largest and best dogs to be found."

Between deer hunts, Tome conducted a profitable business of capturing live elk, exhibiting them to all interested spectators, and later selling them alive for as much as 500 dollars a head. Laying his musket and rifle aside, but with the aid of his dog and a Native American named Billy Fox, he caught several live, full-grown elk by hand along the banks of the Susquehanna. In 1816, according to McKnight's *History of Northwestern Pennsylvania*, Tome captured the largest elk ever secured in Pennsylvania. Using ropes, poles, nooses, horses and four hunting hounds, and after giving chase for 14 strenuous miles, Tome and his party finally brought an elk that "stood sixteen hands high and had antlers six feet long with eleven points on each side" to bay on a large rock and promptly anchored the animal to surrounding trees. Tome successfully managed to get the elk alive to the Allegheny River in sub-zero weather. He then floated the animal on a raft to Olean Point. From there, Tome traveled with the elk through New York State to Albany, exhibiting him for profit; at Albany, Tome sold the elk for 500 dollars.

While at least one historian of hunting likens Tome's white-tailed deer hunting accounts to the famous tales of Baron Von Munchausen, Tome's elk and deer hunting conquests led Chief Cornplanter, a distinguished Chief of the Seneca tribe for whom Tome served as an interpreter, to bestow upon him the title "The Allegheny Elk Hunter." With regard to the strength and physical size of the elk he caught, Tome proudly boasted, "I did not care how large—the larger the better."

In his deer hunting memoirs, Tome reports that in one deer season that lasted from June until mid-January he killed 137 white-tailed deer; during his lifetime he killed more than 1000 deer. He usually averaged 130 big game animals per season. His descendants estimate that at least 500 noble panthers fell to Tome's unerring bullets. These figures almost seem incomprehensible given the rules and regulations of today. Indeed, his yearly deer kill statistics surpass the lifetime expectations of the modern-day deer hunter. Yet, like James Fenimore Cooper and Audubon, contemporary writers on sporting ethics, Tome maintained a strong ethical code with respect to his deer hunting. His code of ethics could have been penned by Cooper or Audubon; it stands as a classic model for the deer hunters of today:

"I never wantonly killed a deer, when I could gain nothing by its destruction. With the true hunter it is not the destruction of life which affords the pleasure of the chase; it is the excitement attendant upon the very uncertainty of it which induces men even to leave luxurious homes and expose themselves to the hardships and perils of the wilderness. Even when, after a weary chase, the game is brought down, he cannot, after the first thrill of triumph, look without a pang of remorse, upon the form which was so beautifully adapted to its situation, and which his hand has reduced to a mere lump of flesh."

These words Tome wrote at the age of 72. Perhaps the flow of time soothed some of the fiery enthusiasm of youth; but nevertheless the sentiment and ethic ring true, thus giving Tome a spiritual kinship across more than a century and a half with the 12 million American deer hunters of today.

Although census data for Corydon Township in Warren County indicates that Tome listed his occupation as a pioneer farmer and lumber man, the wild and thrilling adventures of his autobiography clearly suggest that he was a pioneer farmer turned professional deerslayer, but a deerslayer, like Cooper's Natty Bumppo, with early conservationist leanings, who strongly subscribed to the deer hunting code of ethics of Natty Bumppo in Cooper's *The Deerslayer* (1841):

"They call me Deerslayer. I'll own; and perhaps I deserve the name, in the way of understanding the creature's habits, as well as for the certainty in the aim; but they can't accuse me of killing an animal when there is no occasion for the meat or the skin. I may be a slayer, it's true, but I'm no slaughterer ...I never yet pulled a trigger on buck or doe, unless when food or clothes was wanting."

For more than 60 years, Tome roamed the Pine Creek Valley west to the Allegheny River, east to the west branch of the Susquehanna, south to the Clarion River and north into New York to hunt deer along the banks of the Susquehanna. He often traveled in excess of 20 to 30 miles a day, frequently confronting 450-pound black bears in their dens. He killed bears while asleep and slept in bear and panther dens, when he didn't have time to construct shanties of hemlock brush.

In December of 1818, he started out on a deer hunting expedition with John Campbell, a Warren County deerslayer, Joseph Darling, a sawmill owner, and his Seneca deer-hunting partner, Billy Fox. Before the year ended, this adventurous threesome traveled to Buckville, New York and participated in one of the most famous deer drives in the history of this country. In *Early Times on the Susquehanna* (1870), historian Mrs. George A. Perkins chronicles this massive deer drive, which entailed 200 men armed with hounds, horses, guns, and rifles—some men coming from Pennsylvania and others from New York, but all coming with great gusto:

"Up men! arouse for the chase!
The wild buck is quitting his lair,
The hills are gilded with light,
And there's health in the balmy air."

The drivers formed a circle of men several miles in extent with the "marshals of the day, at the head of their respective commands, and clothed with due authority." The line of the New York drivers stretched from Chemung River, near Buckville, across the hills to Shepard's Creek on the north. As they approached their rendezvous, the woods rang out with rifle shots. In the heat of the excitement, the anxious men shot in every direction and, as Mrs. Perkins notes, "with rashness and recklessness." Many a buck fell, as did one die-hard, Pennsylvania deerslayer himself named "Big Decker." But his wound was only slight and "Big Decker" finished the ordeal in the upright position still riding his horse into battle.

When the belching "smoke pipes" fell silent, the deerslayers dressed, skinned and divided 30 white-tailed deer. As the hunters dispersed to their respective settlements, Tome, Campbell and Billy Fox departed for the "Grand Canyon" of Pine Creek Valley with their hewed-out canoes filled with deerskins and venison.

Philip Tome was no crude, backwoods barbarian. In reading his *Pioneer Life*, a rare book of interest to the American deer hunter and student of pioneer life, we learn that he read extensively and enjoyed a good command of the English language. Historians suspect that in addition to reading the novels of James Fenimore Cooper, that portray deer hunting as a proper mode of ecological consciousness, he also read Sir Walter Scott and Henry W. Longfellow.

He was also a keen student of deer behavior. In addition to his extensive personal experiences with the animal, he probably read the standard work on the subject during his day: Dr. John Godman's classic essay "The Common Deer," published in his popular *American Natural History* (1826), which went through many editions during Tome's life. He also read the leading sportsman journals of the day: the *Spirit of the Times* and the *American Turf Register and Sporting Magazine*.

As an interpreter for Cornplanter and Governor Blacksnake, Indian Chiefs of the Allegheny River, the Seneca Indians placed an implicit faith in his character, integrity and honesty. He was also well acquainted with Red Jacket and Black Hawk. At the early age of 18 in 1790, he recorded verbatim Cornplanter's famous speech to President Washington in Philadelphia. We recognize the names of those who hunted with Tome as well-to-do gentlemen, businessmen and others who emerged in a prominent way in the early pioneer days of Pennsylvania.

Historians of hunting recognize Tome as more than an ordinary deer hunter. Charles Sheldon, a collector and curator of one of the finest libraries ever assembled on North American big game hunting, classifies Tome's *Pioneer Life* as "remarkable and accurate and one of the prize books of my library." Like his friend Sheldon, Theodore Roosevelt believed that no matter how thrilling a deer hunting narrative might be, it did not appeal to him unless it was also great literature. Tome's deer hunting narrative lives up to Roosevelt's exacting standard.

As a work of literature, Henry W. Shoemaker, that prominent chronicler of America's deer-hunting legends, tales and folklore and pioneer Chairman of the Pennsylvania Historical Commission, unhesitatingly recommended it "as the great and outstanding contemporary narrative of the Pennsylvania big game fields ...and one of the most valuable and interesting records of early frontier life and history relative to the State of Pennsylvania."

In the interests of promoting Pennsylvania's heritage, Shoemaker edited and published a new edition of Tome's autobiography in 1928. Not surprisingly, the *Saturday Review of Literature* viewed it as "a source book for the mores of the fringe of the first American frontier." Today the book remains one of the rarest works on the American pioneer hunter and the best example of early, 19th-century life in Pennsylvania's deer woods. This 1928 edition, limited to 500 signed copies, if found today in the out-of-print book market, sells for approximately $500.

An unpublished letter dated October 22, 1855, in the Wisconsin State Historical Society written by Tome's wife, Mary, indicates that the book sold for 72 cents in 1855. Today, few copies of the original edition exist; an original copy is as rare and expensive as a Boone and Crockett, world-class, white-tailed buck, such as the Arthur Young buck, the oldest buck in the Boone and Crockett Club, a 12-pointer shot in 1830 near Norwich in McKean County in the heart of Tome's deer-hunting turf—scoring

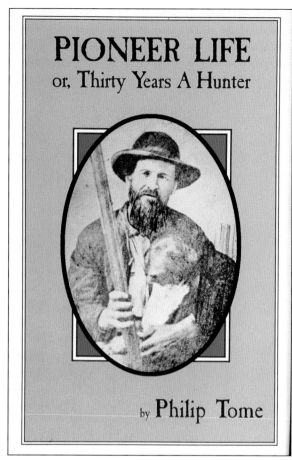

The 1989 Ayer reprint of Tome's classic includes a two-page preface by hunting historian Henry W. Shoemaker and a lengthy appendix by publisher A. M. Aurand.

175 4/8 typical points.

I have collected blue-chip deer books for more than 35 years and have only seen an original copy listed once in an out-of-print book catalogue: Callahan & Company Booksellers' Catalogue #86 published in May of 1996, listed the 1854 Buffalo imprint in original binding for $4500. In 1971, Arno Press and *The New York Times* reprinted the original 1854 edition as part of their First American Frontier series from a rare copy owned by the Wisconsin State Historical Society. Unfortunately, that inexpensive edition is out of print. *Books in Print* (2003), lists the 1991 edition, published by the Reprint Services Corporation, as still in print for $69. A 1989 Ayer reprint is also available on the Internet for $30 from Wennawoods Publishing and Lord Nelson's Book Store.

Towards the end of Tome's life, man still placed venison on the free lunch counters of the better saloons in Pittsburgh and Philadelphia and deerslayers such as Philip Tome kept these free lunch counters well stocked with venison loin. He died on April 30, 1855, in Corydon on the Allegheny at the age of 73. He is buried near Chief Cornplanter in the Riverview-Corydon Cemetery on a hill above the Allegheny Reservoir just below the New York State line. In 1989, several Tome descendants erected a new marker engraved with two white-tailed deer—a buck and a doe eating vegetation along the banks of the Allegheny—as a final tribute to the Pine Creek deerslayer.

According to historian Dan Neal, if you travel the haunted deer hunting grounds of unspoiled areas in the Alleghenies today, you will still hear the footsteps of Tome as he tramps the deer trails that lead to the Allegheny, the Kinzua, the Kettle and the Pine, "For surely this hunter has gone with his Indians friends to the Happy Hunting Grounds." Indeed, Tome loved Native American legend and lore; he learned many lessons while hunting deer with his Native American friends Billy Fox, George Silverheels, Morris Halftown and John Geebuck.

When Tome died in 1855, A. F. Tait issued his famous deer print *Still Hunting on the First Snow: A Second Shot*. Currier and Ives then reprinted it as *Deer Shooting on the Shattagee*. In 1855, Henry W. Longfellow (1807-1882) also published his epic poem *The Song of Hiawatha*. These works of art portray the deerslayer dressed in his yellow shirt of deerskin and buckskin leggings as a cultural hero. In Longfellow's narrative poem, Hiawatha hunts red deer with a bow made from a branch of ash and arrows from an oak-bough. Clad in deerskin shirt and buckskin leggings, like Philip Tome, Hiawatha encounters a roebuck. Had Tome

Courtesy of Wegner's Photo Collection.

White-tailed deer grace the Tome tombstone as a final tribute to the Pine Creek Deerslayer.

lived longer, he would have recited from memory the following lines:

"Then, upon one knee uprising,
Hiawatha aimed an arrow;
Scarce a twig moved with his motion,
Scarce a leaf was stirred or rustled,
But the wary roebuck started,
Stamped with all his hoofs together,
Listened with one foot uplifted,
Leaped as if to meet the arrow;
Ah! the stinging, fatal arrow,
Like a wasp it buzzed and stung him!
Dead he lay there in the forest.
By the ford across the river;
Beat his timid heart no longer,
But the heart of Hiawatha
Throbbed and shouted and exulted,
As he bore the red deer homeward."

Pioneer farmers turned deerslayers such as Philip Tome remain in a class of their own and emerge as heroes in their respective deer-hunting turfs. As long as man tramps the back forty in pursuit of the white-tailed deer, nostalgic memories of their daring feats will linger on: memories of their endless pursuits of mammoth bucks, their victorious conflicts with the "hooves and horns" of their wounded

quarry and the shattering effect of their deer kill statistics.

Although our early American deerslayers killed thousands of deer, as the white-tailed deer became more scarce by the end of the 19th century, they gradually began to react against the savage tendencies of the market hunting prevalent in their day. They now emphasized respect and esthetic appreciation for nature. Combining nostalgia for what they considered the wilder hunting of the past with the moral imperatives of gentle manliness, they championed the general code of sporting ethics called sportsmanship. While they did not regret their commercial hunting of the past, they overwhelmingly proposed a wiser usage of the natural resource towards the end of their lives.

In their writings, they strongly emphasized combining the study of nature with the hunting experience and sought to restrain hunting methods and appetites. The added dimension of communing with nature and scientific curiosity gradually replaced their trigger-itch. While their notions of conservation remained hazy, the blazing-away subsided.

In changing his attitude later in life, Philip Tome de-emphasized the importance of the

American Winter Sports: Deer Shooting on the Shattaggee, Currier & Ives, 1855. In this winter scene, which is based on a painting by Louis Maurer, two deer hunters hide behind a cluster of pines. One takes aim at a group of three deer while an already downed white-tailed buck lies behind them.

kill, or the number of kills, and underscored instead the tonic quality of the outdoor experience and the redemptive and educational aspects of the deer-hunting ceremony and ritual. Deer hunting must become an art, he insisted, an ennobling and instructive ceremony in which the hunter confirms his manhood and self-mastery in the deer forest, but not at the expense of the natural resource.

By the second half of the 19th century, an idealistic type of deer hunter emerged in America called the hunter-naturalist, who viewed deer hunting as the best possible mode of environmental perception. While Tome did not see the development of this movement, he abandoned his market gunning in favor of a firm commitment to conserva-

tion, the hunter-naturalist ideal and the attendant code of sportsmanship. Had he lived longer, he probably would have wandered the deer forest for science and sport like his hunter-naturalist descendants, such as Henry William Herbert ("Frank Forester").

In reliving the adventures of such early American deerslayers as Philip Tome, we do not merely yearn for yesteryear, but we bestow ultimate meaning upon the persons and places of America's deer-hunting heritage—and to some degree its future— upon the 12 million American deer hunters who pursue America's 32 million white-tailed deer with the same enthusiasm and determination of The Pine Creek Deerslayer, Philip Tome.

Long Jakes, The Rocky Mountain Man, by Charles Deas, 1844. Denver Art Museum Collection.

"Everything here is real, useful, yet how showy,

and how more than romantic."

—Henry William Herbert in June 1846 edition of
New York Illustrated Magazine of Literature and Art

Chapter Five

"FRANK FORESTER"

When hunter/naturalist Henry William Herbert (1807-1858), known more popularly under the pseudonym "Frank Forester," arrived in New York City in the spring of 1831, Audubon had just published his essay entitled "Deer Hunting," a colorful and spirited account that induced its readers, Frank Forester included, to course deer on horseback with shotguns, hounds and bugles. The cry of the deerhounds, the sight of galloping horses and the sounds of hunting horns obviously inflamed the author's imagination when he wrote this essay. Forester read Audubon's essay with great delight and responded by saying:

"This is *the sport*, par excellence. He who has ridden once to a good pack, in the open, over a good scenting country, with a well-bred one under him, whether the game be pug in England, or a ten-antlered buck in Carolina, will hold deer driving or deer stalking as mighty slow sport in all time thereafter."

In addition to coursing deer, Frank Forester's deer hunts, like Natty Bumppo's, consisted of floating in a canoe on the lakes and waterways of the Adirondacks. Some of his more complex and challenging still-hunts exceeded distances of 25 miles or

"The Cedars" was the residence of "Frank Forester." According to his biographer, William Southworth Hunt, "no author's dwelling had grown more familiar by name to the world of sporting literature … than was 'The Cedars.'"

Inset: A portrait of Henry William Herbert, who wrote under the pseudonym "Frank Forester."

more. Like Audubon, Frank Forester was a superb shot with his double-barreled shotgun. And like Audubon, his deer hunts usually ended sitting in the glow of the campfire, eating venison steak and indulging in a "brimming bumper or two of port." One can still hear the toasts of his club of good fellows:

"A Club of good fellows we meet once a year,
When the leaves of the forest are
withered and sear;
By the motto that shines
on each glass it is shown
We drink in our cups the deserving alone.
A bumper, a bumper, ourselves right true men,
We'll fill it and drink it again and again!"

Forester arrived in New York at a time when magazines were growing to mass-market size. "Into the hard, hostile publishing environment of New York," his biographer Luke White, Jr. writes, "stepped the twenty-four-year-old Henry William Herbert, a tall, muscular young man, fashionably dressed, who was a charming gentleman when he wanted to be, but an arrogant, overbearing brawler when opposed."

He eventually took up residence in a cozy country retreat called "The Cedars," on the Passaic River, near Newark, New Jersey. According to one observer, "The Cedars" contained more deer antlers than furniture. From the outside, "The Cedars" took on the image of a Swiss chalet. A deer skull hung over the entry hall, together with a vast array of deer-hunting memorabilia. His residence resembled an elegant, monastic, deer-hunting lodge in the best traditions of Europe. It became well known as the home of America's preeminent sportsman. According to another biographer, William Southworth Hunt, "no author's dwelling had grown more familiar by name to the world of sporting literature ... than was 'The Cedars.'"

Due chiefly to the vast volume of his con-

tributions to early American periodicals, this eccentric and engaging figure played an important part in the development of the magazine in America. As an editor and writer of magazine literature, his work soon appeared in John Stuart Skinner's *American Turf Register and Sporting Magazine*, as well as William T. Porter's *Spirit of the Times*. He eventually became Porter's resident naturalist in the *Spirit* and America's most popular nature writer.

He focused his deer hunting tales on Natty Bumppo and the excitement and adventure of the deer hunt. His deer hunting tales exhibited more of a sentimental romanticism than the backwoods realism of Tome and "Miller." He met at the office of the *Spirit* at Barclay Street dressed in deerskins and later at the Appleton's Building at the corner of

Courtesy of Wegner's Photo Collection.

Many of Forester's readers referred to him as "the Shakespeare of sporting literature."

Deer-stalking in the Adirondacks in Winter by Homer, 1871. Frank Forester believed that deer were to be stalked, not shot from platforms overlooking salt licks or driven onto crushed snow.

Broadway and Leonard Street. Here he consorted with editor Porter and such popular writers as William Elliott. When not at the office of the *Spirit*, this tall, muscular man with the heavily matted locks and bushy, shaggy eyebrows hung out at the Dutchman's Tavern near Warwick, New York. This mustachioed, square-jawed deer-slayer preferred the Adirondacks to Broadway, a bout of fisticuffs to the silk attractions of the ballroom.

Born in London and educated in Eaton and Cambridge, Frank Forester, more than any one individual, presented to the American sportsman the accumulated wisdom and ethics of the English nimrod. Forester, known in his day as the father of woodcraft literature, believed that the true sportsman must acquire and develop a specialized language, a code of ethics, fashionable attire and a deep and pro-

found interest in natural history. Many of his readers referred to him as "the Shakespeare of sporting literature."

In sportsmanship, Frank Forester emerged as a man in advance of his times. White-tailed deer, Forester insisted, were to be stalked, not shot from platforms overlooking salt licks and certainly not driven onto crushed snow, where the hunter had all the advantages in his favor. Like Audubon, Forester fiercely denounced deer poachers and fire-hunters.

Frank Forester became one of the earliest proponents of preserving natural areas for recreational purposes and one of the greatest enemies of America's reckless use of natural resources. He viewed habitat destruction and commercial over-shooting as two of the greatest evils facing wildlife of his time. "More than half a century before such thoughts were common currency," George Reiger reports in *Wildlife and America*

(2001), Forester "continually urged his fellow sportsmen to outlaw destructive shooting practices and to enforce wildlife protection laws already on the books."

Indeed, Forester played a very important role in the formative years of American conservation. As an avid deer hunter and popular writer, Forester introduced American sportsmen to a new ethic, an ethic that Gifford Pinchot later labeled conservation. His writings on deer and deer hunting remain important because they established a scientific framework for the identification of deer among sportsmen, dealt with the techniques of deer hunting in a serious manner, and inspired the passage of stricter game laws in several states.

His sporting literature also created a fraternity of sportsmen around the country, who kept alive the gentleman's ideal of the sporting life. His inspiration ultimately led to the founding of the New York Sportsmen's Club on May 20, 1844, that played a very significant role in the early promotion of game protection and hunting ethics.

Writing under the highly successful pen name of Frank Forester, he attempted to popularize sportsmanship. "I have ventured myself," he writes in his popular *Frank Forester's Field Sports* (1848), a book that went through 13 editions between 1848 and 1873 and still remains in print today, "as the champion of American sport and sportsmanship." In doing so, he elevated the title of "sportsman" by shifting the focus to the pristine world of nature and to the romance, excitement and adventure of the hunt.

In the words of his editor David W. Judd, "he aimed to give the word a higher, broader meaning. He believed that if our American men could be drawn from their offices ... to forest and field, to breathe pure air and commune with nature, they would be benefited physically, morally, and mentally, and come to enjoy a larger existence. He expressed this belief in his daily conversations ... "

No one individual better articulates the ultimate excitement, romance, adventure and love of natural history that accompany the pursuit of deer than Frank Forester. In his writings, Forester skirts the boundary lines between the world of fiction and non-fiction, between the nature essay and the fictional sketch. In his articles in the *American Turf Register and Sporting Magazine* and the *Spirit of the Times*, Herbert brings to life the genteel and amiable sportsman Frank Forester and his companion Harry Archer (also based on Herbert himself) and a long list of other colorful characters drawn from Herbert's hunting companions and the literary and social crowd associated with the *Spirit of the Times*.

In doing so, Herbert soon realized the tremendous popular appeal the American

Samuel Washington Woodhouse by Edward Bowers, 1857. American naturalists like Samuel W. Woodhouse, who accompanied government surveys of the Far West in the 1850s, portrayed themselves as backwoods hunters.

public had for the character of Frank Forester, and consequently "played the role of Forester in real life so that this ideal sportsman became almost an alter ego for him," as Stephen Meats observes in the *Dictionary of Literary Biography* (1979). He frequently appeared on the streets of New York dressed in fringed buckskin clothing with his long, wavy, brown hair adorned with a huntsman's cap, and his percussion-lock muzzleloader under his arm. In many ways he resembled the buckskin-clad Audubon himself.

In one of his earliest deer hunting sketches, "The Outlying Stag," originally published in the *American Turf Register* in 1838, we find Frank Forester, Harry Archer, the Commodore and Tom Draw (his hunting friend Thomas Ward) in a quaint, backwoods tavern preparing for a white-tailed deer hunt in the Warwick woodlands of Orange County, New York.

The day starts with a hearty breakfast of cold venison and biscuits in front of a snapping fire, as the deerstalkers enjoy a peculiar mixture of Jamaica rum mixed with sugar and hot milk. Their pre-dawn conversation revolves around their personal preferences in hunting clothes and the effectiveness of their various rifles. Before the sun rises, the deer stalkers are all on horseback trotting at a quick pace toward the last reported sighting of a white-tailed buck in a cherished deer-hunting area called Round Top, which Forester graphically describes in great detail: "Before them lay the high and ridgy head of Round Top, its flanks sloping toward them in two broad pine-clad knobs with a wild streamlet brawling down between them, and a thick tangled swamp of small extent, but full of tall dense thorn bushes, matted with vines and cat-briers, and carpeted with a rich undergrowth of fern and wintergreen and whortleberries. To the right and left of the two knobs or spurs were two other deep gorges, or dry channels, bare of brushwood, and stony—rock-walled, with steep precipitous ledges toward the mountain, but sloping easily up to the lower ridges."

After the standers position themselves along the ridges of Round Top, the drivers soon release the deerhounds. In advance of sunrise, Forester's rifle cracks, announcing to the hunters that a whitetail is afoot, but that shot Frank fired to no avail. All present could now hear "the shrill yelping rally of the hounds ... Fiercer and wilder grew the hubbub! And now the eager watcher could hear the brushwood torn in all directions by the impetuous passage of the wild deer and his inveterate pursuers."

"Bang!" came the report of Tom Draw's large, 10-pound, double-barreled shotgun as the buck passed his

The Hunter's Dilemma, A.F. Tait, 1851. Forester experienced his share of dilemmas while hunting whitetails on the rock walls and steep, precipitous ledges of "Round Top," Forester's cherished deer hunting area.

stand within 15 yards, but that shot only grazed the deer in the ear. Harry Archer finally discharged his "ponderous missile" at the fleeing buck with the ball going clean through the buck's neck.

"Yet ... the stag dashed onward, with the blood gushing out in streams from the wide wound, though as yet neither speed nor strength appeared to be impaired, so fleetly did he scour the meadow." In his escape, the buck once again passed Forester's stand. Forester's double barrel cracked once more. This time a splintered brow tine flew through the air.

"Give him the other barrel!" cried Archer. "The other barrel!" But Frank's gun was empty. In a daring attempt to end this whitetailed buck's career, Archer, in the true spirit of Audubon, spurs his horse and dashes after the galloping wounded buck with the deerhounds in hot pursuit. In his attempt to ride the buck down, he crosses behind the buck and swings himself halfway out of the saddle. He manages to strike the buck with his knife, but suddenly the horse stumbles. Forester describes that thrilling moment in chilling prose:

"Horse, stag, and man, all rolled upon the ground within the compass of ten yards — the terrified and wounded deer striking out furiously in all directions ... To increase the fury and the peril of the scene, the hounds

THE DEER STALKERS.

BY

FRANK FORESTER.

PHILADELPHIA:

T. B. PETERSON & BROTHERS.

The Hunter's Pride was the frontispiece for Frank Forester's *The Deer Stalkers*, published in 1843.

came up, and added their fresh fierceness to the confusion.

"Running in behind the struggling quarry, Archer seized the brow antler, and at one strong and skillful blow severed the jugular. One gush of dark red gore—one plunging effort, and the superb and stately buck lay motionless forever—while the loud death halloo rang over the broad valley—all fears, all perils, utterly forgotten in the strong rapture of that thrilling moment."

One of the most highly-charged deer chases ever recorded in the history of American deer hunting, we find in Forester's *The Deer Stalkers*, published in 1843 after being serialized in *Graham's American Monthly Magazine* several years earlier. In this novel, one of his most famous works of fiction, Herbert tried to imitate Cooper's *The Deerslayer*. The book still remains in print 160 years after its original date of publication. *Books in Print* (2003), lists a 1992 edition by Reprint Services Corporation for $90. In the novel, Herbert transforms a simple deer-hunting excursion into a murder mystery similar to Mark Sullivan's *The Purification Ceremony* (1997), but with a gentleman deer hunter as the hero.

In this stirring portrait of American deer hunting in the southwestern counties of New York, Forester constructs a brilliant sketch of the chase based on the ethical proposition, as he so aptly proclaimed, "that there is not only much practical, but much moral utility in the Gentle Science of Woodcraft."

In this sketch, Forester compares the expert woodsmanship of the mid-19th century deerslayer to the nose of the Bloodhound: "No written instructions can give this lore to the tyro; nothing but long practice, and the closest experience, can give to the eye of man the ability to follow the path of the devious and pasturing deer, through every variety of soil and surface, with a certainty as unerring as that attained by the nose of the Bloodhound."

Herbert's annual deer hunting trips to the woodlands of Orange County and the lakes of the Adirondacks, especially an area known as "Old John Brown's Tract," provide the background for this classic tale unequaled in the annals of the literature on American deer hunting. The following poem sets the stage for Forester's portrait of the early American deer hunt:

"Mark! How they file adown the rocky pass, –
Bright creatures, fleet, and beautiful, and free,–
With winged bounds that spurn
the unshaken grass,
And Swan-like necks sublime, –
their eloquent eyes
Instinct with liberty, – their antlered crests,
In clear relief against the glowing sky,
Haught and majestic!"

Like most deer hunting stories, Forester's account begins with the first flush of autumn as Frank's boys cross the woodland hills in a horse-drawn carriage en route to the Dutchman's Tavern. Through the fast-fading twilight they rattle along—singing, laughing, and jesting all the way, making the deer forest ring with music. Just as the young moon climbs into the sky, they arrive at the little, old, stone tavern nestled so closely into the wooded terrain that its existence remains unsuspected.

Dutch Jake, the owner, opens the door as Frank's boys enter the bar, a large room dimly lit by homemade tallow candles and blazing and snapping hickory logs in the large, open fireplace. Forester describes the shelves of this holy sanctum for us: "They were garnished with sundry kegs of liquor, painted bright green, and labeled with the names of the contents in black characters on gilded scrolls. These, with two or three dull-looking decanters of snakeroot whiskey and other kinds of 'bitters'; a dozen heavy-bottomed tumblers, resembling in shape the half of an hour-glass, set up on the small end; and a considerable array of tobacco-pipes, constituted all the furniture of Jake's bar and promised but little for the drinkableness of the Dutchman's drinkables."

Despite the questionable nature of Jake's snakeroot whiskey for the more refined

"Tis the hound giving tongue! He is driving the deer!" A sketch from Forester's *The Deer Stalkers*.

tastes of Frank's sporting companions, they nonetheless made their way to the bar with the vociferous Fat Tom, a fictional character based on the mammoth and eccentric Tom Ward of the village tavern in Warwick, a well-known man to the sportsmen of New York in those days, hollering, "Jake you darned old cuss, look alive, and make a gallon of hot Dutch rum to rights!" With a burst of laughter the deer stalkers begin to steep their souls in old Dutch Jake's strange compound of Santa Cruz rum, hot water, allspice, brown sugar, and peppercorns.

Following a brace of larded grouse and brazed ham, brought forth with "odoriferous steam" and numerous quart pewter mugs of champagne, imported to the Dutchman's Tavern from New York for the occasion, Frank's boys indulge in yarn spinning until late into the evening. Before retiring for the evening, Forester quotes directly from the gospel of Alfred Street:

"But hark to that sound
stealing faint through the wood!
Heart hammers, breath thickens,
swift rushes the blood!
It swells from the thicket
more loud and more near
'Tis the hound giving tongue!
he is driving the deer!
My rifle is leveled–swift tramplings are heard–
A rustle of leaves–then with flight like a bird,
His antlers thrown back,
and his body in motion
With quick rise and fall
like a surge of the ocean–
His eyeballs wide rolling in frenzied affright–
Out bursts the magnificent creature to sight.
A low cry I utter; he stops–bends his head,
His nostrils distended,
limbs quaking with dread;
My rifle cracks sharp–
he springs wildly on high,
Then pitches down headlong,
to quiver and die."

Shortly after midnight, they remove their tomahawks from their sashes, hang up their stout buckskin leggings, and retire for the evening to dream of shining antlers silhouetted against the eastern sky.

When the kitchen clock strikes four, the deerstalkers are afoot. After a hearty breakfast of venison liver and eggs, "not least, two mighty tankards smoking with a judicious mixture of Guinness's double stout, brown sugar, spice, and toast—for to no womanish delicacies of tea and coffee did the stout huntsmen seriously incline," Frank's boys shoulder their rifles and strike forth while the stars still shine in the sky.

The first flash of dawn in the eastern horizon finds several of Frank's boys, Harry Archer and Dolph Pierson in the company of Smoker, their noble, Scottish, wire-haired deerhound, hunting deer from a canoe while floating down the numerous, narrow streams of the Adirondack country. After miles of floating in an unbroken silence, they suddenly encountered two bucks. Forester recalls the scene for us:

"Under the shade of a birch stood two beautiful and graceful deer, one sipping the clear water, and the other gazing down the brook in the direction opposite to that from which the hunters were coming upon them.

"No breath of air was stirring in those deep, sylvan haunts, so that no taint, telling of man's presence, was borne to the timid nostrils of the wild animals, which were already cut off from the nearer shore before they perceived the approach of their mortal foes.

"The quick eye of Archer caught them upon the instant, and almost simultaneously the hunter had checked the way of the canoe, and laid aside his paddle.

"Pierson was already stretching out his hand to grasp the ready rifle, when Archer's piece rose to his shoulder with a steady slow motion; the trigger was drawn, and ere the close report had time to reach its ears, the nearer of the two bucks had fallen, with its heart cleft asunder by the unerring bullet, into the glassy ripple out of which it had been drinking, tinging the calm pool far and wide with its life-blood.

"Quick as light, as the red flash gleamed over the umbrageous spot, long before it had caught the rifle's crack, the second, with a mighty bound, had cleared the intervening channel, and lighted upon the gray granite rock. Not one second's space did it pause there, however, but gathering its agile limbs again, sprang shoreward.

"A second more it had been safe in the coppice. But in that very second, the nimble finger of the sportsman had cocked the second barrel; and while the gallant beast was suspended in mid air, the second ball was sped on its errand.

"A dull, dead splash, heard by the hunters before the crack, announced that the ball had taken sure effect, and, arrested in its leap, the noble quarry fell.

"For one moment's space it struggled in the narrow rapid, then, by a mighty effort rising again, it dashed forward, feebly fleet, keeping the middle of the channel.

"Meanwhile the boat, unguided by the paddle and swept in by the driving current, had touched upon the gravel shoal and was motionless.

"Feeling this as it were instinctively, Harry unsheathed his long knife, and with a wild shrill cheer to Smoker, sprang first ashore, and then plunged recklessly into the knee-deep current; but ere he had made three strides, the fleet dog passed him, with his white tushes glancing from his black lips, and his eyes glaring like coals of fire, as he sped mute and rapid as the wind after the wounded game.

"The vista of the wood through which the brook ran straight was not at the most above fifty paces in length, and of these the wounded buck had gained at least ten.

"Ere it had gone twenty more, however,

the fleet dog had it by the throat. There was a stern, short strife, and both went down together into the flashing waters. Then, ere the buck could relieve itself, or harm the noble dog, the keen knife of Archer was in its throat—one sob, and all was over."

Although this stirring sketch—written in eloquent prose with a spirited and graphic tone—provides us with a colorful portrait of the chase, in reading his great essay entitled "Deer Hunting" published in 1849, we learn that Frank Forester took a dim view of the general quality of the deer hunting at this time. "Deer hunting proper and scientific, I may say there is none." Too many hunters, in his opinion, were waging promiscuous havoc on the deer herd by not respecting the seasons, age, or sex of the animals.

This charge was certainly not an exaggeration, for such famed New York deerslayers as Elisha Risdon, who hunted deer in Parishville Township in St. Lawrence County during the years 1804-1833, reportedly killed 579 white-tailed deer over this 28-year period. Other famous Adirondack deerslayers such as Thomas Meacham (1777-1850) killed 2550 white-tailed deer during his lifetime. Two noted deerslayers of the Mohawk Valley, Nick Stoner (1762-1850) and Nat Foster (1767-1840), also recorded incredible lifetime, white-tailed deer kills, which they accomplished with their $70 rifles called "double shooters" made by Willis Avery of Salisbury. Yet, the New York white-tailed deer herd remained at an all-time high during Frank Forester's life.

Of the two most popular modes of deer hunting during the 1840s, driving and still-hunting, Forester favored the latter. "It is by far," he writes, "the most legitimate and exciting, as it demands both skill in wood-craft, and endurance, on the part of the hunter; whereas driving requires only the patience of Job, added to enough skill with

"The buck gazing down the brook." Illustration by Henry William Herbert.

the gun to knock over a great beast, as big as a Jackass, and as timid as a sheep, with a heavy charge of buckshot."

Like Audubon, Forester condemned fire hunting as a mode of deer hunting. His critique of this form of deer poaching resounded throughout the deer forest like the sudden crack of a rifle on a quiet, crisp November day:

"There is nothing of fair play about it. It

is a dirty advantage taken of the animals; and, apart from its manifest danger, ought to be discountenanced. It is utterly unsportsmanlike, and butcherly. The great drawback to this species of sport ... is that other animals than deer often approach the treacherous blaze; and instances are not uncommon of hunters shooting their own horses and cattle—nay, every now and then, their own companions, sisters, and sweethearts."

Forester also denounced deer hunting parties often numbering 20 to 30 guns, presenting a situation in which, as he exclaims, "the odds are, perhaps, a hundred to one against so much as even hearing the distant bay of a hound." Whether or not we agree with these odds, I am sure that many conservationists can relate to his final assessment of the sport of deer hunting:

"Here there is no work for the featherbred city hunter, the curled darling of soft dames. Here the true foot, the stout arm, the keen eye and the instinctive prescience of the forester and mountaineer, are needed; here it will be seen who is, and who is not the woodsman, by the surest test of all—the only sure test—of true sportsmanship and lore in venerie, who can best set a-foot the wild deer of the hills, who bring him to bay or to soil most speedily, who ring aloud his death halloo, and bear the spoils in triumph to his shanty, to feast on the rich loin while weakly and unskillful rivals slink supperless to bed."

Frank Forester viewed the American deerslayer in heroic terms. He dedicated his chief work, *The Field Sports of the United States* (1848), to that wild and adventurous deerslayer of the "Wild Woods" plantation of South Carolina, Colonel Wade Hampton III (1818-1902). Hampton was surely one of the finest horseback riders in America to ever course deer and hunt bear. Herbert referred to him as "The First Sportsman in the land."

In describing deer hunting in this classic book, Forester declared "to enjoy deer hunting in anything like perfection ... we must go into Virginia, into the Carolinas, Louisiana and Mississippi. There we find the gentlemen of the land, not pent up in cities, but dwelling on their estates; there we find hunters, *par amours*, if I may so express myself, and packs of hounds maintained regularly, and hunted with all legitimate accompaniments of well-blown bugle and well-whooped halloo; with mounted cavaliers, fearlessly riding through brush, through briar, over flood, over mire ... as desperately, for the first blood, or kill, as they do in old England, in Leicester or Northampton, to the Quorn hounds, or the Squire's lady pack. This is *the Sport*, par excellence."

Several years before the publication of this book, Charles Deas' oil painting *Long Jakes* (1844) and his pen and ink on paper *The Hunter* (1845) struck Henry William Herbert like a thunderbolt. In these dramatic images of the red-shirted and bearded hunter and the masculine lines of the buckskin-clad deer hunter astride a gallant stallion, Herbert saw the very epitome of the American deerslayer.

Herbert became so enamored with the image of Long Jakes that he wrote one of the most emotional essays ever written in the history of hunting, "Long Jakes, the Prairie Man," which was published in June of 1846 in the *New York Illustrated Magazine of Literature and Art* and accompanied with Henry Jackman's engraved illustration of the painting. In this epistle of hyperbole, Herbert characterized Jakes' attire as perfect: "Everything here is real, useful, yet how showy, and how more than romantic."

In his fictive biography, Herbert imitated his great literary hero, James Fenimore Cooper, by portraying the frontier deer hunter as the epitome of manliness and independence. Long Jakes, like Natty Bumppo, Audubon, "Miller" and Tome, was a man whose "untrammeled sense of individual will and independent power" opposed the decadent corruptions of modern civilization. Indeed, Herbert and the American public ultimately embraced Long Jakes, the Prairie Man, as a political symbol of independence.

"That is the picture of a *man*. A man emphatically and peculiarly a man, at an epoch when manhood is on the decay throughout the world; when individuality and personal characteristics and personal influence are yielding everywhere to the pre-eminence of masses. A man of energy, and iron will, and daring spirit, tameless, enthusiastic, ardent, adventurous, chivalric, free—a man made of the stuff which fills the mold of heroes...

"Hurrah! then for the prairie horse; Hurrah! for the Prairie Rider! both children of the wilderness! both nobler, stronger, braver, and more faithful than the pale offspring of society! both

Are America's peculiar sons,
Known to no other land!"

An early sketch of "Long Jakes" by Charles Deas, May 23, 1835.

The Life of a Hunter: Catching a Tartar, A.F. Tait, 1861.

"If a man undertakes a dangerous enterprise with

a determination to succeed or lose his life, he will do many

things with ease and unharmed which a smaller degree of

energy would never accomplish."

–Meshach Browning, in
Forty-Four Years of the Life of a Hunter, 1859

MESHACH BROWNING

With his faithful deerhound called "Gunner" and his trusty percussion Pennsylvania long rifle, now reposing in the Smithsonian's National Museum of American History, Meshach Browning (1781-1859), the famous American pioneer turned deerslayer, roamed the vast, Appalachian wilderness of Maryland. He especially favored the area of the Youghiogheny and Castleman River watersheds, now known as Garrett County, Maryland, as well as the surrounding region of West Virginia. Here the buckskin-clad Browning pursued "those wicked fighting bucks," as he called them, with a vigorous tenacity unmatched in the annals of American white-tailed deer hunting with the possible exception of the thrilling exploits of his contemporaries: Audubon, Tome, "Miller" and Frank Forester.

Born in Montgomery County, Maryland, in March of 1781, this pioneer Marylander carved a living for himself and his family of 12 out of the Maryland wilderness much like Philip Tome had done in the hills of Pennsylvania. Whitetails provided him not only with meat and hides but with a source of income as well. At that time, venison sold for 12-1/2 cents a pound. What he could not use for his family, he sold. The money raised

The Meshach Browning cabin at Sang Run, which Browning built in 1820. This photo was taken in 1920 after the cabin had been abandoned for many years. It no longer exists.

Inset: The only known formal portrait of Meshach Browning. "He was very positive and strong in his nature, as ever line in his rigid face show. He was a powerful man in physique."— Jacob Brown, *Brown's Miscellaneous Writings*, 1896.

eventually enabled him to create a small farm at Bear Creek Glades and later establish a gristmill at Sang Run. Like Philip Tome, deer hunting represented not only Meshach's favorite pastime, but his basic source of livelihood as well.

"I could sell deer-skins at any time in the old settlement; for in those days many men, and almost all the boys, wore buckskin pants and hunting-shirts; which made skins bring a good price. I used to take my skins to the mill, and leave them there, and the farmers would leave me their value in grain and for bear-meat I received four dollars a hundred."

Dressed in a buckskin hunting shirt and buckskin pants and moccasins, Browning still-hunted and hounded white-tailed deer in such sacred places in Garrett County as the Big Gap of Meadow Mountain, Campbell's Saw Mill, Hoop-Pole Ridge, Roman Nose, Negro Mountain, Marsh Hill, Deep Creek, Muddy Creek Falls, Little Crossings, Browning's Bear Hill, Glade Cabin, and the Big Youghiogheny River, all religiously recorded on William W. Hoye's 1823 map of

Browning's hunting grounds published in the 1942 edition of Browning's autobiography, *Forty-Four Years of the Life of a Hunter.*

"This was his kingdom," writes historian Charles Hoye, "and its wild tribes of bear, deer, wolf, cat, and turkey—all paid tribute at the crack of his trusty rifle and the bark of his faithful dogs." The entire area known today as Thousand Acres comprised his deer-hunting turf. The fog banks along Holy Cross and the tremendous sunsets on Deep Creek Lake furnished the most beautiful scenery for his deer hunts and were, as Henry Herbert might have said, "more than romantic."

Browning's deer hunting grounds can surely be described as a "hunter's paradise," for the streams were heavily populated with brook trout and the woods with turkeys, grouse, rabbits, and squirrels, as well as deer, bears, wolves, wildcats and panthers. Like Audubon, Buckskin Browning repeatedly enjoyed gourmet, backwoods cuisine such as stewed hen turkeys

C. STABLER. DEL

VAN INGEN-SNYDER

Hunter's Camp on Meadow Mountain, a plate from Meshach Browning's *Forty-Four Years of the Life of a Hunter*, 1859. From left to right, we see Francis P. Blair, Joseph Friend, Wm. Browning, eldest son of Meshach Browning, Edward Stabler, and John L. Browning, also a son of Meshach Browning.

with potatoes and turnips and venison tenderloins basted with fresh, sweet butter over oak coals.

The elevation of his hunting grounds ranged from 1400 to 3400 feet above sea level. He often had to deal with sudden shifts in temperature of 50 degrees in 24 hours and 18-inch snowfalls. "His hunting expeditions," R. Getty Browning, Meshach's great-grandson reports, "must have been seriously affected by these sudden climatic changes and the difficulties in traveling on foot through the snow for long distances in zero weather must have demanded the greatest resolution and endurance, even for one so strong and active as he was." Transporting deer from six to 15 miles from his cabin at Sang Run must have been a difficult matter in and of itself.

In his autobiography, Browning lists four amusements and occupations that he loved dearly: moving hay in the glades, killing deer, catching trout and shooting wild turkeys. Like other American pioneers of the backwoods, he could equate occupations with amusements, an equation lost to modern society. In his history of Maryland, *Brown's Miscellaneous Writings* (1896), Jacob Brown describes Browning's humble abode at Sang Run as the seat of hospitality and generosity, and characterizes Browning, the man:

"He was entirely free from vice; honest and direct as any man could be and greatly respected. He was very positive and strong in his nature, as ever line in his rigid face show. He was a powerful man in physique and occasionally, but only occasionally, would have a combat with a man of known metal when it would not be manly to avoid it. He had a noted battle in early life at Selbysport with a man by the name of Shannon. The contest began on an old-fashioned saw mill, and ended below among the water-works. The ducking they received in the fall had the good effect to cool the ardor of the contest-

ants. But no man more despised the ruffian and bully than he."

Since this legendary, pioneer deerslayer had to carry everything on his back, he reduced his load to the barest necessities: salt and bread, his rifle, powder horn, and bullet pouch, plus his hunting knife, punk, flint and steel for fire-making and his tomahawk. It seems remarkable that in a lifetime spent in the wilderness, he never suffered from illness or accident.

Like Tome, "Miller" and Audubon, Browning pursued white-tailed bucks for days on end as he traveled through the great virgin forests of hemlock, white pine and spruce sometimes regaling himself "with a stout horn of good old rye whiskey" at one of the quaint, 19th-century taverns that served as the social centerpiece of the deerslayer tradition, as well as the local post office. He sometimes went without food for a day in his relentless pursuit of deer, and slept wherever he found himself. He frequently spent weeks at a time alone in the forest miles from home. Of one night's memorable experience, he vividly wrote as follows:

"It was dark and a heavy cloud was coming up with thunder and lightning, and every appearance of a dreadful storm. Seeing a large fallen tree, I took poles, and, laying one end of each on the ground, I placed the others on the log, and spread my bear's skin over them, with the greasy side upwards ...by the time I had seated myself under my shelter, the rain was pouring down in torrents, accompanied by vivid lightning, and such appalling peals of thunder that the earth seemed to tremble under me. Two trees were torn into splinters within a few rods of my lodge."

On one hunt to the headwaters of the Potomac, he went all day without eating. That night he sat alone in a virgin stand of white pines. While spending the night sitting against a large pine tree, he watched it rain and then snow. He had done this many times before, and knew he would survive, as long as he still had some Dupont's rifle-powder, balls in his 9-inch, buckskin pouch and a horn of salt. When he awoke the next morning, he found his long hair frozen tight to the tree against which he slept.

Like Tome and "Miller," Browning didn't shoot deer; he "put their lights out!" He often accomplished this feat with the plunge of the fatal blade of his knife into the neck of the struggling buck. He always carried his "fighting" knife, a weapon with a 10-inch blade honed to a razor sharp edge and kept that way. The "Green River," made by E. Barnes and Son in Greenfield, Massachusetts was one of the best known knives of his era. It seems likely that Browning carried a "Green River." "I always took the knife in a close contest." Indeed, the young Browning had many opportunities to practice and master his knife-wielding act while chasing whitetails and bears.

In the Foreword to the 1942 Tenth Edition of Browning's autobiography, his great-grandson describes the typical manner in which the great deer hunter confronted his quarry: "Approaching up-wind he generally succeeded in getting close enough for an effective shot with his flintlock rifle, the accuracy and penetration of which were so uncertain that he was obliged to get close to the game and deal a fatal first shot if possible. If he failed, his especially bred and carefully trained dogs took over the battle and when necessary he settled it with a thrust of his knife rather than risk another shot which, in the confusion of the fight, might kill a dog. His dogs were a cross between the large English Bull and Greyhound and were exceedingly courageous, active and powerful."

On a typical day's deer hunt, Browning would see from 10 to 12 deer, sometimes securing as many as five to six. On one particular day, he got 13; on another, he shot three bucks with three shots. For 44 years he tramped the Maryland wilderness in pursuit of white-tailed bucks and bears.

"I began to hunt in 1795, and pursued the chase every fall till 1839, — a period of forty-four years, — and in a country where game was exceedingly plentiful. During this time, I think I found out as much about the nature and habits of the wild animals of the Alleghenies as any other man, white, red or black, who ever hunted in those regions."

Browning studied the white-tailed deer for many years and acquired an accurate knowledge of its social habits and feeding grounds. He understood the whitetail's habitat; he knew their mating season, gestation period and browse preferences. He called, grunted, and decoyed deer as early as the beginning of the 19th century. Like many pioneer deerslayers, he used candles in bark reflectors to spotlight them at night while floating down streams in his canoe. On the subject of deer hunting he

An illustration of Meshach Browning and his deerhound "Gunner," 1928. Illustrator unknown.

Like many pioneer deerslayers, Browning used candles in bark reflectors to jack deer at night while floating down streams in his canoe.

wrote: "If a man undertakes a dangerous enterprise with a determination to succeed or lose his life, he will do many things with ease and unharmed which a smaller degree of energy would never accomplish."

Even though his livelihood depended upon venison, he claimed to live by a certain ethical code toward whitetails suggesting, in much the same way as did Tome, Audubon and Herbert, that the chase is more important than the kill. Ultimately, he insisted that self-reliance is vital to anyone who would hunt the white-tailed deer in the wild.

Since the rifles of his day were so inaccurate and the powder so poor that even at 30 yards they lacked killing power, the 6-foot, 185-pound, muscular Meshach frequently confronted his quarry with knife in hand. On one of his first white-tailed deer hunts we find Meshach and a friend following a buck's track on a freshly fallen snow in October of 1795. As darkness approached, the 14-year-old boy suddenly spotted the buck. "I took aim, let drive, and off went the buck." In his autobiography, Meshach recalls the ensuing events:

"As he made off, we set on our dog, who was trembling with eagerness for the chase. Off went Gunner and we soon heard him at full bay. Who should be up first was then the question to be decided. Jump and jump we went, side by side, till my strength and long wind prevailed, and I ran up first. But in running through the bushes, some snow having fallen on the lock of my gun, wet the powder, and it would not fire. Here we were, with no means of helping poor Gunner, or of keeping him from being injured by the buck's sharp horns. At length, while the faithful dog was holding the buck by the nose, I drew my hunting-knife from my belt and made a desperate pitch at the heart of the infuriated beast, which laid him out dead in the creek, where he had expected to be able to defend himself in the water."

For the next 24 years, Browning took up the chase each fall beginning in October, with the hunting season ending in January. Each of these annual deer hunts turned into highly spirited, momentous events. But the deer hunt of 1819, Meshach clearly never forgot. In October of that year, the 28-year-old Browning decided to hunt deer on the west side of the Great Yough River. Upon reaching the river, he took off his buckskin pants and moccasins and waded across.

After he had gone a short distance, he discovered the tracks of a very large buck searching out company in the heat of the rut. In several hours of tireless tracking, he soon encountered a 10-pointer. After badly wounding the buck with a heavy charge of buckshot, his half-breed Greyhound took to the heels of the animal and drove him into the river, where the dog and the buck engaged themselves in a desperate battle. Due to the river's deepness, neither hound nor deer could get a foothold. In his chilling memoirs, Meshach tells us what happened:

"I concluded to leave my gun on shore, wade in, and kill him with my knife. I set my gun against a tree, and waded in—the water in some places being up to my belt, and in other places about half-thigh deep. On I went until I came within reach of the buck, which I seized by one of his horns; but as soon as I took hold, the dog let go, and struck out for the shore, when the buck made a main lunge at me. I then caught him by the other horn, though he very nearly threw me backwards into the river; but I held on to him, as I was afraid of our both being carried into the deep hole by the swift current. I dared not let him go; for if I did I knew he would dart at me with his horns. I must kill him, or he would in all probability kill me; but whenever I let go with one hand, for the purpose of using my knife, he was ready to pitch at me. I called and called the dog, but he sat on the shore looking on, without attempting to move.

"After awhile, it occurred to me to throw him under the water, and drown him; whereupon I braced my right leg against his left side, and with my arms jerked him suddenly, when down he came with his feet toward me.

Gunner's Victory from Browning's *Forty-Four Years of the Life of a Hunter*. Meshach's faithful deerhound was crucial in his success as a deerslayer.

Then it was that my whole front paid for it, as his feet flew like drum-sticks, scraping my body and barking my shins, till ambition had to give way to necessity, and I was not only compelled to let him up, but even glad to help him to his feet again, though I still held on to his rough horns. From the long scuffle, my hands beginning to smart, and my arms to become weak, I took another plan.

"I threw him again, and as he fell I twisted him around by his horns, so as to place his back toward me and his feet from me. Then came a desperate trial, for as this was the only hope I had of overcoming him, I laid all my strength and weight on him, to keep him from getting upon his feet again. This I found I could do, for the water was so deep that he had no chance of helping himself, for want of a foothold. There we had it round and round, and in the struggle my left foot was accidentally placed on his lowermost horn, which was deep down in the water.

"As soon as I felt my foot touch his horn, I threw my whole weight on it, and put his head under the water, deeper than I could reach with my arm. I thought that was the very thing I wanted; but then came the hardest part of the fight, for the buck exerted all his strength and activity against me, while I was in a situation from which I dare not attempt to retreat.

"I was determined to keep his head under, although sometimes even my head and face were beneath the water; and if I had not been supported by his horns, which kept me from sinking down, and enabled me to stand firmer than if I had no support, that stream might have been called, with great truth, 'the troubled water'; for I know that if it was not troubled, I was, for often I wished myself out of it. I know that the buck would have had no objection to my being out; though he probably thought that, as I had come in to help that savage dog, he would give me a punch or two with his sharp points, to remember him by. Indeed, that was what I most dreaded; and it was my full purpose to keep clear of them, if possible.

"In about two minutes after I got my foot on his horn, and sank his head under water, things began to look a little more favorable; for I felt his strength failing, which gave me hopes of getting through the worst fight I had ever been engaged in during all my hunting expeditions.

"When his strength was but little, I held fast to his upper horn with my left hand, and keeping my foot firmly on his lower horn, I pressed it to the bottom of three feet of water and, taking out my knife, when his kicking was nearly over, I let his head come up high enough to be within reach, when at a single cut I laid open the one side of his neck, severing both blood vessels. This relieved me from one of the more difficult positions in which, during all my life, I had been placed for the same length of time."

After reading Browning's stirring account of his buck fight in *Forty-Four Years of the Life of a Hunter*, A. F. Tait (1819-1905), the great Adirondack artist/deer hunter, created a painting in 1861 of Browning grappling with the unexpectedly formidable opponent titled *The Life of a Hunter: Catching a Tartar*. In the same year, Currier and Ives published a hand-colored lithograph of Tait's black and white painting of Browning's buck fight in the Yough River, thus immortalizing the famous incident. Tait varied the scene a little by adding another hunter in the background instead of a dog, and shifting it to the banks of the river. The illustration of this buck fight by Browning's editor, Edward Stabler (1794-1883), is historically more accurate, although less dramatic.

In 1857, Jacob A. Dallas engraved a deerman skirmish for the frontispiece for S. H. Hammond's *Wild Northern Scenes* (1856). Tait undoubtedly knew of this engraving as

Edward Stabler's engraving of Browning's famous buck fight in October of 1819.

well as others. A similar life-and-death struggle between a man and a wounded white-tailed buck was also reported near Milford, Pennsylvania, at this time. Indeed, during the 19th century, numerous and similar deer-man skirmishes repeatedly occurred as a leitmotiv in the sporting literature of the time.

Several years later, while hunting again on the west side of the Big Yough River, near that fine tract of deer country called "The Land Flowing with Milk and Honey," Browning encountered a tremendous white-tailed buck traveling on hard, frozen ground with head down in aggressive pursuit of estrous does. Browning could hear the animal's footsteps as he pursued the rutting buck. When the buck walked, Browning walked; when the buck stopped, Meshach stopped. The great, Maryland deerslayer remembers the event on that cold, cloudy November day:

"By this means I kept getting nearer and nearer; and after a while, finding a bush full of dry leaves, he went to it, and rushed his great horns into it; making such a noise round his own ears, that I took advantage of

it, and while he was pleasing himself by fighting the bush, I ran up as near to him as I wished, took my stand, and waited until he was done amusing himself, when he walked a few steps and made a full stop, with his side fairly exposed to me. Then it was that my heavily-loaded rifle belched forth fire and brimstone, sending a heavy ball through his heart, killing him so quickly that he had not time to see who had done it."

Browning's first wife, Mary McMullen Browning (1781-1839), loved the sweet taste of venison and always encouraged her husband to take up the chase. One day when the family was in dire need of venison, she reminded him to "put the little end foremost" the next time he sees a deer. After hearing this rather humorous remark, Browning grabbed his gun and started for the deer woods with his dog. He traveled for about eight miles to a place where the woods had been previously burned over. Here he knew that deer fed on the lush, new vegetation. As he trudged along that day, he encountered a whitetail feeding on sumac: "I said, 'little end foremost,' and unerring leaden messenger," and added a fifth whitetail to the bag. "I put the 'little end foremost' five times that afternoon, and got a good deer every time the little end flashed fire and brimstone."

After this extremely lucky hunt, he traded his gun for a different rifle and traveled to see a gunsmith in Monogahela County, Virginia, where he requested that the gunsmith do some repair work. The gunsmith apparently failed in the repair work, for Meshach hunted for the next week and shot many times but to no avail. After doing some target practice, he discovered that his ball struck about 18 inches above the mark. He then became his own gunsmith:

"This gave me the fidgets; and putting the gun between the forks of a tree, I gave it a bend downward, which made it very crooked. I put it in again and again, until by frequent twisting I got it so that it would shoot a ball within six inches of a mark. I then concluded to try if I could kill with it in that condition."

Having finally gotten his rifle in working order, confidence returned, overtaking Browning's "fidgets." Returning once again to the burned-over area, he found evidence of where two large bucks fought a bitterly-contested battle, a battle fought over a quarter acre of ground. In his autobiography, he notes if he had caught them while so engaged, that he would have gotten both of

Courtesy of Wegner's Photo Collection.

In this image by Ralph Crosby Smith, Meshach travels to see a gunsmith in Monogahela County in Virginia.

creeping up as near as I wished to be, I shot and killed it."

He then discovered the tracks of a large, white-tailed buck, which he followed. After several hours of tracking, the buck suddenly came galloping directly toward him. He fired at the distance of eight steps and laid him down. He then proceeded on his course. Before the day ended, he again fired twice more, securing two does. As darkness descended, he once more "sent forth his them. Indeed, the barrel-bending Browning had great faith in his whizzing leaden messengers!

On his 1836 deer hunt one mile from Negro Mountain, one of his cherished deer hunting turfs, Browning shot three large white-tailed bucks with three shots. He jumped the first buck from his bed and dropped it within a few yards. When he fell, two more bucks came running along and stopped where the first buck laid. A second ball went whizzing through one of these and before the third buck vanished in the brush, Meshach's rifle belched fire once more, making the final score three bucks for three balls—all done during a desperate wind storm, and before breakfast.

After many years of successful deer hunting, Browning decided in the winter of 1836 to create a deer park. With his deer hound fitted with a leather muzzle and Browning with snowshoes, they caught deer in heavy snow by hand for the Browning Deer Park, America's first deer park, created to preserve deer for purposes of observation and research.

Not much is known about this deer park, except that it existed for six years and preceded the 200-acre deer park established by Judge John Dean Caton (1812-1895) in Ottawa, Illinois, in 1858 and the more famous 1,000-acre deer park established in 1871 in Pike County, Pennsylvania, by the Blooming Grove Park Association. Browning was not alone in his attempt to catch deer by hand; Audubon and Tome were also catching deer by hand at this time. Browning's colorful account of trying to capture a mature, white-tailed buck for this deer park needs to be preserved in full:

"I walked close up, bade him good morning, and told him that I had a summons for him to make his appearance forthwith at Browning's Deer Park. But the haughty animal raised his head high up, threw up his tail, his hair all standing out, and came boldly up to the attack. As he came he reared on his hind feet, and made a pass at my head; but as I saw what he intended, I stepped to one side and seized him round the neck, when into it we went, round and round so fast, that it looked as if we were dancing Fisher's hornpipe. We danced and pranced till I threw him down in the snow; when, as he commenced kicking, my front underwent a complete raking. I bore it until I could endure it no longer, and was glad to let him up again; when we took another dance, and after two or three rounds I threw him again, and tried to tie him; but when I would relax my hold he would rise and lead me another dance. At last, becoming as mad as he was, and the fight becoming desperate, I got him down, and was determined to tie him at all hazards.

"He continued to kick until he had so raked my front, that I felt as if covered with a blister plaster; after which he drew himself up, and with the points of his hinder hoofs caught my pants, and tore them from the seam of the waistband, taking one-half of my pants clear off to the ankle, leaving me half-naked, on a cold day and in the midst of snow.

"Maddened at such an insult, I ran into him with desperation, and threw him down in the deep snow. By this time I was so worried and heated, that I felt no inconvenience from the snow and the cold; for I was smoking like a coal-pit. On my part, the fight had not been carried on with much vigor and determination, until I lost my pants; but after that happened, I became furious, and determined to conquer him, if it took me until the moon rose; and I did not thereafter suffer him to rise to his feet until the fight ceased. When he found that he could not rise, his whole aim was to get the rope off his neck, which by hard labor I had tied round it.

"He would get his hind feet in the rope, and drag at it until he choked himself; and

Left: Dust jacket of the 1942 Tenth Edition of Browning's classic autobiography, which originally appeared in 1859.

Right: Various editions of Browning's classic book, which was penned by quill under the dim candlelight at Sang Run.

when I pulled them out, in a moment he would be in the same fix again. So it continued until he caught the points of his hoofs in a wrinkle of the loose hanging skin of his neck, and tore just half of it from his shoulder, as far up as the rope could go towards his ears. This looked so bad, that I loosened the rope, pulled the skin down again, and let him rise to his feet. Finding that he was still inclined to fight, I told him that he was a brave fellow, but a big fool, for he might have known that I did not mean to take his life; but as he was so selfish, he might go and do as he pleased; whereupon he walked off slowly into a thick laurel, and I saw him no more."

In an article published in the *Baltimore Sun* on September 6, 1900, 64 years after Browning established his deer park, one correspondent named "Eyrie" told readers that Deer Park, Maryland, existed as the natural and inevitable outcome of Browning's idea.

By the end of this backwoodman's adventurous life, Browning had acquired a great deal of land in Maryland, including one tract called Browning's Manor. Meshach Browning, farmer, miller, author, and one of America's foremost deerslayers, died of pneumonia on November 19, 1859, at the village of Hoyes at the age of 78. At his bedside the night of his death, one member of the family briefly commented on the vast abundance of chestnuts that autumn. Before serenely passing into the Happy Hunting Grounds, the stricken, old hunter roused himself in bed and boldly said, "The bears will be there!"

That same year saw the publication of his classic autobiography, penned by quill under the dim candlelight at Sang Run, and published by the prominent Philadelphia publisher J. B. Lippincott & Company. Rebecca Harding, a reviewer of this historic account of American pioneer life, wrote as follows in *Harper's New Monthly Magazine*:

"He lived to an extreme old age, and told the history of his life shortly before he died, in the rude, marrowy pioneer's vernacular. It fills a certain gap in American literature, being not only a picture in detail of the savage youth through which every one of the States has passed in turn, but of a man of the woods, simple and honest as Esau, in whom the senses and the hunting instinct were as keen and strong as in a sleuth-hound."

One reviewer in the *Baltimore Sun* praised Edward Stabler, Browning's editor, for saving the book from the "stupid revisions of the literary fellow and the meticulous tinsel of the tinkers in style." Writing in *The Glades Star*, published by the Garrett County Historical Society, another reviewer called the book, a classic in its field. "For eighty years this book has been entertaining and instructive reading for sportsmen, historians, and the general public."

Historian Charles Hoye described it as a vivid picture of pioneer life. One commentator in *Gray's Sporting Journal* reported that "the period illustrations are wonderful, portraying both the normal incidents of the frontiersman's life and such odd incidents as chasing a turkey stark naked. I particularly liked the detailed accounts of animal's habits which combine sound natural history with odd superstition."

The publisher of the 1965 edition refers to the book as "a classic example of non-fiction, outdoor composition unsurpassed in American literature." Historian James Casada agrees: "It is a classic in every sense of the word." Researcher and publisher Ivan Rowe of Appalachian Background, Inc., says, "Meshach Browning's keen observations and commentary on hunting, woodcraft, wild animal behavior, and habitat together with his roughly written down descriptions of Maryland folkways and settlement life, have long established this book

as an important 19th-century classic."

In her study, "Images of the Hunt in Nineteenth-Century America and their Sources in British and European Art," art historian Ruth Weidner observes that "the autobiography of Meshach Browning suggests that the typical subsistence hunter was courageous, knowledgeable, and principled, a genuine wilderness hero."

This extremely popular book went through various editions and numerous printings before the end of the 19th century, and several editions and numerous printings during the 20th century, remaining almost consistently in print for the past 143 years in one edition or another with 26 different publication dates listed for the various editions and reprints. An original 1859 edition in fine condition will probably cost as much as $4000 in the out-of-print book market. *Books in Print* (2003) lists a Reprint Services Corporation edition (1991) for $79.00. As of this writing, cheaper editions can still be located on the Internet.

Browning's backwoods style and peculiar phraseology hold great historic and nostalgic appeal. For the connoisseur of deer books, it serves as a rich compendium of American deer hunting lore of the first half of the 19th century. If you are interested in backwoods Americana and in the heroic, picturesque adventures of fighting with bears, wounded bucks and catching deer barehanded in the snow, you will want to read this exciting, rustic volume of early pioneer life in the Alleghenies. It includes everything from a classic love story to in-depth descriptions of minerals, geography and the habits of animals.

This frontier woodsman was indeed one of America's greatest deer hunters. He stands in the cavalcade of such individual hunters as Daniel Boone, John James Audubon, Philip Tome, "Frank Forester," William Elliott, Oliver Hazard Perry and Theodore Roosevelt, who greatly appreciated Browning's autobiography. Browning could read the deer forest and its signposts better than any man—dead or alive. This legendary highland outdoorsman could outrun his dogs during the chase, jump 27 feet, sneak up on a sleeping white-tailed buck and kill it with his knife, as well as kill black bears in their den with a knife and a candle. "The harder the fight the better I like the fun," he admitted.

In Charles Hoye's history of the Browning family, Meshach's great grandson, R. Getty Browning, compares Meshach's hunting adventures with those of other pioneer characters:

"It is my feeling that he undoubtedly killed more game than any other except perhaps Buffalo Bill. For the reason that he not only hunted in what was truly a hunter's paradise, heavily stocked with deer and bears, but he had the incentive as well as the desire to kill a great deal of game.

" ...In all his hunting experiences it is easily seen that he was a sportsman as well as a hunter and that he had a keen appreciation of everything that made life in the wilderness attractive."

After reading Browning's autobiography, Colonel William Kilgour, the silver-tongued orator of Montgomery County, Maryland, said, "as I lingered over his thrilling descriptions of the wilder portions of the deep, frightful and illimitable forest through which he hunted I could not but feel that vast, unbroken and indescribable solitudes ...magnificent sunsets bathing in flood of light the ragged cliffs of the innumerable chains and spurs of mountains; the gloomy grandeur of the deep shadows creeping down the mountainside, the music of the streams as they went dashing down the dark and almost inpenetrable ravines ...the mighty roar of the winds ...the low murmurs of sinking blasts."

When first read, his deerslaying tales seem implausible, overdramatized, unreal and unbelievable, but when re-read, studied, and placed in their cultural perspective, that is, compared with the adventures of his contemporaries and the deer hunting epistles of the time as recorded in John Stuart Skinner's *American Turf Register and Sporting Magazine*, published in Baltimore, and William T. Porter's *Spirit of the Times*, published in New York, Browning's daring adventures ring true with a great deal of historic authenticity.

In a letter dated March 7, 1859, Judge Thomas Perry of the Fourth Judicial District of Maryland writes, "no one doubts the truth of the many interesting incidents narrated by him." Browning's editor and friend, Edward Stabler, an illustrator and engraver, agrees: " ...although many of the incidents here given may, to the minds of some, savor of romance, yet no doubt whatever is entertained of their entire truthfulness and reliability." Browning once solemnly said of himself that he never "departed from the known truth."

In his Preface to the autobiography, Stabler applauds Browning's genuine humor, his enduring energy and perseverance, and "the most undaunted firmness," when engaged in hand-to-hand combat with primitive beasts of prey and fighting white-tailed bucks: "Meshach Browning's life may be deemed an eventful one, considering the almost constant risks he ran of losing it in his many dangerous conflicts with bears, panthers, wolves, and wounded white-tailed bucks; for the latter are scarcely less to be feared than the former, as their sharp horns and keen, cutting hoofs, are wielded with as much strength and skill, both in attack and defense, as are the teeth and claws of the beasts of prey."

Browning estimates that during his 44 years of hunting, he shot 1800 to 2000 deer, 400 bears, 50 panthers and scores of wolves and wildcats. Browning was often referred to as a man of sterling integrity, as one of nature's noblest works, and as a prominent figure among America's stalwart mountaineers.

One thing is certain, writes E. Lee Le Compte, a Maryland State Game Warden, in the Introduction to the 1928 edition of Browning's tome: " ...few, if any of us, will ever have such sport as the hardy pioneer, Browning, enjoyed in search of his supply of winter meat, hunting bears armed with an old flintlock or at times only with a knife, catching deer barehanded in the snow and lying out under the cold stars in his meagre blanket."

Historian Jacob Brown referred to Browning as a farmer by occupation and a deer hunter by taste and passion. Meshach Browning traveled the deer forest with "a light foot and a willing mind," as he himself acknowledged, believing that a man will live for a long period of time under the impetus of a high fever. Browning knew of no higher fever than that which excited him by the prospects of engaging in a buck fight, or of chasing down and securing a half-dozen, sleek, fat, white-tailed bucks. "Meshach had a fever and a flair for hunting," publisher Ivan Rowe notes. "He approached it almost religiously. This was his grace."

In his hot cast bronze ($5200), artist Wayne Hyde captures the ultimate masculinity and heroic wrath of this legendary deerslayer/bear hunter and his faithful deer hound "Gunner."

Lee Teter, a contemporary researcher and painter of Meshach Browning, best summarizes the ultimate historic importance of this great American pioneer: "This man is unique among men. It is he who embodies the spirit of us all who partake of the bountiful pleasure of the forest. Within him dwells the soul stirring spirit that has for ages prompted man to a dog and gun; the 'Spirit of the Hunter.'"

The Hunter's Wrath, a hot cast bronze by Wayne Hyde, 2001. Like artist Lee Teter, Wayne Hyde presents Browning in this sculpture as the courageous, masculine hunter in the tradition of Natty Bumppo.

Lee Teter 1987   Artist's Proof Lee Teter

The Spirit of the Hunter, Lee Teter, 1987. Meshach Browning's rugged lifestyle as a legendary deerslayer has inspired artists like Lee Teter.

This photo, by Leonard Lee Rue III, shows a white-tailed buck swimming a river, a common escape tactic for the South Carolina bucks that William Elliott chased during the 1800s.

"Whether he swam the Combahee, as he had before swam the

Chee-ha; whether he here escaped from the hounds, or was

devoured by them; whether he was a deer of flesh and blood,

or the phantom buck of legend—we cannot decide."

–William Elliott, *Carolina Sports*
by Land and Water, 1846

Chapter Seven

WILLIAM ELLIOTT
"VENATOR"

During the late 1820s, William Elliott ("Venator," 1788-1863), a lifetime planter, politician, poet, and one of the most widely read authorities on Southern sports during his day, chased white-tailed deer in the Chee-Ha area of South Carolina with the enthusiastic gusto of starry-eyed generals engaged in sylvan warfare. With hounds and drivers ("whippers" he called them) moving the deer, this Harvard-educated deerslayer spurred his horse on until gaining a position near the deer's flank. If the deer was wounded, whether shot with the double-barrel or struck in the head with the armed heel of his boot, Elliott would often fling himself upon the struggling animal and bury the fatal blade of his knife into the whitetail's throat.

Elliott referred to deer drives as "raids against the deer!" in which the hunters would marshal their forces for a week's campaign and use "all the appliances of destruction at their beck." Those "sleek-skinned marauders," as Elliott called them, had to be eliminated, for they were ruining his crops—the beginnings of our modern-day pest-control policies. Consequently, Elliott waged havoc against deer in general and bucks in particular, especially old, over-grown bucks that had the insolence to baffle

"Oak Lawn," William Elliott's plantation on the Edisto River in Beaufort, SC, 1863.

Inset: A formal portrait of William Elliott (1788-1863), from the painting by Thomas Sully, 1822.

Elliott and his boys. Before the hunt ended, he quoted verbatim his favorite deer-hunting carol, *Sound the Horn*:

> *Sound the horn—sound the horn,*
> *O swiftly flies the deer,*
> *Torrent and steep alike they scorn,*
> *For the prize—for the prize is near.*
> *See, the hounds on his track are gaining;*
> *Swiftly he flies thro' the valley and wood,*
> *By horse, and huntsman, and horn pursued.*
> *Speed—speed—ere noon has seen the sun,*
> *The prey must be caught—the game be won—*
> *The noble game be won.*
> *Then heed not the river, and spurn the spray,*
> *To the chase—to the chase away.*

This planter of the noblest South Carolina breed carried the deer drive, Southern-style, to its ultimate climax. Once spotted, a buck had to be pursued until its death; he viewed killing deer as a habit to be developed to the utmost. After watching one of his hunting buddies, a backwoods ruffian named Geordy, finally kill a deer after wounding six, Elliott cried out in one of his wild utterances, "Done like a sportsman, Geordy, one dead deer is worth a dozen cripples. I remember—once, your powder was too weak; and next, your shot was too small; and next, your aim was somewhat wild; and one went off bored of an ear; and another nicked of a tail. You are bound to set up an infirmary across the river, for the dismembered deer! You have done well to kill—let it grow into a habit."

Driving deer became an intense habit of mind: The noise of the shotguns, the aroma of gunpowder, the baying of the hounds, and the echoes of the huntsmen's horns set his heart to pounding and his mind to the issuance of wild utterances as he galloped on

A Good Shot by Winslow Homer, 1892. "Go, thou fool, no better than Napoleon, hast thou known the fitting time to die! The *devil* take thee, for thou has needlessly kicked and thrust thyself beyond the reach of *a blessing*!" William Elliott, *Carolina Sports by Land and Water*, 1846.

The deerslayers moving through the nearly impenetrable southern cane jungles in pursuit of whitetails.

through the deer forest. Although he loved his hounds and horses as well as the deer, when the hounds lost the trail, he cursed the "laggards of the pack, the cold of nose, and the slow of foot."

When one wounded buck miraculously escaped into the depths of the rapidly flowing Chee-Ha River, after fleeing the hounds and evading buckshot, Wild Willie stood along the shoreline and vented his frustration by hollering at the buck, "Go, thou fool, no better than Napoleon, hast thou known the fitting time to die! The *devil* take thee, for thou has needlessly kicked and thrust thyself beyond the reach of *a blessing!*" And with that grotesque verbiage, the Harvard-educated deerslayer spurred on his horse and disappeared from the scene of ultimate disappointment only to find partial consolation later over venison steak at the campfire, where Elliott decried all bucks as "luxurious rogues and the greatest epicures alive!"

Elliott took to white-tailed deer during the day on horseback with guns, knives, trained dogs, and a complete retinue of servants. Unlike his Northern contemporaries, Oliver Hazard Perry, Philip Tome, and Meshach Browning, Elliott hunted deer for sport, not out of necessity. His deer hunts were manly, animated affairs—an affirmation of masculinity—done with great gusto. He refers to Chee-Ha deer shooting as "delicious uproar." Chee-Ha is the name of a river that flows into the Combahee River 10 miles east of Beaufort where Elliott was born in 1788. Today, it is spelled Chehaw.

Elliott hunted deer for amusement with great intensity of feeling. He became totally involved and loved to be at the scene of action. Deer hunting for old Venator became a profound passion, a way of life, not just a hobby. His hair-splitting pursuits were daring to the point of recklessness. Elliott remained a die-hard buck hunter the likes of which America has not seen before or since.

The Return from Hunting: The Halt in the Woods, A.F. Tait, 1855. Like the famous artist/deer hunter A.F. Tait, pictured here on the right smoking a cigar, William Elliott loved to pursue whitetails with horses and hounds. This historic painting depicts deer-hunting camaraderie as the three deerslayers enjoy a moment of relaxation deep in the deer woods near Chateaugay Lake, Franklin County, New York.

When one reads his accounts of deer hunting in *Carolina Sports by Land and Water* (1846), one is reminded of Francis Parkman's comment on the early 19th-century deerslayer in his book *The Oregon Trail* (1849): " ...in the recklessness of the chase, the hunter enjoys all the impunity of a drunken man, and may ride in safety over gullies and declivity's, where, should he attempt to pass in his sober senses, he would infallibly break his neck."

No one in the history of American white-tailed deer hunting ever chased whitetails at a more furious pace. This naturalist and gentleman farmer admired the athleticism involved in the ritual; at Harvard he emerged as the fastest runner in his class. What prompted this self-conscious aristocrat and scholar to become such an avid deer hunter? His own answer was heredity. This man of wealth and leisure inherited the tastes of his grandfather; deer hunting was his birthright. In commenting on his own abilities as a deer hunter, Elliott acknowledged that "my forte lay in quick firing; and it resulted from this, that in deer-hunting, I was eminently successful; when the chance was fair, I seldom had occasion to fire the second barrel ...I indulged myself in a Westley-Richards 14 gauge."

Venator's deer hunts followed a prescribed manner. Hunters took stands while drivers and a pack of hounds set out to move the deer and drive them towards the standers. The standers kept their horses ready, for after they shot a deer, they saddled-up and joined the chase. They then pursued the wounded deer on horseback along deer trails until they brought the quarry down. Both William Faulkner and Archibald Rutledge described the same method a century later.

Prior to the Civil War, South Carolina harbored some of the most enthusiastic deer-hunting devotees in America; William Elliott was one of them

and eventually became one of the most popular deerslayers of his day. His Chee-Ha deer-shooting exploits greatly influenced the religiosity of Archibald Rutledge's later South Carolina deer-hunting campaigns, as well as the deep-seated, mysticism of William Faulkner's classic deer hunts in the "Big Woods" of the Mississippi Delta near Vicksburg and the philosophical agony of James Kilgo's more recent deer hunts in the Savannah River Swamp of South Carolina.

In his book, *Man and Nature in America* (1973), cultural historian Arthur A. Ekirch, Jr. describes deer hunting as "both a ceremonial cult of gentlemen and the simple pleasure of humbler folk." This definition accurately characterizes deer hunting during William Elliott's time, a period of time when deer hunting was an essential part of everyday life, when the deer hunting epistles appeared in print next to cultural reviews of classic music, drama and literature. Deer hunting was part of mainstream American culture.

Elliott, like many Southern planters, greatly valued horsemanship as an essential ritual of the chase. "H." of Chatham County, North Carolina, best summarizes the importance of this ritual in the October 1830 issue of the *American Turf Register and Sporting Magazine*, a popular sporting magazine that Elliott read with great delight: "In the part of the county in which I reside, deer are not killed with the view of wholly to venison, nor that the lucky huntsman should add to his count, but we are only emulous in superior horsemanship in heading the deer oftenest before he is run into by the dogs, or in dexterity in shooting."

In 1860, Daniel R. Hundley defined deer driving in his *Social Relations in our Southern States* "as a royal sport." More recently, Clarence Gohdes, a professor of American literature, labels deer driving as the top-ranked field sport of the Old South. Elliott, like deer hunters everywhere, hunted for the joys of camaraderie, for pleasure and the excitement of the chase. For planters like Elliott, the chase itself, the very process and procedure of the hunt, was considered the most important component of hunting. The process produced a sense of belonging to nature. But above all, Elliott insisted, it must be exciting; it must include the thrill of danger and intensity! In his writings, Elliott evoked the highest level of emotional excitement that deer hunters can experience in their pursuit of this animal.

This Harvard alumnus was extremely well-read in the sporting literature of his day and greatly relished Audubon's colorful essay entitled "Deer Hunting," which encouraged its readers, including Elliott, "to go driving the light-footed deer in the western and southern woods." Indeed, Audubon's spirited account of driving whitetails on horseback not only induced Elliott to take up the chase and drive whitetails, but provided him with a classic model for high-spirited writing about the experience.

Like Audubon, Elliott combined his interests in natural history, romance and adventure with his prodigious skills as a hunter. He believed that the hunter was, essentially, a man of nature. Participating in the hunt not only puts man in the realm of nature, but also demands that he acquire a basic knowledge of natural history in order to succeed in the deer hunt. He hunted deer to maintain an intimate connection between his code of sporting etiquette and a proper understanding of nature.

With one barrel loaded with buckshot and the other with birdshot, Elliott tells of a deer hunt on one fine October day in 1837, when four bears were started unexpectedly. Venator quickly fired the barrel with buckshot and killed two bears with one barrel. After one of Elliott's entourage, a neophyte identified as "Splash," accused him of being lucky, Elliott, the Squire of Oak Lawn (the name of his estate on the Edisto River), indulged in some light-hearted and joyous boasting about his skill with the shotgun:

"What a damper!—to tell a man who was priding himself on having made a magnificent shot, that it was nothing but luck.

"I'll tell you what, Splash, said I, to have met the bears, was my good luck, I grant you; but to have disposed of them, thus artistically, excuse me!—and my wounded self-love led me into a recital of incidents perfectly true, yet so nearly akin to vain glorious boasting, that even now I redden beneath my visor at the recollection! It was by good luck then, that I once killed two bucks with one barrel! Loveleap you saw this! By good luck, that, at another time, I killed two does with one barrel!—then, too, you were present. By good luck that I killed, on a two days hunt, five deer in five shots—not missing a shot! By good luck that I killed thirty wild ducks at a fire!

"It is by good luck, I suppose, that I throw up a piece of silver coin, and batter it while in the air, into the shape of a pewter mug!—or, laying my gun upon a table before me, fling up two oranges successively before I touch the gun, then snatch it up, and strike them both before they reach the earth, one with each barrel! Luck—luck—nothing but luck! Be it so; but when you have beaten this shot, and killed three bears with one barrel, let me know it, I pray you, and I will try my luck again! But while we waste time in talk, the scent gets cold. There are two other bears which took that foot-path there; let us pursue them—and *good luck* to the expertest sportsman in the field. I shall not fire another shot today!"

William Elliott's skill as a deer hunter with a heavily loaded shotgun was well known. He took great pride in marksmanship and said that "the report of a gun went unquestioned, in our sporting circle; it was in a manner axiomatic, in woodcraft mysteries,

A Deer Drive in the Texas "Cross-Timber," a drawing by Frenzeny and Tavernier that appeared in Harper's *Illustrated Weekly*, 1874, shows a typical Southern deer drive.

and passed current, with all who heard, for this much—*a deer is killed!*"

In an unpublished letter, his grandson, Ambrose Elliott Gonzales, remembers his prowess:

"A few weeks before his death in February of 1863, when I was five and a half years old, a servant came up to the house to say a covey of partridges was in the briar thicket near the pond, two hundred yards away. He called me, took his gun, walked up to the birds and killed one with each barrel. I picked them up and we were back at the house within five minutes. He was a very fine shot to the last, and in his seventy-third and seventy-fourth years made some remarkable bags—partridges, snipe and woodcock, which at the close of the day's shooting were always spread upon the big silver waiter and brought into the hall by the butler, as was custom, for the ladies to see. About this time, too, I remember seeing three beautiful bucks laid out at the back steps, two of which my grandfather had killed with two barrels—a double shot."

But not all deer hunters of Elliott's era cherished the shotgun for deer. A good number of hunters in the frontier areas, such as Kentucky, regarded the use of the shotgun as "beneath the dignity of the genuine backwoodsman," as one hunter commented in the August 25, 1832, issue of the *Spirit of the Times*, the leading sportsman's journal of the period. But Elliott, like Audubon, nevertheless, remained a life-long advocate of the double-barrel shotgun for shooting deer.

The Chee-Ha area in which he hunted was generally referred to as the best deer hunting grounds in South Carolina. Deep swamps traversed the rich land confined to the rivers. In these swamps whitetails sought secure retreats and Elliott pursued them with a vigorous energy unmatched in the annals of American deer hunting.

One fine February day in 1837, Elliott decided to hunt with a select body of hunting friends in the area near the ruins of Col. Barnard Elliott's plantation along a road between the Ashepoo and Combahee rivers about 40 miles southwest of Charleston. "We turned out, after breakfast with a pack of twelve hounds, and two whippers, or drivers, as we call them. The field consisted of one old shot besides myself, and two sportsmen who had not yet fleshed their maiden swords."

As the deer drive began to unwind, a long, deep note from a hound named "Ruler" announced the fact that whitetails were up. Minutes later, the whole pack agreed with further "querulous" announcement. The whitetail headed for the backwaters with the hounds yelping at his heels. After infinite toil in tangled, forested grounds, the deerhounds brought the deer past "Tickle," one of the young sporting neophytes, who had yet to flesh his maiden sword. "Crack!" "Crack!" went the double barrel. And the deer hit the forest floor. Elliott recalls the event:

"We all rode to the spot, to congratulate our novice on his first exploit in sylvan warfare—when as he stooped to examine the direction of his shot, our friend Love-Leap slipped his knife into the throat of the deer, and before his purpose could be guessed at, bathed his face with the blood of his victim. This, you must know, is hunter's law with us, on the killing of a first deer—his face glaring like an Indian Chief's in all the splendor of war paint—Robin the hunter touched his cap and thus accosted him.

"Maussa Tickle, if you wash off dat blood dis day—you neber hab luck agen so long as you hunt.

"Wash it off! cried we all with one accord—who ever heard of such a folly. He can be no true sportsman, who is ashamed of such a livery."

With Tickle's face stained with the blood of victory, with the "blood baptism" of his first killed deer complete, the drive resumed, or as Elliott reports, they continued to "beat up the ground." Before this Chee-Ha deer drive would end, Elliott would become involved in one of the most spirit-stirring incidents ever recorded in the history of American deer hunting.

In the afternoon of that splendid February day, the Harvard-educated Venator suddenly heard a rousting noise from the whole pack announcing that another whitetail was up. While riding his horse named "Boxer," Venator saw a buck dash along at top speed before the hounds. Elliott notes, "the distance was seventy-five yards—but I reined in my horse and let slip at him."

He fell in the thick underbrush, but soon recovered and disappeared with the hounds following furiously behind in hot pursuit, as the buck plunged into a canal and climbed the opposite bank. Later in the day, Venator again heard the lone cry of "Ruler," that prince of hounds, about a half-mile from where he first shot the buck. Elliott gave spur to Boxer and headed in that direction to cut him off. Elliott documents the event with this outburst of aristocratic rhetoric:

"It was now sunset, and the white outspread tail of the deer was my only guide in the pursuit, as he glided among the trees. 'Now for it, Boxer—show your speed, my gallant nag.' The horse, as if he entered fully into the purpose of his rider, stretched himself to the utmost, obedient to the slightest touch of the reins, as he threaded the intricacies of the forest; and was gaining rapidly on the deer, when plash! he came to a dead halt—his fore legs plunged in a quagmire, over which the buck with his split hoofs had bounded in security. What a balk! 'but here goes'—and the gun was brought instantly to

the shoulder, and the left-hand barrel fired. The distance was eighty yards, and the shot ineffectual.

"Making a slight circuit to avoid the bog, I again push at the deer and again approach—'Ah, if I had but reserved the charge, I had so idly wasted!' But no matter, I must run him down—and gaining a position on his flank, I spurred my horse full upon his broad-side, to bear him to the ground. The noble animal refused to trample on his fellow quadruped; and, in spite of the goading spur, ranged up close along side of the buck, as if his only pride lay in surpassing him in speed. This brought me in close contact with the buck.

"Detaching my right foot from the stirrup, I struck the armed heel of my boot full against his head—he reeled from the blow and plunged into a neighboring thicket—too close for horse to enter.

"I fling myself from my horse, and pursue on foot—he gains on me: I dash down my now useless gun, and freed from all encumbrance, press after the panting animal. A

Historic illustration of Elliott engaged in a dramatic deer-man skirmish taken from the 1918 edition of Elliott's classic *Carolina Sports by Land and Water*. These deer-man skirmishes were not only a leitmotiv of the deer hunting literature of the time, but also a common occurrence due to the primitive nature of the weapons used and the fear of shooting the deerhound instead of the deer when confronting the wounded animal at close range.

large fallen oak lies across his path; he gathers himself up for the leap, and falls exhausted directly across it. Before he could recover his legs, and while he lay thus poised on the tree, I fling myself at full length upon the body of the struggling deer—my right hand clasps his neck, while my left detaches the knife, whose fatal blade, in another moment, is buried in his throat. There he lay in his blood, and I remained sole occupant of the field.

"Other hunting matches have I been engaged in, wherein double the number of deer have been killed; but never have I engaged in one of deeper or more absorbing interest, than that which marked this day at Chee-Ha."

While hunting deer on horseback at Chee-Ha, Elliott boldly dashed through the deer woods at the risk of ending his own life, for tree branches sometimes tore the rider from his horse. He sometimes discharged his double barrel from horseback at full speed with the reins abandoned on the neck of the mount. In his two-volume *History of South Carolina* (1809), historian David Ramsay characterized deer hunting in South Carolina as war in miniature as mentioned earlier: "To the inhabitants of cities, it is a matter of astonishment with what ease (these deerslayers) who reside in the country can force their way at full speed through the thickest recesses of the forest. Impediments apparently insurmountable are readily got over. Dangers that seem to threaten life and limb—to tear riders from their horses, or horses from them, are escaped without injury."

On another deer hunt at Chee-Ha, while in the saddle at high speed, a white-tailed deer suddenly appeared directly under Boxer's nose. While poised in mid-air, the deer grazed Elliott's knee in his descent. When the deer touched the earth, Venator brought his double-barrel, Westley-Richards 14

gauge down, pistol-fashion, and sent a whole charge of buckshot through the animal's backbone. The deer tumbled over Boxer's heels.

Elliott dismounted and quickly dispatched the deer with exquisite, knife-wielding artistry. Before Elliott could stand up, a second deer followed directly in the track of the first deer, and passed so closely between him and Boxer that Venator could have bayoneted him. As the white tail flashed from the scene, Elliott unloaded the second barrel and "another deer is mine!" he cried. Two deer downed in less than five minutes. In surveying the saddles of choice venison, one thought came to his mind: "Morsels more savory smoke not upon a monarch's board!"

Indeed, venison was the choice source of food for the antebellum South. Elliott loved nothing better than venison tenderloins cooked over oak coals, or ribs grilled over hot coals, and consumed with the sweet taste "of the sparkling glass." A basic element of the underlying ideology of Elliott's deer hunting frequently included a gala evening with a holiday venison dinner at his Oak Lawn Plantation. His deer hunts became part sport and part social extravaganza. A day in the deer woods best ended with a meeting of the minds over the "sparkling glass" to fight the buck battles over and over again with one's deer-hunting comrades. Although he "drank his share of fine wines and brandies," historian Theodore Rosengarten tells us, "he did not guzzle or touch corn liquor to his lips."

His entourage often baked a deer's head in a forest oven—a hole dug in the ground with a fire constructed over it. They wrapped the head in moss and placed it in the hole under the embers of the fire. After it was cooked, they removed the skin, and placed the smoldering meat on a board. After a sprinkling of red pepper, it was meat fit for a king.

While feasting on venison in front of the campfire, Elliott's thoughts often turned to the great, phantom, white-tailed buck of mythic and cosmic proportion, as they often did at a later time for Archibald Rutledge and William Faulkner. On one Chee-Ha deer hunt, a man called "Laird" wounded a deer, which they could not find. Laird claimed he found a bit of marrow from the deer's leg. Later that night, Elliott put forth the following theory:

"His seeming to be shot, yet moving as if unhurt!—his losing a leg, yet running off without it!—his bloodlessness!—his disappearance at 'May's Folly'—the confusion of the hounds—and the unaccountable dispersion of the pack!—impress upon my mind the possibility of this being no deer of flesh and blood—but the 'Specter Buck,' of which we have heard traditionally, but which I never supposed had been met by daylight!

"Sometimes this milk-white buck is seen, by glimpses of the moon, taking gigantic leaps—then shrouded in a mist wreath, and changed in a twinkling, into the likeness of a pale old man, swathed in his grave clothes—then melting away slowly into air! At other times, the 'Specter Buck' starts up before one's eyes, pursued by phantom hounds, which rush maddening through the glades—yet utter no sound, nor shake the leaves, while they flit by like meteors!"

Elliott's planting domain on which he hunted deer consisted of five plantations in Charleston, Colleton and Beaufort counties. The fifth of these plantations, Oak Lawn, was located near the village of Adams Run. It could only be approached through a classic avenue of magnificent, moss-covered oak trees. It remained his favorite winter residence. Many people considered this oak avenue one of the most scenic spots in the Low Country. It faced the old "King's Highway" connecting Charleston with Savannah.

South Carolina conservationist James Rice called Oak Lawn "one of the noblest seats on the entire coast." Surrounded by 10 acres of rose gardens, this mansion, constructed in 1730 of English brick, sported a staff of 23 servants. Here Elliott became known as the "aristocrat of Oak Lawn."

His home contained one of the largest libraries on the East Coast. The complete works of the classic authors lined the shelves of the oak bookcases. The structure housed a concert hall equipped with a complete array of musical instruments on which Elliott entertained himself. In front of the massive stone fireplace he read Xenophon's *Cynegeticus* and came to view hunting as a means of scholarship and virtue.

Gaston Phoebus's *The Hunting Book*, one of the oldest and most famous hunting books written in France in 1391, remained on his bedside table. In conversations held in the library with fellow deer

An illustration of the phantom buck from the 1859 edition of Elliott's *Carolina Sports*.

Courtesy of Wegner's Photo Collection.

hunters, he quoted passages therefrom with great gusto:

"When autumn comes, the hunter sets out in quest of the deer's tasty flesh; the hunt becomes a battle of wits and instinct, along the paths trodden by the deer. It is a difficult animal to flush out, forever moving in circles rather than taking flight. How many hours do the hunters and hounds spend on the trail of the deer, which is expert in the art of escape, and which can always throw off a scent with the greatest of ease."

The Oak Lawn library also contained the complete works of Sir Walter Scott (1771-1832). While presiding over many Oak Lawn Christmas Day dinners, Elliott quoted Scott's great poem *The Lady of the Lake* (1810), which contained some of the most remarkable poetry ever written on man's endless pursuit of deer:

"The Monarch saw the gambols flag,
And bade let loose a gallant stag,
Whose pride, the holiday to crown
Two favorite greyhounds should pull down,
That venison free, and Bordeaux wine,
Might serve the archery to dine."

Elliott loved to read the classic hunting literature at Oak Lawn with the accompaniment of fine Bordeaux wine. Indeed, Elliott's epicure's taste for the choicest wines available prompted him to order the best wines from all around the world.

Like his ancestors, Elliott took part in the political arena throughout his life, even though he viewed politics as "this scene of petty intrigue and triumphant mediocrity." In 1814, he was elected to his father's seat in the lower house of the South Carolina State Legislature and served there until 1832. He also served one term in the United States House of Representatives.

Throughout his life, he politicked for game laws and took a strong stance against fire-hunting—a practice that entailed light-

ing a fire and placing it in a bark reflector, thus allowing the hunter to shoot blinded deer from canoes at close range. "The practice of fire-hunting," Venator writes in his short story, "The Fire-Hunter," "forbidden by the laws, is nevertheless but too much pursued in certain parts of the country. It is the author's aim ...to expose the dangers to property and to life, attendant on this illicit practice. It is nearer akin to poaching, than to legitimate hunting." Horses, cows, and humans were often shot as a result of this procedure.

In 1784, North Carolina passed a law prohibiting fire-hunting deer under the penalty of 39 lashes. The state of South Carolina was one of the first states in America to ban the practice with a series of laws (1769, 1785-1788, 1789). But these early laws did not stop the practice. On May 27, 1856, Venator published an article entitled "Preservation of Deer" in *The Charleston Mercury* in which he argued that the early laws against fire-hunting were not enough to prevent its practice; he proposed a closed season from April through August, when any hunting of deer would be an offense punishable by law.

In his deer hunting narrative, "The Fire-Hunter," Elliott raises some very profound questions with regard to propriety and ownership, as Stuart Marks points out in discussion of Elliott's narrative: "Who owns the deer? What right does the planter have to reserve the deer for his own purposes merely because he owns the land? Why should an absentee landlord have the right to prevent those who live on the land from reaping its fruits?" These difficult questions call to mind today's paradox of managing a public resource, such as the whitetail, on private property. These questions raised by Elliott as early as 1846, still go unanswered in American society to the great embarrassment of many state wildlife resource managers.

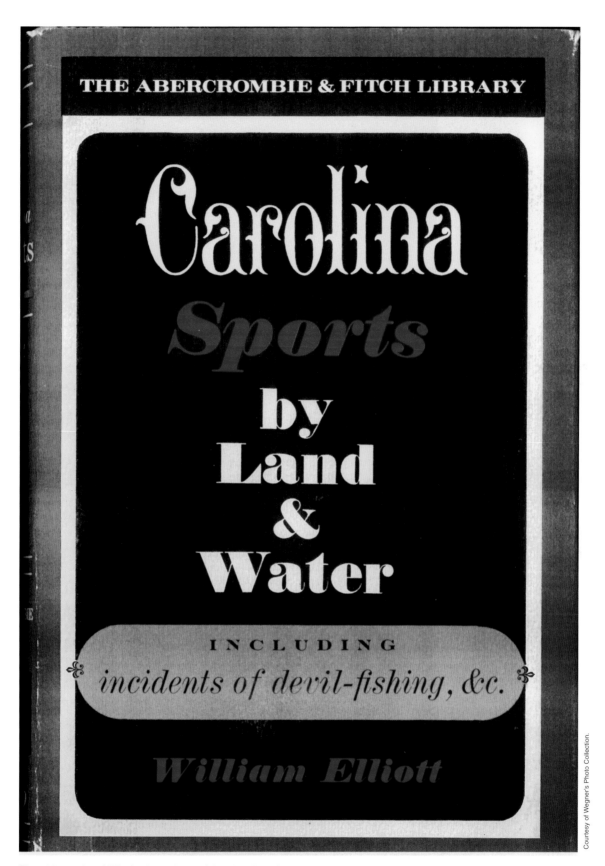

THE ABERCROMBIE & FITCH LIBRARY

Carolina
Sports
by
Land
&
Water

INCLUDING
❧ *incidents of devil-fishing, &c.* ❧

William Elliott

The 1967 reprint of Elliott's classic book of deer hunting adventures.

In 1846, Burges & James of Charleston published Elliott's *Carolina Sports by Land and Water*. Several of the deer hunting sketches had already been published under the signature of "Venator" in the *Southern Literary Journal and Magazine of Arts* and the *American Turf Register and Sporting Magazine* in the 1830s. This classic book of adventure remains one of the few early American sporting titles that stayed in print almost without interruption since its first days of publication. It went through 10 editions, the latest one being a paperback edition published by the University of South Carolina Press in January of 1994, with a new Introduction by historian Theodore Rosengarten. As of this writing, the book remains out of print. A copy of the original sells for $375-$450 in the out-of-print book market.

Elliott's deer hunting sketches are intense, brazen, graphically accurate, humorous and filled with comic relief. Most critics praised his ability "to convey the dash of the chase." In reading them, one literally hears the classic hunting music of Hayden's *The Hunt Symphony* and Wagner's *The Flying Dutchman*. The book served as an indispensable manual for the disciples of Natty Bumppo for generations and continues to do so as we enter the 21st century.

One of his strongest champions wrote in the *Library of Southern Literature* that "...much of the charm of the volume lies in its familiar personal tone and the genial vein of philosophic reflection which at intervals interrupts the stories of adventures." In style, it is highly charged and extraordinarily animated. Elliott concludes his volume on Carolina sports with an optimistic commentary in which he speculates that the future enforcement of deer legislation will lead to the preservation of deer and the perpetuation of "the healthful, generous and noble diversion of deer hunting." Elliott yearned for the ethical code of the hunter-naturalists that would emerge later in the century in the life and writings of Theodore Roosevelt, William Faulkner, Archibald Rutledge and Aldo Leopold.

Elliott's *Carolina Sports* received widespread favorable reviews during the past century and a half. Writing in *The Southern Quarterly Review* in July of 1847, one reviewer of the original edition says that Elliott "gives us no second-hand accounts from the observations of other men, but genuine reports of things actually seen and done, in which he was himself an important actor. This imparts to them a dramatic effect and an accuracy of detail, which no mere narrator who was not a doer also, could hope to attain. His narratives have a truthfulness about them not to be mistaken. His pen is the faithful coadjutor of the line, and his hits in description and in the chase are equally palpable and numerous."

In reviewing the third enlarged edition published in 1859, the *Boston Bulletin* noted that these sketches by "a scholar as well as a sportsman will afford very agreeable entertainment to the reader."

More recently, historian Lewis Pinckney Jones says in *The Journal of Southern History*, "it still can be read profitably by one seeking excitement and entertainment in hunting and fishing tales ...his entertaining and well-phrased letters are replete with evidence of a broad and classical education, practical knowledge, and a lively, keen observation." Charles R. Anderson, another reviewer, agrees in *The Georgia Review*: "*Carolina Sports*, following an old English tradition of the literature of hunting and fishing, is still an entertaining book even after the lapse of a century."

After reading Elliott's deer shooting adventures, Theodore Roosevelt years later called them "admirable." Archibald Rutledge and William Faulkner—both greatly influenced by Elliott's religious gusto for the deer hunt—agreed with

Roosevelt's assessment, and further developed the cosmic and spiritual dimensions of the deer hunt as they inherited it from Elliott's graphic and inspiring accounts of chasing white-tailed deer. Most recently, the publisher of the 1994 paperback edition of *Carolina Sports* reports that "Elliott's captivating sketches preserve a bounty of natural history and local wisdom, and just as important they provide insight into a Southern way of life that would soon end in Civil War."

In a postscript to *Carolina Sports* entitled "Random Thoughts on Hunting," Elliott, like his Northern contemporary, "Frank Forester," denounced the wanton and uncalled-for destruction of forests and the professional market hunters who supplied the tables of luxurious hotels with venison. In his eloquent defense of hunting, Elliott pleas for the imposition of British hunting ethics and issues an urgent call for game conservation. In this postscript, old Venator underscores the basic and essential qualities and values of the deer hunter, as he understood them:

" ...the *punctuality*, that observes the hour and day appointed—the *observation*, that familiarizes itself with the nature and habits of the quarry—the *sagacity*, that anticipates its projects of escape—and the *promptitude* that defeats them!—the rapid glance, the steady aim, the quick perception, the ready execution—these are among the faculties and qualities, continually called into pleasing exercise; and the man who habitually applies himself to this sport, will become more considerate, as well as more prompt—more full of resource—more resolute—than if he never had engaged in it!"

These great cultural values hold true for the white-tailed deer hunting aficionado of today, even though Elliott articulated them almost a century and a half ago. We need to listen to our great mentors, especially this sportsman's sportsman, if our white-tailed deer hunting heritage is to be preserved. Elliott not only touched on the mythical qualities of the white-tailed deer and its incredible ability to disappear like wood smoke, but underscored the need for a metaphysics of deer hunting that all Americans can understand and appreciate—non-hunters and hunters alike. No one in the history of American white-tailed deer hunting more enthusiastically embraced the spiritual brotherhood of the American deer hunt and its inherent cultural values than did William Elliott, a giant among deer hunters.

On Wednesday, February 4, 1863, R. B. Rhett, Jr., editor and publisher of the *Charleston Mercury*, wrote as follows in response to the death of the Hon. William Elliott: "As a sportsman, we hazard little in saying that, on land and water, his equal has rarely, if ever, been seen in this country."

William H. H. "Adirondack" Murray in a poster for Saranac Gloves, ca. 1878.

"The pleasure of the sportsman in the chase is

measured by the intelligence of the game and its

capacity to elude pursuit and in the labor involved

in the capture. It is a contest with sharp wits where

satisfaction is mingled with admiration for

the object overcome."

–Judge John Dean Caton,
The Antelope and Deer of North America, 1877

JUDGE CATON

No student of white-tailed deer behavior studies the natural history of this animal or the hunting of them without first consulting the life and work of John Dean Caton (1812-1895), that prominent Chief Justice of the Supreme Court of Illinois and one of the most distinguished "deer doctors" America ever produced. Setting the tradition followed by modern-day deer Ph.Ds, Caton systematically studied the natural history of the whitetail and made the hunting of them his favorite leisure-time diversion. Although Judge Caton claimed to be an amateur naturalist, he nevertheless maintained that severe and systematic study and discipline so indispensable to the professional scientist. No one in the history of American deer hunting so intimately combined the hunting of deer with the science of natural history.

Although trained as a jurist, he studied the whitetail throughout his life not only in books and research reports, but in the grandest school of all—the realm of nature, where he pursued his quarry with gun and pen in hand. Like his contemporaries Theodore Roosevelt, T. S. Van Dyke and Carl Rungius, Caton participated in the stirring excitement of the chase so he could learn even more about the whitetail's habits, especially its

The Caton home located in North Bluff, Ottawa, Illinois.

Inset: Judge John Dean Caton (1812-1895), one of the most distinguished "deer doctors" America ever produced.

breeding characteristics during the rut. Like Van Dyke and Roosevelt, Caton believed the deer hunter, even more than the scientist, has the greatest opportunity to study the white-tail's habits, ways and capabilities, for he spends more time in the deer forest.

Throughout his life, this famous deer hunter/naturalist combined with great religiosity the study of the natural history of the white-tailed deer with the thrilling incidents encountered in the hunting of them. As his great and lasting contribution to the study of white-tailed deer and deer hunting, he not only published the first scientific treatise on the subject, *The Antelope and Deer of America* (1877), but also created America's first deer park in 1858, a 200-acre enclosure established solely for observing and studying the various kinds of deer he held in captivity with special preference for his favorite species, *Odocoileus virginianus*. His enthusiasm for deer remained infectious; at the conclusion of reading his work and studying his life, you wonder why everybody does not turn to keeping deer and studying their habits.

Caton was born on a small farm near the Hudson River in Orange County, New York, in 1812. By the time he was four years old, his mother became a widow struggling to feed and clothe her four small children. The young boy spent most of his youth as an apprentice to farmers and harness makers while continuously striving to get an education. He was aided by persons who befriended him, admiring his ability and perseverance. However, his mother was able to keep the boy in the district school only with the greatest of difficulty, for he maintained a reputation for being a mischievous boy. "I preferred," Caton later wrote in his unpublished memoirs, "an active outdoor life, running, jumping, wrestling, and hunting."

The farmers he worked for never wearied of relating their deer hunting experiences to him, and the boy never wearied of listening to them. "Their hunting experiences when deer, bear and wild turkeys were so abundant as to be almost nuisances, fairly transported me to the wild woods and wild scenes and the exciting chases which they so graphically described; and I longed for the time to come when I should be old enough to carry a rifle, and when I might wend my way to a new country such as they described, where I too might revel among game which had scarcely ever been alarmed by civilized man."

After studying at Grosvenor High School in Rome, New York, and spending an apprenticeship in the law offices of Beardsley and Matteson in Utica, young Caton not only secured a legal education in the spring of 1833, but was introduced to the wild adventures of the famous Unadilla Deer Hunting Club in central New York by Levi Beardsley (1785-1857), judge, President of the New York Senate, buck hunter and hunt master incarnate. Here the young lad experienced the day-long deer hunts with hounds and horses that culminated in "boisterous mirth" in the evening at the Village Inn, named "Hunter's Hall." After one November week, 31 guns brought down 40 bucks. One member of the club, Old Towser, toasted the communal deer shoot in a poem entitled "The Unadilla Hunt: Or Oxford Chase:"

> *Forty stags are brought down,*
> *at forty rods how they fall!*
> *Forty bucks are made venison*
> *by the long shots and ball,*
> *Forty saddles now smoke*
> *on the plentiful board,*
> *Forty corks are now drawn*
> *from Bachus' hoard,*
> *Forty sportsmen club-wits,*
> *every man in his place,*
> *Forty stories are told of*
> *the grand Oxford chase.*

Caton would never forget the celebrated, grandiose adventures of this deer hunting club, the cries of the deer hounds, their vociferous and discordant yells, the curling smoke of rifles, and the great hunters' feasts that followed with saddles of venison, Susquehanna pike and wine and brandy "that were not unsparingly proffered," as Beardsley described it in his *Reminiscences* (1852).

These were indeed times that enlivened and enlarged the souls of men. Speaking of these arduous Unadilla deer hunts, Col. Clapp, a member of the club, said "they generally lasted four or five days, and resulted in the capture of 20 or 35 deer. I have seen 19 fat bucks and does lying side by side, in the ball room of our hotel, in Unadilla. The glorious scenes in the chase, and the many remarkable deaths that occurred; the music of the dogs, and the excitement of the sportsmen, are indelibly impressed on my memory." Twenty years later Caton would re-enact these joyous moments of coursing deer, but this time on the "Grand Prairie" of Illinois.

Tales of the daring life in the great wild West, heard from the lips of a Dutchman named Detmore, another member of the Unadilla Deer Hunting Club, fired Caton's burning desire to emigrate to the western country in search of his fortune. His bold start for the West was spontaneous; his precise destination quite unfixed. The Erie Canal took him to Buffalo; a steamer called the "Sheldon Thompson" to Detroit; a stagecoach to Ann Arbor; and a horse-drawn wagon to White Pigeon, Michigan, where he began to live off the land on grouse, wild turkeys and venison, which sold for a half-penny per pound in Illinois in 1831.

In June of 1833, the 6-foot, well-proportioned outdoorsman arrived in the small hamlet of Chicago with his cherished flint-lock rifle called "Old Hemlock" in hand and 14 dollars and some odd cents in his pocket.

His favorite rifle, an old Springfield flint-lock musket in 54 caliber, eventually burned in a fire at his cabin on his farm in Plainfield, Illinois. He later remounted it and gave it to a friend going to California in 1848, who lost it in a fight with bandits on the Gila River in New Mexico.

The young, boyish, enthusiastic lawyer from Rome, New York, who was destined to become one of the great deer men of the 19th century and a multi-millionaire businessman, stopped for the first night in Chicago at a log tavern at Wolf Point kept by W. W. Wattles thoroughly prepared to set his stake and commence the business of life. By February of 1834, he had opened the first law office in Old Chicago and as an "old resident" of nine months, the 21-year-old back-woodsman with a heavy black beard stood before 250 inhabitants and proceeded to authorize a village incorporation under the general laws of the State of Illinois.

Chicago, at that time, consisted of merely a few log houses clustered around Fort Dearborn, a range of sand hills covered with cedars and willows along the shoreline of Lake Michigan. To the south and west was an endless stretch of prairie. Virgin pines bordered the lake north to the Chicago River. Dense shrubbery forests clothed the east sides of both branches of the river.

The winter of 1832, Caton recalls, was the hardest winter ever for deer. Four feet of snow covered the northern half of the state of Illinois. In 1833, he hunted deer in the Grand Prairie and did not see a single deer. By 1835, however, "many were met with and in 1838, they were as abundant as ever ...In that year I counted over 60 in one drove, only 16 miles from Chicago, and you could cross a prairie nowhere without jumping deer."

When Caton arrived in Chicago, he found the whole area occupied as the deer hunting grounds of the Pottawatomie Indians. He soon formed the acquaintance of many of their chiefs, acquaintances that ripened into

Trappers at Fault, Looking for Trail, A. F. Tait, ca.1852. Although Caton enjoyed hunting various species of deer in other locations and participated in almost every mode of deer hunting imaginable, he always returned with great joy to the Grand Prairie of Illinois to hunt whitetails on horseback.

cordial friendships. He found they possessed a great deal of information resulting from their careful observations of deer, and he traveled with them over the prairies in pursuit of deer. "I hunted and fished with them, I camped with them in the groves, I drank with them at the native springs of which they were never at a loss to find, and I partook of their hospitality around their campfires."

Whether group-hunting deer with the Pottawatomie Indians, coursing them with greyhounds, floating the waterways with his old friend John Stockton or still-hunting them, all of Caton's deer hunts became exercises in acquiring and recording practical information about the whitetail's senses and habits.

On one of his earliest recorded still-hunts in December of 1847, documented in the pages of the *American Naturalist*, Caton followed a large, antlered buck from daylight until around four o'clock in the afternoon over the bluffs of the Vermilion River near his farm in Ottawa. After tramping through six inches of dry, hard snow all day—"as difficult to walk in as dry cornmeal"—he stopped on a bluff. Too fatigued to track much farther, he rested his 45-caliber flintlock rifle, "Old Hemlock," made by Paul Smith of Franklin County, Kentucky, against a tree, feeling deeply chagrined at the dimming chance of getting the deer. Suddenly, he heard a twig crack and the buck stopped not more than 30 feet from him, but the brush was too thick for a shot. Caton tells us what happened:

"The buck stared at me some seconds, as if something told him of danger; but at length he seemed to become reassured and bounded along in his original course as if he was in somewhat of a hurry, but not in manifest alarm. As I anticipated, on his third or fourth bound he gave me a chance, and I fired as he was descending. His heels flew into the air with a snap as if his hoofs would

Two deer arrive in camp in their classy, horse-drawn hearse as B. F. Charlton celebrates the event with some sort of hearty libation. This photo was taken by George Shiras III at whose White Fish Lake deer camp Caton hunted on occasion.

Michigan's famous Deerfoot Lodge was owned and operated by that well-known sportsman, editor, author, and traveler, the Hon. Chase S. Osborn, ca. 1897. From left to right, Barney, the deer camp cook, Governor Osborn and two unidentified deer hunters. Caton frequently hunted here with Osborn.

fly off, and he fell all in a heap. There was something in the size of the deer and his antlers, the way in which his hind legs, as quick as lightning, stretched almost perpendicularly in the air, and the mode of his falling, which produced a thrill of delight which I have never before or since experienced."

Despite a busy career as a jurist and businessman, Caton tramped the broad prairies of Illinois in search of whitetails during every free day he could spare, thus making the study of these animals and the hunting of them his main recreational activity. In 1853, the state of Illinois passed its first deer law establishing a 6-month deer-hunting season. Caton made the most of it. Although he enjoyed hunting various species of deer in California, Wisconsin, Michigan, Canada, and the Adirondacks of New York, among other places, and participated in almost every mode of deer hunting imaginable, including jack lighting on the waterways, he always returned with great joy to the Grand Prairie of Illinois to hunt whitetails on horseback with his friend Mr. Buchanan of Ottawa and "Old Speed," "the fastest, smartest and most knowing greyhound I ever saw," as Caton characterized him in an article in *The Rod and Gun*. This type of deer hunting afforded him the most varied and exciting experiences. The white-tailed deer, he once remarked, "has an intelligence which enables it to resort to expedients to baffle its pursuer, and it possesses a vitality which enables it to escape with wounds which would prostrate the other species at once."

Caton found the prairies of Illinois the proper theater for coursing, for running deer with greyhounds by sight, not scent. In commenting on this exhilarating mode of chasing deer, he classified it, like William Elliott and Frank Forester, as by far the most dangerous, especially for the inexperienced rider, for if he returns with a sound horse and a sound body, he may consider himself fortunate. With a lunch of bread and cold venison steak in his pocket and a double-barreled gun in hand—one barrel a rifle and the other for buckshot—Caton raced across the prairies urging his steed to the utmost to keep up with the expert greyhounds as they drew near to their quarry. "To be the foremost in such a chase," Caton admitted, "to keep even with the leading hound, and see that each stride lessens the intervening space between the pursuers and the pursued, is the culmination of excitement only known to the ardent sportsman."

Although Caton preferred coursing deer to all other modes of hunting, like his friend, T. S. Van Dyke, he also loved to still-hunt in the pine woods north of Chicago, but with the added element of the silent and sagacious deer dog. "The best dog I ever owned for the still hunt was a pointer. Though not so fleet or so powerful as the greyhound, his fine nose and great sagacity compensated for all else. He would take the track of the deer and follow it by the scent just as fast or slow as directed, and as still as a cat. When he brought a wounded deer to bay, he would give tongue as furiously as one could desire, and hold him at bay with great pertinacity; but, of course, he never seized the animal."

Throughout his lifetime, the great debate raged on over hounding deer versus still-hunting them, and became the major motif of the deer hunting literature of the time. Caton took the unusual position of doing both with equal fervor. On the one hand, he understood and loved the great excitement of hunting deer with dogs: "Rifles are cocked, not a whisper is breathed, not a twig is broken, not a leaf is stirred. Every wandering thought is summoned back and absorbed in the excitement of the moment. The course of the hounds may be traced by their voices, each listener calculating the chances of their arriving at his stand."

Yet, he also understood the avid still-hunter who argued, "What business has a man got in the woods who can't take home a piece of venison to his shanty without scaring all the deer for ten miles around before he gets at it? The flesh of the poor creature is worth nothing neither, after their blood is heated by being driven to death with dogs!"

Even though Caton loved to hunt deer with dogs as well as the silent still-hunt, he readily acknowledged that "the sublime stillness of silent nature in the solitude of the dark forest is broken by the noisy bay of great packs of hounds as the deer goes rushing through the woods... "

As the deer herd began to decline in Illinois during the 1870s, Caton shifted his focus to hunting deer in Michigan and northern Wisconsin. In October of 1873, he purchased a Winchester Model 1873 carbine in 44-40 caliber with a 20-inch barrel—the rifle Jimmy Stewart later immortalized in the film "Winchester 73." The Model '73 was indeed special, for it shot special cartridges—centerfires. Theodore Roosevelt, Caton's friend, had a Winchester Model 1873 among his many "ranch rifles" for deer and loved it. The Model 1873 became the best-known custom gun in the history of Winchester Arms.

With this famous sporting rifle and a copy of James Low Jr.'s classic *Floating and Driving for Deer* (1873) in hand, the Illinois judge traveled to northern Wisconsin to hunt deer with his friend John Stockton and his Indian guide John Komoska. They set up their deer camp tent along the banks of a small lake near Pike River, Wisconsin. During the day they fished for black bass and floated for deer toward sunset. One day, while heading their canoe from camp at sunset, they heard a pack of wolves in the woods. Suddenly they saw a large buck—a 10-pointer—leave the woods and enter the

lily pads in the shallow water. The white-tailed buck with the "great branching antlers" stood in the water and listened to the yelping noise of his pursuers unaware of the deer hunters in the canoe. Komoska stopped paddling the canoe. Caton describes the scene:

"Not a breath of air was stirring, and the water was as smooth as a mirror, while the bright declining sun cast the shade of the tall pines on shore far out upon the lake. 'There,' said Stockton, 'is the first full realization I have ever seen of Landseer's glorious picture *The Monarch of the Glen.*' And so it was. The ideal of the great artist stood before us in all his magnificence, an actual verity. There stood the monarch of the forest in the border of the quiet lake, where the deep solitude is rarely broken by invading man, not dreaming there were enemies before him more dangerous than those behind, of escape from which he now felt assured."

But escape he did not; for the buck suddenly plunged into deep water and swam directly toward Caton's canoe. Within 50 yards of the canoe, Caton's Winchester '73 spoke, and the trophy 10-pointer was secured, thanks to the wolves along shore. After towing the buck to shore and examining the shot, the Judge found "a great warrior," whose broken antler tines gave evidence of many scars from the rigorous battles of the rut. The old warrior weighed 250 pounds dressed and remained the largest whitetail buck Caton ever shot.

Caton also hunted deer at Michigan's famous Deerfoot Lodge, owned and operated by that well-known sportsman, editor-author and traveler, the Hon. Chase S. Osborn, Governor of Michigan; as well as at the White Fish Lake deer camp of George Shiras III, the father of deer photography whose deer photos Caton greatly admired.

Caton considered Sir Edwin Landseer's *The Monarch of the Glen* the most famous deer painting in the world, 1851.

Most of Caton's deer hunts, regardless of where he hunted or his mode of deer hunting—whether still-hunting or dog hunting or canoeing the waterways of Wisconsin—ended in camp by aging and weighing the harvested deer and preparing the skins and other parts of the skeleton for mounting and research purposes. "After our camp work was done," he wrote in his journal while deer hunting in the secluded valleys of California's Gaviota Pass, "we enjoyed a most leisurely feast of venison prepared in all the different modes most approved of in camp, sweetened by long absence and hard toil."

The incidents of the day were then recounted in Caton's deer camp with such extravagant embellishments as were deemed necessary to enable each companion to outwit the other with his own dazzling stories. The soothing influence of the burned herb and a dash of good old port eased the disappointments and heightened the accomplishments. But before turning in on beds formed by rank, wild oats, all comrades agreed with the Judge when he insisted that "an old buck is as cunning as a fox, but if you understand his ways, it is possible to circumvent him, and to do so is the very essence of sport."

Caton not only studied deer while hunting them in the wild and sharing the experiences of others in his deer camp, but by way of daily contact with them in his 200-acre deer park, he carefully observed and documented their social behavior and physiology, especially the nature and function of antlers and glands. At his deer park, he kept 50 to 60 deer in captivity, including all of the American deer except the moose and caribou. Here he measured, drew, photographed, studied, and collected deer antlers with all the obsession and furor of the current American antler craze. Indeed, he was perhaps the first American deer hunter to "romance the antler." In his numerous writings, he described their system of nutrition, mode of growth, maturity, decay and rejection, the effects of castration and, finally, their uses.

Not content to merely study and examine the American species, in both captivity and the wild, he traveled to Norway to study red deer and reindeer for comparative purposes. When visiting Europe a second time, he studied the deer of England, Ireland and Scotland as well. He also went to China and Japan to learn about the unique deer of China, Pere David's deer, and the Japanese Sika deer. In the fall of 1872, he hunted and studied the habitat of wild animals in Nova Scotia. In America, he hunted and traveled through every state of the Union except Montana and Idaho, extending his hunting tramps into Manitoba and British Columbia.

From these foreign excursions and vast tramps across America, he brought home to his farm in Ottawa a remarkable collection of deer prints, photographs, antlers, deer droppings, tails, glands, skins, ears, hoofs, plus sundry deer memorabilia, and he constantly received specimens in the mail from deer hunters around the world. From Scotland he returned with a copy of Sir Edwin Landseer's "The Monarch of the Glen," which he considered the most famous deer painting in the world. In return, he shipped various species of American deer to Scotland, France, Belgium, and Germany. In his billiard room, he hung the heads of the trophy bucks he shot while on these excursions—"the greatest sporting events of my life." In February of 1886, Caton's magnificent, world-class antler collection and the most complete library on deer and deer hunting in existence were unfortunately destroyed by a major fire at his summer residence in Ottawa.

The final outcome of his sporting events, his patient and industrious study of deer in captivity, and his vast travels to foreign countries resulted in the publication of *The Antelope and Deer of America* (1877), a book dealing with the life history of these animals and the various methods of hunting them. It took a deer hunter to write this great book, which still remains in print 125 years later, for in it, Caton brought to life the world of deer in general and the whitetail in particular, with the same vitality and enthusiasm that prompted him to carry his rifle in daily pursuit of them.

The book became an immediate success. *Forest and Stream*, the leading sportsman's journal of its time, called it "the most important publication ever printed on the subject; indeed it is so comprehensive in its scope and exhaustive in detail that it may justly be termed the only one." *The New York Times* highly recommended it for sportsmen because it "contained the exact experiences of a deer hunter who has a direct interest and a practical acquaintance with the subject he exhaustively treats." *The Atlantic Monthly* called his deer book "the best work on the subject ...in many respects, a model for all writers of natural history." All of the reviews in the scientific journals and the newspapers praised the book without reservation, thus making it the standard authority of its day on the subject. President Theodore Roosevelt said no deer hunter could be without it.

In this classic deer book, Judge Caton insisted that a complete knowledge of natural history and whitetail woodcraft meant many things. It entailed knowing in an intimate way the habits and movements of deer, being skillful in whatever weapon you choose to use, being able to prepare shelters along the trail and hearty venison meals in the field, and in general, creating and maintaining a deer camp as a school for the young beginner where he or she may learn many things besides just the mode of pursuing and capturing the animal. The hunter, above all others, Caton believed, can study the habits of the animals he pursues and captures, and in the process, gather a fund of knowledge that he can pass along to the novice that will also be of untold value to the scientist as well, who frequently studies deer only in the laboratory, library and penned enclosures. "The hunter, who seeks and takes the game in its native fastnesses, may thus, I say, give the scientist valuable assistance."

But above all else, woodcraft for Caton revolved around ethics in the field. Shortly before his death, he published a classic essay entitled "The Ethics of Field Sports" in one of the great sporting books of his day, *Big Game of North America*, edited by G. O. Shields (1890), in which he urged us to go to the deer forest with partners whose tastes are congenial with our own, for companionship remains indispensable for the full enjoyment of life in deer camp. Indeed, friendship and good feelings always prevailed in Caton's deer camp. "Between us there at once grew up a fraternal feeling; a cord of sympathy was drawn out between us which made us brothers and would have prompted us to make great sacrifices for each other, if need had been."

Caton only shot deer when he needed venison, or when others needed it or when he needed the animal for research purposes. He rightly argued that we must associate utility with the activity of deer hunting. "If the deer cannot be utilized, a pang of regret takes the place of gratification in the breast of the true sportsman." If you don't utilize the animal to the fullest—eat the venison, tan the hides, and mount the antlers—don't hunt. In conclusion he wrote: "Let me beseech all sportsmen to maintain the dignity of the craft to which they belong and to exert all their influence to elevate

the standing of that craft and to preserve our game."

Like his contemporaries T. S. Van Dyke and Theodore Roosevelt, who were also lawyers, deer hunters, and avid students of white-tailed deer, Judge Caton loved to leave the noise and legal hassles of city life to set his face toward the green wild-wood where whitetails and nature reign supreme. He went to the deer forest with men whose tastes were congenial to his own. His deer camp became a school of learning where he instructed many a tenderfoot about the ways of the whitetail and the marvels of natural history. He loved to pitch his tent deep in the forest "beside a fountain gushing from the living rock as if some Moses in former times had touched it with his wand," as he so elo-quently described it. There the music of its waters would soothe the Judge to sleep after a hard day's chase of great-antlered bucks. Before falling into the deepest repose, he would think to himself, "Oh, how delightful are such scenes! Their very remembrance is a joy renewed."

When the Judge shot a deer, he examined it with tremendous vitality, as he would a book full of knowledge and information. As an amateur naturalist with a vivid imagina-tion and profound persistence, he selected and solved many of the earliest scientific natural-history problems dealing with deer. He encouraged sportsmen in their outdoor publications to rely on science and natural history and set a remarkable example himself in popularizing science in this regard in his own writings on deer and deer hunting.

As he examined his downed quarry, a vibrant thrill flashed through every fiber of his massive, rugged, 240-pound frame. We have no finer guide and mentor than this all-time giant among American deer hunters. As long as the white-tailed deer roams the forests of this country and man pursues this marvelous and unique creature, we will

Chicago's premier deerslayer, John Dean Caton.

always remember Judge Caton's measure of what a deer hunt is all about:

The pleasure of the sportsman in the chase is measured by the intelligence of the game and its capacity to elude pursuit and in the labor involved in the capture. It is a contest with sharp wits where satisfaction is mingled with admiration for the object overcome.

Judge Caton, Chicago's premier deer-slayer, lived a life full of honors and accomplishments; his life reads like a Horatio Alger story. Beginning life as an impoverished farmhand, he later corresponded with such dignitaries as Charles Darwin, Abraham Lincoln and Theodore Roosevelt. After retiring from the Illinois Supreme Court, he presided over the Illinois &

Mississippi Telegraph Company as its president, controlling all of the telegraph lines in the state of Illinois and amassing a colossal fortune in the process, listed at more than two million dollars at the time of his death.

When this pioneer lawyer, popular judge, die-hard deer hunter, Honorary Member of the Boone and Crockett Club and enthusiastic naturalist died at his home in Chicago on July 30, 1895, Charles Hallock, the famous editor of *Forest and Stream* wrote the final tribute:

"Judge Caton was in his day a tireless sportsman, a fine shot and a most observing student of all things afield. His *Antelope and Deer of America* would alone have assured him recognition, and we believe that it was in matters of sportsmanship and of natural history that he took his chief pride and main enjoyment."

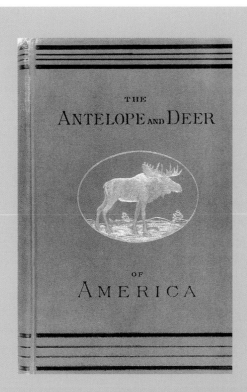

A BLUE-CHIP DEER BOOK

Front cover of the 1877 first edition of *The Antelope and Deer of America* by John Dean Caton. This classic, blue-chip deer book, a favorite of Jack O'Connor, Theodore Roosevelt and Aldo Leopold, still remains in print 125 years after its date of original publication. An original edition sometimes appears in the catalogues of out-of-print booksellers specializing in outdoor literature for $250-$400. Theodore Roosevelt believed that no deer hunter should be without this book; it formed the cornerstone of TR's hunting library, which now reposes as a Special Collection in the Library of Congress. Roosevelt's mother gave it to him as a Christmas gift in 1877, when he was 19 years old. TR cherished Caton as the final authority on deer and deer hunting.

The Trapper's Last Shot, Currier & Ives, undated.

"For durability, buckskin is as important as it is to the hero

of a sporting romance."

–T.S. Van Dyke, 1882

"THE

Chapter Nine

T.S. VAN DYKE
STILL-HUNTER"

When *The American Field*, the most prestigious sporting journal of its time, serialized 30 articles entitled "The Still-Hunter" in 1881, it became immediately apparent that Theodore Strong Van Dyke (1842-1923) adeptly communicated the universal qualities of the deer-hunting experience to his readers, especially the uncertainty and unpredictability of still-hunting deer. The serialization generated a host of letters to the editor.

One gentleman told the editor that Van Dyke "sums up in a single sentence an argument which a less compact mind would have spread over pages." Another reader named "Evergreen" commented that Van Dyke "moves over the subject with the passionless strength of a rifle ball." "Peep Sight," an even more enthusiastic reader, admitted while reading Van Dyke's articles, he wiped his eyes many a time.

Old deer hunters, practical sporting men and writers on the art of woodcraft who read the early portions of Van Dyke's classic book as serialized in *The American Field*, gave unsought testimony to its great value. J. C. Rossler, a medical doctor, observed that while "I have still-hunted deer for thirty years, I know of nothing more admirable in the way of scientific exposition than Mr. Van Dyke's articles on this subject." Fred Pond ("Will Wildwood"), the editor of Frank

Van Dyke guarding the Daggett Community Jail House with his Winchester '73.

Inset: Portrait of The Still-Hunter, T. S. Van Dyke, 1842-1923.

Forester's work and a well-known outdoor writer of his time, joined in the chorus of triumphant praise: "After carefully reading the current sporting literature of America for many years, I must confess that Van Dyke's work comes the nearest to my ideal."

One backwoods deerstalker named "Mack" wrote the editor saying, "Mr. Van Dyke is a trump! I can almost imagine after reading his articles on still-hunting that he had followed me through the woods when I first began to hunt deer. He depicts exactly the greenhorn's mistakes and trials." The author Ned Buntline perhaps best summarized the reader's enthusiastic response by calling for the publication of the articles in book format: "I have as fine a collection of works on hunting and fishing as can be found in any library, but it will lack the best, the very best, deer-hunting treatise till Mr. Van Dyke's book stands most prominent of all before my eyes."

In responding to these comments of praise and the many inquiries and letters to the editor, Van Dyke completely revised and rewrote the material. On December 20, 1882, Fords, Howard and Hulbert of New York published the book that was destined to become the greatest classic in the history of American deer hunting. It sold for two dollars.

Entitled *The Still-Hunter: A Practical Treatise on Deer Stalking*, the book went through 14 editions and numerous printings between 1882 and 1944. In 1987, 1988 and again in 1995, I edited and revised three different editions of the book. All three of these editions are out of print. It remained an all-time favorite of President Theodore Roosevelt, who referred to it as "a noteworthy book which for the first time, approached the still-hunter and his favorite game, the deer, from what may be called the standpoint of the scientific sportsman. It is one of the few hunting books which should really be studied by the beginner because of what he can learn there from in reference to the hunter's craft." In his *Hunting Trips of a Ranchman* (1885), TR crowed, "No ranchman who loves sport can afford to be without Van Dyke's *The Still-Hunter!*"

In 1882, the New York *Spirit of the Times* called his book "the best, the very best work on deer hunting." *The New York Evening Post* agreed: "Altogether the best and most complete American book we have yet seen on any branch of the field sports." Sir Henry Halford, one of England's foremost hunters and anglers, characterized it as "by far the best book on the subject I have seen – in fact, the only really good one." *Forest and Stream*, the leading outdoor journal of the time, categorized it "as a well written primer on still-hunting, a valuable book which gives us a general theory of deer hunting. It serves to impress upon the student who is venturing into this new and difficult field of research, the importance of the three cardinal principles by which success may be attained: caution, patience and deliberation. It deserves high praise." In 1904, *The New York Times* observed that "lovers of paradox, still hunters of subtleties in the expression of truth, will rejoice by the manner in which the author conveys instruction in the art of deer hunting."

Outing Magazine reported that "so lifelike is the action that the reader is charmed in the imaginary pursuit and shares the exultation of the capture." *The New York Herald* called the book "very entertaining and intensely practical." Writing in New York's *Turf, Field, and Farm*, one reviewer labeled it as "a classic in the sporting literature of America." *The American Field* referred to the book as "the best work from the pen of this fluent and graceful writer. The information contained in it, is as exhaustive as it is possible to make it." When Charles Sheldon, one of America's most famous big game hunters, annotated his copy of *The Still-Hunter* for his magnificent world-class library on sport and travel, he wrote in the inside cover: "The best book ever written on still hunting."

In my opinion, the book represents a very successful attempt to combine the interest of a deer-hunting novel, which is all too rare in our time, with the more practical features of an authoritative work on deer hunting methodology. Even with the passage of time, one can hardly dispute the early evaluations. Indeed, Van Dyke's basic philosophy of still-hunting as formulated in 1882, remains pretty much intact today. Even after more than 120 years of intensive deer hunting in America and after a tremendous amount of theorizing on the subject, the principles of still-hunting according to T. S. Van Dyke have received little or no embellishment. Giants among deer hunters such as Judge Caton from Illinois, William Monypeny Newsom from New York and Paulina Brandreth from the Adirondacks recognized their own contributions to the study of deer and the art and science of deer hunting as but modest footnotes to the works of Van Dyke.

The book awakens our enthusiasm for deer and deer hunting, for Van Dyke uses the pen as skillfully as the gun. The work is crisp and readable throughout. His powers of observation and ability to picture graphically what he experienced while in the field remain unsurpassed. He wrote the book as though he were talking to some fellow deer hunter, recounting as we never tire of doing, exciting incidents in the field which have their date in history but which renew their life in vivid recollections. I think that no better praise can be bestowed upon this blue-chip deer book than to say that the sportsman who reads it will vividly relive his own deer-hunting days. In short, its spirited and life-like descriptions will make every deer hunter who has ever found enjoyment in still-hunting white-tailed deer tingle with the delight of pleasant recollections. A classic!

Consider the wild and high-spirited dis-course on the deer shooting adventures of Dr. Belville, a young physician from San Francisco:

"Bang! goes the Winchester rifle as he sweeps through the shrubbery, and the ball, whizzing through the place he has just left, hisses harmlessly away over the great Temecula canyon far below. *Bang!* goes another shot aimed to catch him as he rises; but he never rises twice alike, and as he clears a bush with slanting spring the ball splashes itself to pieces against a rock by his side. Vainly Belville tries to hold the rifle on the point where the buck will touch ground; for now he springs fifteen feet ahead and five to one side; now five feet ahead and five to the other side; now going down behind some rock, from the top of which the ball sings over the depths beyond; now flashing

A Good Shot, a Carl Rungius illustration from the 1923 edition of Van Dyke's *The Still-Hunter*.

full on high with his whole shining body in the bright sun, clear above brush and rocks, falling as the ball spins over him, and glancing up again from the hard ground as he strikes – all the time fast nearing the top of the ridge. Over he goes in a high curve, clear-cut in outline against the western sky, a beautiful mark if it only stayed long enough. The rifle cracks as the figure clears the climax of its bound, and a foreleg dangles useless on the buck.

"Thanks to the light moccasins, which never slip, Belville skipped along the tops of the boulders and reached the farther edge in about a minute. A wild mass of steep confusion, chaotic with rocks and scraggy brush, lay before him, and the buck – stopped? Yes, as the rocket when it is once fairly started stops when the stick breaks. Fast as before, but more erratic in his twist, he went down the rocky slope, smashing through brush like a circus rider through papered hoops, bounding as high as if he had gained another leg instead of losing one. *Bang! whang! bang! whang!* went the swift repeater with desperate energy. The bullet sank glancing from the rocks into the bluish-green abyss below, or spattered into leaden spray against their granite side. *Bang! bang! bang!* in quick succession sounds the rifle; and at last a faint spat is heard; the bound changes to a lumbering canter; the buck no longer clears the brush, but smashes headlong through it with his momentum; he still steers clear of the rocks and bushes, crashing onward for several yards, when suddenly he lunges,

Still Hunting on the First Snow: A Second Shot, A.F. Tait, 1855. As a young boy, Van Dyke frequently stared at this classic deer hunting painting at the Van Dyke mansion at Green Oaks in New Brunswick, New Jersey.

staggers, rolls heavily through a bush, which is crushed beneath his weight, and the dust rises from his scuffling feet as he turns a somersault on the dry ground among the rocks."

Van Dyke was born in New Brunswick, New Jersey, in 1842. His father, John Van Dyke, was a lawyer and jurist, a member of the United States House of Representatives and a long-standing friend of Abraham Lincoln. Like his father, young Theodore was born, raised and educated in the woods, and emerged as a student of the white-tailed deer. "From the earliest days the woods were to me the greatest of attractions. My home was in the corner of a 20-acre piece of forest on the edge of town, which connected with woods upon woods reaching the groves that I started when school was out and there most of my vacations and Saturdays were spent. Frequent trips to New York were mainly to explore the game departments of the museums and the novelties of the gun stores, and I always returned with a pitying contempt for the city boys who knew nothing of the woods."

The young boy dreamed of becoming a mighty deer hunter. In the family's three-peaked mansion at Green Oaks among the idyllic countryside of wooded terrain and rich farmlands, two large paintings caught the boy's attention several times a day: A. F. Tait's *Still Hunting on First Snow: A Second Shot* (1855), and William Ranney's *The Trapper's Last Shot* (1850). As he stared at these classic and dramatic paintings of the hunt, which inspired many sportsmen, he saw himself as a son of the frontier, as an ardent follower of Audubon and James Fenimore Cooper's Natty Bumppo.

As an avid outdoorsman and a lover of books, the young lad went to Princeton University, receiving a B.A. in 1863 and his M.A. in 1866. In the latter year, he was admitted to the bar. In his autobiography, Van Dyke's younger brother John C. notes that Theodore "went through Princeton College with a dog and a gun, as my father said, and to this day there lives at Princeton the tradition of his wonderful shooting with a dueling pistol with bullfrogs as targets. 'A Van Dyke Shot' was synonymous with a bull's eye."

After graduating from Princeton University, the young Van Dyke moved to the woods of Wabasha, Minnesota, in 1867, where he practiced law for the next eight years. Here he lived in a home on a bluff overlooking the Mississippi River. After establishing residency there, he later became a member of the Minnesota State Assembly. During this time, Van Dyke became so enamored with still-hunting whitetails, both in Minnesota and northern Wisconsin, that his deer hunts generally lasted for several months. Dressed in moccasins and deerskins, he hunted deer in the big pines. Like Audubon and Natty Bumppo, he shot, tanned and lived in buckskin and believed that "for durability buckskin is as important as it is to the hero of a sporting romance." He hunted deer in the sparsely settled state of Minnesota with the Sioux Indians and learned about their deer-hunting ways from frequent conversations in their tepees.

Following the code of the ethical sportsman, he always considered deer hunting more of a charm than mere shooting; wild game that knew how to get away always remained his first choice of pursuit. By the time he was 25, he had 13 years of deer hunting experience behind him. As he put it in an autobiographical essay, "I was distinguished for keenness of sight and skill with pistol, rifle and gun at an early age, even among far older companions. Since childhood I had seen deer run before hounds and helped shoot many of them with buckshot. I was a natural still-hunter that needed only opportunity."

At the age of 25, he roamed the finest shooting grounds of Minnesota at every possible opportunity. Yet he always longed for bigger and wilder forests, not the pinewoods, but the old hardwood timber that Daniel Boone so admired. After years of longing, the opportunity arose in 1867 when an obstinate case of ague gave him an excuse for spending seven months in the great virgin forest of northwestern Wisconsin. He recalls the event in an essay entitled "The Forest Primeval."

"A dim wagon road wound 40 miles into the north, on which were five new settlers, each going eight or ten miles beyond the last, looking for something better. Like them I wanted the last and best and started for the end of the line with nothing but a rifle and blanket. As I left the lovely oak openings and the heavy timber closed in around me, I felt like the prince in a fairy tale, just come to his own."

He so enjoyed the northern forests that when ill health struck again in 1875, he sought solitude and tranquility, but this time in the mountains and wilderness of southern California. There, he lived 60 miles from anything that could even be called a village, in one of the wildest parts of the country. During this time he lived among game, camping daily and loafing or walking in its haunts. Morning, noon and night, he was rarely out of sight or sound of deer, for amidst the trees where he wrote, read and dozed, they trotted about within a few yards of him.

"Often when no venison was needed, I spent the day in the tumbling hills on the trail of the deer just to study the habits and tricks of this most mysterious of big game animals. No book is more interesting than the record of his daily life when you have cultivated the eye to the point where you can read it on dry ground and follow it through dead grass and fallen leaves. And when at last you find where the deer has lain down

for his siesta, there is almost as much pleasure in seeing the dust fly from his plunging hoofs as there is in stopping them with the best of modern rifles."

In California, when hunting quail with his shotgun became too easy, he took to shooting them with his bow and arrow and his 22-caliber rifle, but freely admitted in a superb essay on the ethics of hunting that he never really mastered the inherent difficulties of this "fine sport."

Van Dyke was, incidentally, one of the early American bow hunters. Even the famed Thompson brothers, Will and Maurice, the patron saints of American archery, were admirers and careful readers of Van Dyke's philosophy of deer hunting. Like the Thompsons, during his early days, he too roamed the woods and sent many an arrow after every squirrel and rabbit that crossed his path. From early childhood on, he loved bow hunting as dearly as he loved his dog and gun. With regard to bow hunting in the mountains and wilderness of California, he has this to say:

"Where the bow can be used with any reasonable chance of hitting, as on hares, etc., and without danger of losing too many arrows, it will afford much more pleasure than the gun to that class of sportsmen whose pleasure lies not in a big bag, not in the tickling of the almighty palate, and not in mere murder, but in the skill required, the scenery and association of the chase, etc. That class, too, is fast on the increase. I joined it years ago, and have no disposition to leave it. On the contrary, the changed taste grows upon me. Year after year I care less for game and count, and more for the way and manner of securing a little. And herein lies I believe the truest pleasure of hunting."

Like other sportsmen before him, he soon became so enchanted with the hunting opportunities of southern California that by the summer of 1876, he decided to make San

Diego his future home. Thus, with bedroll, bow and rifle in hand, he took to the back-country of San Diego County. For the next 10 years, he lived outdoors most of the time. The image of the lone hunter/trapper turning his back on civilization and riding off into the pristine wilderness of the West with Winchester rifle enclosed in a buckskin scabbard strikes a deep cord in American cultural history.

Although Van Dyke killed his first deer with a 40 Maynard and held that rifle in high esteem throughout his life, his favorite deer rifle remained the Winchester Model '73. The Winchester '73, carried in a buckskin saddle holster, went with him as a constant companion; it provided his venison and defended his life and possessions. He said this about his favorite deer rifle: "The combined ingenuity of Earth, even assisted by light from on high, could not improve upon the quintessence of perfection for big game hunting known as the Winchester of '73." For Van Dyke, the Winchester '73 possessed occult virtues far surpassing those of any other rifle. Judge Caton also chose this classic rifle as his first choice for deer hunting, and as Van Dyke once said about Caton, "His opinion is of more value than that of all the hunters in California!"

Throughout his life, Van Dyke not only enjoyed the truest pleasures of hunting, but remained a prolific writer. As he tramped the primeval forests of southern California, he used his eyes and ears, his pencil and notebook, and gave to the sporting world the vivid results of his wildlife observations. His writings in this regard combine a rich blend of natural history, adventurous fiction and unmatched, empirical perception. Indeed, between 1880 and 1895, he wrote nine books on outdoor pursuits.

In March of 1881, he published his first book, *Flirtation Camp, or The Rifle, Rod,*

and Gun in California, which described in a technical way California's wild game – afoot, afloat and on the wing. This technical description was placed in the context of a sporting romance with just enough lovemaking woven together with the wildlife adventures to give it additional zest. His popular treatise on still-hunting came out in the following year. In 1886, another fascinating outdoor book appeared; entitled *Southern California,* it gives us a great variety of information on southern California's mountains, valleys and streams, its animals, birds and fish, as well as hunting, fishing and camping in this area.

In 1902, he published *The Deer Family,* one of several books for The American Sportsman's Library, which he co-authored with Theodore Roosevelt and others. The book soon emerged as a standard work in the field. It consisted of an instructive collection of essays about the natural history of deer, as well as an interesting aggregation of stories about the adventures of deer hunters. After reading the book, John Spears rightly observed in *The New York Times,* "Van Dyke is always intensely amused when he thinks of the tenderfoot, with his brand-new shiny outfit and his obtrusive helpless imbecility, and yet he is the tenderfoot's best friend. The backwoodsman snorts when told that books can teach a tenderfoot anything, but Van Dyke's writings have made sportsmen of some of the most helpless tenderfeet that ever hit the trail." In 1903, he also co-authored several other volumes for The American Sportsman's Library on the waterfowl of the Pacific Coast and on the hunting of upland game birds.

During the first decade of the last century, he continued to write many articles on small and big game hunting that appeared in such popular magazines as *Outing* and *Collier's.* He also frequently contributed articles to *The American Field* and *Forest and Stream.* To accompany these articles on hunting, he created his own wildlife illustrations and pen sketches. Although he first went to southern California in poor health at the tender age of 34, he soon found a perfect cure in turning his undivided attention to outdoor pursuits, especially still-hunting for deer and writing about his outdoor adventures.

In addition to writing books and articles on hunting and various aspects of natural history, Van Dyke continued to practice law in the courts of California, and wrote many articles and several publications promoting San Diego County. He also established himself as an irrigation specialist. Indeed, Van Dyke became the first American to give substance to the idea that the importation of water was essential to the early prosperity of San Diego. By the 1890s, he emerged as one of the prime movers in construction of the great Flume Company that first brought

decent water to San Diego from Lake Cuyamaca. This technical experience as an irrigation engineer led him to a systematic study of not only the water requirements of human endeavor, but also of mammals and water's relationship to movement patterns of wildlife.

After a thorough study of the basic element of water, Van Dyke formulated some perceptive remarks about hunting deer at waterholes in wooded terrain. First of all, he observed that deer would frequently go a day or more without water even in the hottest and driest weather. Actually, they can dispense with water altogether when browse is succulent. When deer approach waterholes, however, they are quick drinkers, generally wasting little or no time—especially if heavily hunted. Secondly, Van Dyke noticed that in counties where water was scarce and

Whitetail Deer by Carl Rungius, a friend of Van Dyke. Rungius' artwork accompanies much of Van Dyke's work.

White-tailed Buck by Carl Rungius. Van Dyke studied the habits of deer when going to and coming from waterholes.

Courtesy of Wegner's Photo Collection.

the season especially dry and hot, deer would generally seek water right at daybreak. But he hastened to add that "how a deer will act in going to water or leaving it, as well as his time of watering, are things that cannot be reduced to a rule." Thirdly, Van Dyke discovered that deer frequently postpone drinking water until after feeding, and when going to water at this time, they generally walk quickly and stop infrequently. After many years of watching whitetails at a small waterhole in the North, I found this particular observation quite true. Yet Van Dyke continually reminds us not to place too much reliance on the whitetail's daily water requirements.

Van Dyke left San Diego in 1901 and moved to a 1200-acre ranch one mile east of the small community of Daggett, a rambunctious, wild and woolly frontier town filled with raucous silver miners, land speculators and famed characters such as Death Valley Scotty. Daggett was indeed a town of bizarre roisterers as Peter Wild observes: "There, a murder one night in the crowded Bucket of Blood Saloon had no witnesses. And when sinful Old Sally died of dissipation, folks genuinely grieved, if perhaps for themselves."

In this town of swindles, cow drives and shootouts, Van Dyke not only hunted deer on horseback in the hills, valleys and along the streams of the Calico Mountains, but he also entertained such distinguished naturalists as John Muir and John Burroughs at his ranch, while acting as justice of the peace for the Town of Daggett and its wild, barbarous desperadoes getting in trouble down at the Bucket of Blood Saloon. When he needed help on the ranch, he would go to town and round up drunks at the Bucket of Blood Saloon and hobos at the local railroad station. This free-wheeling behavior does not seem extraordinary given the very unusual nature of the law at this time in such isolated areas as Daggett.

In his delightful book, *Theodore Strong*

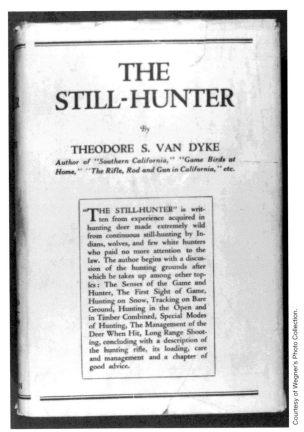

THE
STILL-HUNTER

By

THEODORE S. VAN DYKE

Author of "Southern California," "Game Birds at
Home," "The Rifle, Rod and Gun in California," etc.

"THE STILL-HUNTER" is written from experience acquired in hunting deer made extremely wild from continuous still-hunting by Indians, wolves, and few white hunters who paid no more attention to the law. The author begins with a discussion of the hunting grounds after which he takes up among other topics: The Senses of the Game and Hunter, The First Sight of Game, Hunting on Snow, Tracking on Bare Ground, Hunting in the Open and in Timber Combined, Special Modes of Hunting, The Management of the Deer When Hit, Long Range Shooting, concluding with a description of the hunting rifle, its loading, care and management and a chapter of good advice.

Courtesy of Wegner's Photo Collection.

The 1923 edition of Van Dyke's classic. The deer hunter who reads this book will vividly relive his or her own days afield. The book's spirited and lifelike descriptions will make every reader who has ever found enjoyment in still-hunting whitetails tingle with the delight of pleasant recollections.

Van Dyke (1995), author Peter Wild described Van Dyke's situation in Daggett:

"As the justice of the peace, known as Judge Van Dyke, he occupied an honored, if at times dicey, position in a community that could turn nasty on Saturday nights when miners coming down from the hills joined forces with Daggett's assorted ruffians for a collective toot. Facing such circumstances boldly, Theodore was a respected person, holding court on the verandah of his ranch, where malefactors brought to the bar of justice had a clear view of the sturdy plank jail Theodore kept at his ranch. He brooked no sass from thugs, but, softening when appropriate, he offered counsel to troubled souls needing avuncular guidance."

The Van Dyke Ranch, located near Sidewinder Mountain and Calico Ghost Town, hosted the Daggett Community Jail House, a primitive 10x12 wooden shack made of 2x6 timbers bolted together with wrought iron rods – preserved and still standing in Daggett as I write this book. Van Dyke often defended the Jail House with a double-barreled shotgun loaded with buckshot against attempted breakouts by ruffian friends of the inmates. In this frontier town of barrooms, brothels and shoot-outs, Judge Van Dyke stood ready to dispense justice with Winchester firearms, if need be. H. W. Keller, a prominent citizen of Los Angeles and one of Van Dyke's hunting companions, once asked Van Dyke, "if Daggett was not a tough town. Van Dyke said no. I told him it was the toughest-looking place I had ever been in. He insisted that it was a quiet, peaceful town. The night I left he escorted me to the railway depot with a double-barreled shotgun."

On this estate in the Mohave Desert, he again put his specialized knowledge of water to use and became a pioneer desert alfalfa grower. At the age of 67, he worked out-of-doors six or seven hours a day, paying no attention to the temperature. "I was not in any way obliged to do this, but I found my health better always for exercise, and I learned many years ago that the best way to endure heat is the same as enduring cold – to keep yourself strong with exercise and a good appetite."

Daggett and San Diego never forgot Van Dyke. The family name still applies to streets in East San Diego and Del Mar. American deer hunters never forgot Van Dyke either. His classic text on still-hunting stands as a giant on the American sportsman's bookshelf, a text one returns to with great delight. Theodore Strong Van Dyke, keen and observant naturalist, pioneer American still-hunter, engineer, farmer, writer and lawyer, died on June 26, 1923.

During his lifetime, Van Dyke was often referred to as "one of the first authorities in the sporting world" and as "that prince of a Sportsman." Indeed, he exhibited all of the qualities of the true sportsman, and these qualities are vividly revealed in his book *The Still-Hunter*. First of these was his passionate love of nature in every form and phase, which continually prompted him to study her patiently and faithfully. Consequently, he knew every tree and flower in the regions he hunted and fished, not only by their names, but also by their minutest features. He had the same familiar acquaintance with the animals he pursued. "In the saddle at four o'clock and miles into the hills by the time it was light enough to shoot – such were the requirements," of the deer hunter Van Dyke believed, if he were ever to learn the habits of this unique animal.

Second of these sportsman-like qualities was his esthetic appreciation of the woods. After searching for deer in the woods of the East Coast, and after pursuing them in the old hardwood timber of Minnesota and Wisconsin, as well as in the wild forests of Oregon, Mexico and California, Van Dyke gradually formulated a spiritual statement on what the woods meant for the deer hunter. The woods, he maintained, give scope and deeper satisfaction to the hunter who values game more for the skill required to bag it, than as a thing to eat or boast of.

In 1907, he wrote, "no wonder Bryant called the woods God's first temple. For nowhere else can you feel the mysterious power that rules all. Not upon the prairie, though there are few places where you feel smaller than on its vast sweep of loneliness. Nor on the sea with its still more certain proof that there is no fellow man within many miles. Nor yet on the mountain top where you can see even more plainly what a trifling link you are in the mighty chain of

being." Like his contemporaries Judge Caton, Paulina Brandreth and Archibald Rutledge, Van Dyke viewed man as one of the smallest minorities in the whole superstructure of life's many forms.

This idea is no more evident than in his conception of the final stage of deer hunting, the ultimate stage he hoped all deer hunters would reach – sooner or later. In this stage, the mere act of killing, though it requires the highest skill, merely becomes an inferior factor in the pleasure of those who really love the woods and hills. "In this stage there is more real enjoyment than in any other. I never saw the time when I cared a cent for records or anything of the sort and have always despised the trophy business, which too often means beastly murder. I never had an Indian or a guide hunt any

Where a Man's a Man, Philip R. Goodwin, 1904. Goodwin read the works of Van Dyke as he prepared his classic portraits of the American sportsman.

game for me to pull the trigger on, and would far rather do the hunting and let the Indian pull the trigger. What I wanted from a deer hunt was not that particular bit of meat or that head of horns, but to know whether I could get that buck or he get me. The pleasure in resolving this problem begins with the very first attempt to play your wits against the wits of the game." The number of hunters who reach this stage, Van Dyke acknowledged, is greater than many suppose and many reach it early.

In *The Deer Family* (1902), which he coauthored with President Theodore Roosevelt, he described this final stage of deer hunting in his own personal context. It bears repeating: "From 1875-1885, I lived where deer were so plentiful that going out to find fresh tracks was like going to the corner grocery. In the greater part of the section there were no hunters but myself, and deer so abundant that I made my own game laws, with no one to protest. Compelled to spend most of my time in the hills to regain lost health, I had little to do but study nature; and many a deer have I tracked up without a gun, and many a one have I let go not shot at simply because I did not want it, enjoying the hunt just about the same. In this way I knew many a deer clearly as well as if he were hanging under the tree at the house, for I rarely troubled those nearby, but kept them for emergencies, short hunts, and hunts without a gun." Shooting deer with the aid of today's excessive technological gadgetry would have disgusted Van Dyke, as it did Aldo Leopold.

In the tradition of Leopold and Judge Caton, Van Dyke grounded his theory of still-hunting in a broad conservation ethic that emphasized man's relationship with his environment and revealed an in-depth understanding of conservation history, the loss of wildlife habitat through defor-estation and draining swamps, while cele-brating large tracts of wilderness as national treasures. Like Caton and Leopold, Van Dyke believed man must live with nature according to nature's terms. If he monkey-wrenches nature to fit his own outrageous delusions, he will be doomed for his wrong-headed thinking. He believed in hard work and good stewardship. Man must accept nature on its own terms, he argued, and work within its limitations.

As a deer hunter, Van Dyke always believed he belonged to a hunting fraternity with a well-defined code of conduct and thinking. In order to obtain membership in this ideal order of true sportsmanship, he believed one had to practice proper etiquette in the field, give game a sporting chance and possess an esthetic appreciation of the whole context of the sport, which included a com-mitment to its perpetuation. He encouraged deer hunters above all to improve their "mental furniture," to avoid drawing hasty conclusions from an insufficient number of instances and to avoid inaccuracy of state-ment. As he put it in *The Still-Hunter*, "it's always and eternally that 'old buck' or 'big buck' that a writer kills (with his quill), until in the interest of philosophy one is almost tempted to offer a reward for any reliable information about the killing of a small doe or fawn."

He also came down hard on the braggart, on the man who talks of placing a bullet wherever he wishes to place it in a running deer and at any distance, or at one standing beyond 150 yards. This type of fellow deer hunter Van Dyke labeled as "an ignoramus who takes his listener for a bigger fool than he is himself." Mockery of the blockhead and self-mocking humor remained a major motif in all of Van Dyke's writings. Indeed, he greatly mocked Greenhorn mediocrity in deer hunting, especially with regard to poor shooting skills. Consider, for the example, the following passage:

"Bang! bang! bang! goes your rifle again,

Philip Goodwin watercolor, ca. 1907. "Bang! bang! bang! goes your rifle, and still the brown goes on."—T. S. Van Dyke in *The Still-Hunter*.

and still the brown goes on. Stop. Save your cartridges. He is wounded, and if you empty your rifle-magazine he may get out of this ravine before you can load again. It is evident that you are now too excited to hit anything; and therefore you had better take a few moments' time to cool down. And in the mean while fill up the magazine of your rifle, for you may need all the shots it will hold."

Or consider this choice piece of self-mocking humor with regard to a handkerchief waving a mocking farewell to hope and wringing a chicken's neck in the moonlight:

"You wind your way homeward over the oak ridges, and through the darkening timber see a white handkerchief or two beckoning you on, and hear once or twice the sound of bounding hoofs. But you reach home without seeing anything upon which you can catch sight with your rifle. You have seen plenty of deer today, but all going, going, going, glimmering through the dream of things that ought to be. Yet somehow you feel a supreme contempt for the exploit of your friend who last year sat by a saltlick and bagged two in one night with a shotgun. You feel rich in a far higher and nobler experience, and feel that to him who has within the true spirit of the chase there is far more pleasure in seeing over a ridge or among the darkening trunks a flaunting flag wave a mocking farewell to hope than in contemplating a gross pile of meat bagged with less skill than is required to wring a chicken's neck on a moonlight night."

It would be difficult to adequately summarize his basic principles within the scope of this chapter; it took Van Dyke one volume or nearly 400 pages to do so. I would like to recall some of the highlights of his theory, however. To begin with, Van Dyke points out that still-hunting is an extremely puzzling and mystifying affair. The intensity of concentration demanded by this type of hunting produces a total commitment and awareness to the natural environment around you. For many deer hunters, it's almost like a mystical experience. "When you have mastered it, you will say it is the deepest and most enduring of all the charms the land beyond the pavement has to offer." Van Dyke attributed its popularity to this mystifying aspect and to the fact that you tend to see more deer while still-hunting as opposed to stand hunting. My own data indicates he was correct in this assessment. Based on an analysis of Stump Sitter Data Sheets during the early years of the *Deer & Deer Hunting* magazine, I found that on the average, stand hunters saw 433 deer per 1000 hours of hunting, whereas still-hunters saw 554 deer per 1000 hours, or an increase of 28.2 percent.

Van Dyke's list of basic precepts that all still-hunters should follow is long indeed.

Here are a select few:

- "Avoid noise while walking by selecting trails, easing off brush with your hands, going around it, crawling through it, etc.

- Avoid going downwind.

- Keep on high ground as is consistent with quiet walking and wind direction.

- Keep the sun on your back.

- Beware of shortcuts in still-hunting.

- Positively no hurrying, for in still-hunting, Hurry is the parent of Flurry.

- In still-hunting, you never have an advantage to spare.

- If patience ever brings reward, it is to the still-hunter.

- You can scarcely have too strong a pair of binoculars or use them too thoroughly – though you should not use them until you have first given a careful and extensive sweep of the area with the naked eye.

- When greatly pursued by hunters, whitetails drift into a state of chronic suspicion of their back track.

- Everyone who still-hunts should get his feet accustomed to buckskin moccasins.

- A fair percentage of failures in still-hunting come from leaving in your net a few loose knots to tighten which could have cost you only a trifle more of work, care and time.

- The simpler and lighter you dress the better – the most valuable knowledge in the world is to know what we can dispense with.

- In scarcely any branch of life is one more apt to draw wrong conclusions from hasty observation than in still-hunting white-tailed deer.

- In no other branch of the field sports are there such an array of exceptions to nearly every rule."

Interwoven amidst these basic precepts, we find two major themes running throughout his theory of still-hunting: learned ignorance and the necessity of seeing deer before they see you. "We are never so wise," Van Dyke once wrote, "as when we know what it is that we do not know." For example, there are many movement patterns of whitetails that remain impossible to reduce to rules, since the animal is frequently governed by the caprice of the passing moment. But just as there are doctors who will never admit ignorance on any complication, so too do we encounter a host of deer hunters who "have ever on their tongue's end an exact explanation of every movement of deer." As a former editor of a specialized magazine on deer and deer hunting, I agree with what Sir William Hamilton once said: "Contented ignorance is better than presumptuous wisdom." This axiom certainly applies to the field sport of still-hunting whitetails, whether with bow, gun or camera.

Van Dyke lived according to this axiom throughout his hunting career, and continually studied errors committed while in the field. No matter how many years of experience you have in still-hunting, "make it your custom whenever you lose a deer to study how you lost him. This may occupy a little time at first, but in the end it will repay you. Few things are so fatal to ultimate success as an early germination of the idea that you are a pretty smart chap on deer. The teachers you need are disappointment and humiliation. If these cure you of still-hunting it is well; for it proves you were not born for that, and the sooner you quit the better. But if there is any

Van Dyke's boys bringing home the bucks on their 1912 Model T "Runabout." As E.B. White said in *One Man's Meat* (1941), "If Hitler had ever spent a fall … watching the bucks go by on the running boards, he never would have dared reoccupy the Rhineland!"

of the true spirit in you, defeat will only inspire you. You will learn more from your failures than many do from success, and they will arouse you to double care, double energy, double keenness and double hope. The analysis of errors is a far better source of instruction than the analysis of truth. For this reason you should at first study failures more than successes. And this will be rendered all the more easy by the fact that at first you will probably have little beside error to study." It is safe to say that during his deer-hunting career, Van Dyke studied errors in a prodigious manner in which not one in 1000 hunters has either the humility of soul or the patience to do.

Even at the risk of being tedious, Van Dyke continually emphasized the idea of seeing deer before they see you, and the extreme difficulty, in the majority of cases of doing so. This theme runs throughout his book and his hunting adventures, and remains a basic principle the still-hunter must never forget. "The advantage that one of two persons or animals at rest has over the other one moving is immense." Once a whitetail gets this advantage, you will rarely get him. "Nothing in the whole line of hunting is so important as to see the deer before he sees you; and there is scarcely anything else so hard to do. In this more than in almost any other one thing lies the secret of the old and practical still-hunter's success."

Van Dyke's classic text contains much valuable information not only on the secrets of still-hunting, but on all phases of deer and deer hunting, on everything from the myth of the waiting game after you hit a deer, to the mythology of solunar theory—all given in an engaging and entertaining manner. At times the passages are so inspiring with their charming description that they will send you to your deer shack at any time of the year, even if only in an imaginary sense. Indeed the wizardry of words frequently assumes a tinge of poetry. In an unpublished letter dated March 19, 1952, his son, Dix, tells us that his father always cherished a desire to

The White Flag, Carl Rungius, 1899, *Forest and Stream*. Van Dyke stressed the importance of seeing the buck before he sees you. If you fail to do that, this is what you can expect to see.

be a poet, and even wrote a book of poetry that apparently remained unpublished. Consider, for example, the following poem Van Dyke aptly entitled *A Dilettante Sportsman*:

"Twas on a clear and frosty morn,
When loudly on the air were borne
Those weird and deeply thrilling sounds,
The clanging tones of clamorous hounds.
"How sweet," said he, "that music floats
And rolls in wild tumultuous notes;
Now ringing up the mountain's side,
Now waxing, waning, like the tide,
Or swinging loud across the dell
Like Pandemonium's carnival."

Hot bounds his blood in swift career,
When bursts the uproar still more near,
And hope and fear alternate play
With bounding joy and dark dismay.

As louder, nearer, bays the pack,
Cold shivers dance along his back;
From tip to toe his nerves all tingle,
All on his head each hair doth scramble;
He feels his heart erratic beat,
He nearly melts with inward heat,
And grasps with quivering hand the gun
As nears the pack in rapid run.

And now there comes an ominous sound
Of hoofs that fiercely spurn the ground,
Close followed by a sudden crash,
As through the brush with headlong dash
There bursts in view a lordly buck.
"Ye god!" he chattered, "oh, what luck!
But oh! Ain't he a splendid sight!
Those spirit-eyes! How wildly bright!

What graceful form! What glossy vest!
What massive neck! What brawny chest!
What proud defiance seem to shed
Those antlers o'er his shapely head
How in the sun they flash and shine
From rugged base to polished tine!"

In the final analysis, still-hunting, more than any other type of deer hunting, requires a great deal of field experience before the tyro reaches a practical realization of the simplest principles. Van Dyke frequently compared this type of hunting with the game of chess; both games keep you at your wit's end. Still-hunting, he rightly argued, is both an art and a science. After 35 years of deer hunting and 20 years after the publication of his book, Van Dyke wrote a fascinating article entitled "Hunting the Virginia Deer" for *Outing* Magazine. In this article he again addressed himself to the subject:

"This subject is so vast that I can give but samples of what one must learn to realize the highest pleasure that can be drawn from still-hunting. With the wild Virginia deer it is the farthest from murder of all that is done with rifle or gun, the finest game of skill man ever plays, finer even than he plays against his fellow man. In *The Still-Hunter* I thought I had treated the subject too fully, but in looking it over 20 years after publication, it seems as if I had not said enough. The vast range of the subject, the many ways in which you may be left alone, the intense care, eyesight and knowledge of the game and the woods necessary for much success, make still-hunting the Virginia deer a joy to thousands who would not touch a gun for any other purpose, for beside it all other hunting is tame and even the pursuit of the blacktail and the mule deer often ridiculous in simplicity."

A familiar sight at the Brandreth Tract: a classic deer hunting rifle, the Winchester Model 1894 25/35 caliber, and antique Coleman camping gear.

Photo courtesy of William N. Headrick.

"The deerskin on our study floor, the buck's head

over the fireplace, what are these after all but the

keys which have unlocked enchanted doors and

granted us not only health and vigor, but a fresh

and fairer vision of existence?"

–Paulina Brandreth,
Trails of Enchantment, 1930

Chapter Ten

PAULINA BRANDRETH

In 1930, publisher G. Howard Watt of New York published a very unique book on white-tailed deer and deer hunting by Paul Brandreth entitled *Trails of Enchantment*. In the Introduction to the book, naturalist and explorer Roy Chapman Andrews (1884-1960) noted that Brandreth knew the white-tailed deer as few hunters know any game animal. He ranked the book as a standard contribution to the natural history of the animal.

I recall my enchantment when I first encountered this blue-chip, white-tailed deer book in the early 1980s, 50 years after its publication, and how I read, re-read, and cherished the great one liners found therein. I also recall my surprise when, after a great deal of deep-digging research, I learned that Paul Brandreth was the pen name for Paulina B. Brandreth (1885-1946), a deer hunter from the Adirondacks who not only loved to shoot big bucks with such noted deer hunters as Roy Chapman Andrews, General "Black Jack" Pershing (1860-1948) and famed Adirondack guide Reuben Cary (1845-1933), but who also loved to photograph deer, illustrate them for her own writings and tramp the deer yards at every opportunity to observe and study them in every detail.

That a woman should have penned one of

Camp Good Enough at Brandreth Lake.

Inset: Paulina Brandreth with her cherished old Model 40-65 Winchester.

Got Him, a Hy S. Watson lithograph from 1909.

the first classic, blue-chip deer books should, perhaps, come as no surprise when we realize the Greek Goddess Artemis, Goddess of the Hunt, first introduced deer hunting into Western civilization in the eighth century B. C. The first sentence of the 27th Homeric Hymn to Artemis reads as follows: "I sing of Artemis of the golden shafts, the modest maiden / who loves the din of the hunt and shoots volleys of arrows at stags."

The deer-huntress Artemis, whom the Romans called Diana, appeared throughout the ages in deer-hunting attire made of deer-skin with a silver bow and a quiver of arrows on her back and often in the company of a deer. Dressed in deerskins, Artemis pursued deer in groves called "deer-gardens," (German *Tiergarten*), which after the hunt became the scene for popular venison feasts in the first century A. D.

Paulina read deeply into the mythology of the deer-huntress Artemis and quoted from it extensively in her writings on hunting and conservation. One of the three major camps on the Brandreth Tract, owned by General Edwin A. McAlpin, who married a Brandreth, was known as Trophy Lodge. Trophy Lodge contained the finest collection of mounted big game heads in the country at the time and a very extensive book collection on the classic hunting literature, which gave Paulina access to the hunting adventures of Diana.

The young girl also received intellectual stimulation about the deer hunt from the learned conversations at the other two major deer camps at Brandreth Lake: "Camp Good Enough" and "Camp As You Like It." The very word "deer" dominated the geography of Hamilton County: Deerfoot Lodge, Deerhurst Camp, Deer Head Lodge, Deer Island, Deerland Hotel and Deerland Grove.

As a poet, naturalist and conservationist, Brandreth was a woman way ahead of her time. By the age of nine, she already

published articles on whitetails and wolves in Charles Hallock's *Forest and Stream*, the most prestigious sportsmen's journal of its time. Editor Hallock listed her material as coming from "Camp Good Enough, Brandreth Lake" and considered her to be "one of the most skillful of the *Forest and Stream* family of hunter/naturalists." Her poems appeared in *Harpers*, *The Atlantic* and *Scribners*. In 1910, she published a book entitled *Plays and Poems* and another in 1911, *The Hour of Sunset*.

Although a good number of women hunted deer at the turn of the century and although the early issues of various outdoor magazines such as *Forest and Stream, Outing* and *The American Field* offered stories about or by these modern Dianas, Brandreth remained isolated in this male-dominated recreational activity. Not wanting to be an outsider, she chose to write with the pseudonym of Paul Brandreth, which undoubtedly facilitated the publication of her byline. Of the more than 2000 books written on the subject of deer and deer hunting in my library, only five are written by women. Not only is *Trails of Enchantment* the best of this group, but it also is perhaps one of the best books ever written on the subject of white-tailed deer and deer hunting.

In addition, the book remains a very rare, first-hand account of adventures deep in the Adirondacks during that period of time Dorothy Plum calls "The Rise of Recreation, 1916-1945." The book, somewhat similar to Henry Abbot's birchbark books, reveals one woman's profound love of the deer forest and of the sacred and secret places seen by few humans, but enjoyed mostly by white-tailed deer. In reading it, one is reminded of New York conservationist Paul Schaefer's delightful reflections of Adirondack deer hunting during the 1920s and 1930s at The Old Log Cabin (*Adirondack Cabin Country*, 1993).

Brandreth and her deer hunting companions. From left to right on top of the buckboard: Reuben Cary, Frank Cary, Mary McAlpin and Barbara McAlpin. Paulina is standing against the buckboard with her cherished 40-65 Winchester. Kempton Adams and Adam Lafoy kneel beside her.

Brandreth was born in Ossining, New York, in 1885. In 1848, her grandfather, Dr. Benjamin Brandreth, a wealthy pharmaceutical manufacturer, bought Township 39 in the Town of Long Lake in Hamilton County for the exclusive purposes of fishing and hunting. It consisted of 24,000 acres, for which he paid 15 cents an acre. The area became known as the Brandreth Tract and contained Brandreth Lake.

As lumber operations prospered in this area, the white-tailed deer population responded and eventually exploded. Within this well-known deer hunting mecca, the young buck hunter came of age while hunting white-tailed deer with her father, Colonel Franklin Brandreth, and two prominent Adirondack deer hunting guides: Wallace Emerson and Reuben Cary.

At her grandfather's deer hunting lodge at Brandreth Lake, she read the classic deer and deer hunting tales of Meshach Browning, Philip Tome, T. S. Van Dyke, Judge Caton and Archibald Rutledge. Antlered bucks graced the walls of the lodge as did the classic deer photos of George Shiras III and the great deer and deer hunting paintings of A. F. Tait and Winslow Homer.

Like T. S. Van Dyke and William Monypeny Newsom, two of her contemporaries, Brandreth preferred to still-hunt white-tailed bucks. She compared deer drives and stand hunting to catching speckled trout with bait; she clearly preferred fly fishing and still-hunting and did both with a great deal of style, energy and enthusiasm. Outwitting and overcoming a white-tailed buck's tactics of escape gave her the ultimate satisfaction of beating them at their own game. She admiringly viewed the white-tailed buck as "a shadow lurking in a shadow." Like all die-hard still-hunters, she loved the elements of expectancy and uncertainty that still-hunting whitetails affords.

No one in the history of American deer hunting ever better defined the true art of still-hunting white-tailed deer than Paulina Brandreth:

"There is a charm about still hunting that no method of circumventing the wiles of the whitetail can compete with. It requires patience, skill, fore-thought, good judgment and often a sort of subtle intuition that brings into play the ancestral hunter that is in you. It is an active red-blooded game with the odds greatly in favor of the hunted. Time and again you will suffer disappointment, or be done out of a good shot by some infinitesimal slip, or lack of proper fore-sight. Yet, the difficulties encountered—an ill chosen gust of wind, a branch cracked underfoot, a trail on freshly fallen snow lost in a maze of other tracks—only serve to increase your energies and add fuel to your enthusiasm. And sooner or later, the desired opportunity will present itself and another ten-or-twelve pointer be added to your collection."

Under the expert tutelage of Reuben Cary or "Rube" as she called him, Brandreth learned the business of still-hunting white-tailed bucks as she followed in the footsteps of this tall, picturesque figure with the silvery beard and the penetrating blue eyes. Of this memorable Adirondack guide and caretaker of the Brandreth Tract, Brandreth wrote as follows in her deer hunting journal: "Unhurried and tranquil, full of dry humor and witty sarcasm, his personality and companionship form an indispensable part of our trips."

On one of her more memorable still-hunting trips through the woods one November day with old Rube, Brandreth came across the track of a good-sized buck along a ridge that overlooked North Pond. Although somewhat discouraged as a result of a long day's still-hunt coming to an end, the size of the track seemed to put new life in the two weary hunters. Both Rube and Brandreth always believed in the possibilities of last chances.

"Never cuss yer luck till yer git home," Rube remarked.

The wisdom of that remark soon became a reality. As the hunters reached the top of the ridge, Rube suddenly stiffened and stood still, gazing ahead for a patch of gray, the flicker of a white tail or the glimmer of an antler. "The buck is here somewhere," Rube insisted! Brandreth explains what happened:

"Suddenly we glimpsed a mighty set of horns as the buck burst cover and fled up the ridge. He did not bound, but seemed to slip like a shadow over the ground, his head carried low, his great dusky antlers laid back on his shoulders. Twice we obtained a fair view of him, and twice I tried to get a shot, but each time with almost uncanny precision, he managed to put a barrier of lopped tree tops between us. The thing happened so quickly that we just stood there and looked at each other."

Refusing to accept defeat, Rube and Brandreth ran down into the valley in an attempt to get the wind in their favor. In *Trails of Enchantment*, she describes the taking of this white-tailed buck:

"With his keen eyes covering the woods ahead, Rube fell into a swinging gait. There was no chance for any puzzy-footing or cautious still hunting. It was getting dark too fast. Coming to a skid trail which led down the hill, he followed it a short distance, and then striking a logging road, turned to the left again. Just at that moment I caught the outline of a deer moving at a walk down the ridge in our direction.

"The next few seconds were crammed with excitement. Looking back on the experience, it seems always to assume more and more, an element of the ridiculous. Certainly it proves like many other incidents, that the game of hunting is more often than anything else a game of chance. Here were we, the hunters, being literally hunted by the deer which a short time previous we believed had given us the slip. In other words, we had been whisked around within fifteen minutes from the extreme of bad to the extreme of good luck.

"Side by side, we knelt in the snow, waiting for the buck to appear from behind the intervening trunk of a big birch. The suspense was harrowing. And then at last he loomed suddenly before us.

"Enough of daylight still remained for us to see him in detail, and certainly he was a magnificent creature. He came at a swinging walk, his head lowered, his nose close to the ground. There was something almost formidable in his appearance, and I believe that, not having winded us the first time he was scared out, he had gotten the idea that another buck was in his area, and was therefore returning to administer a sound thrashing to the intruder.

"I have seen a number of large heads during the years I have spent in the Adirondack woods, but the head of this buck overshadowed all the others. The horns were so massive they made the animal look top-heavy. As he came towards us, he swung them from side to side with motion similar to that of a belligerent bull.

"When he had passed a few feet beyond the birch, I gave a loud whistle. Instantly he froze into rigid suspicion, and threw up his head. He stood facing us, slightly quartering and offered a deadly shot. At the crack of my rifle he plunged forward in his tracks, struggled a few paces, and just as Rube fired a second shot, rolled over stone dead."

The buck carried 13 tines, several of which were heavily palmated. The blunt tips of the tines suggested that the old warrior had done a good deal of rubbing and thrashing. The buck weighed 245 pounds dressed.

When Roy Chapman Andrews examined the buck as a possible addition to the American Museum of Natural History's col-

Guide Reuben Cary poses with Paulina's magnificent 13-pointer.

A cathedral-like deer camp in the heart of the Brandreth Tract.

lection, he concluded the buck had the largest and heaviest antlers of any whitetail he ever observed. Apparently, this buck was never scored for the Boone and Crockett record book, nor is its current location known. Many of the deer on display at the Museum of Natural History during that era were shot by Andrews on the Brandreth Tract. The backgrounds for the whitetail displays were made by Brandreth's brother Courtenay, a well-known bird painter and ornithologist.

Brandreth and Rube generally breakfasted under the stars and traveled from sunup to sundown. During the deer season, they roamed for miles each day in the vast and picturesque wilderness of the Adirondacks. "Being young and enthusiastic," she confessed, "I wanted to eat up the miles, and eat them up we did in spite of Rube's argument against such overstrenuous methods." In their travels they found many unique places on which they put a stamp of ownership by constructing a special deer hunting camp on the site. One of her cherished deer camps was located near a sheet of water called "Panther Pond."

Its unique character never faded from her mind: "In shape it resembled a large Indian tepee. Great rolls of spruce bark had been ingeniously wrapped around a framework of poles, and a wide opening in front faced the fireplace. In many ways it was warmer and more comfortable than a lean-to. Inside three people could sleep without crowding on the thick fragrant mat of balsam boughs.

"The tepee stood on a knoll sown thick with big balsams. They were not the kind that snapped off easily in a windstorm, but were trees of antiquity, and their aromatic spires towered high above the camp. On the south side of the knoll at the bottom of a shallow ravine coursed a clear spring-fed brook, which emptied and lost itself a little farther on in the heart of a dense black spruce swamp. Beyond this swamp a spacious beaver meadow reached to the brink of Panther Pond and extended for almost the entire length of its easterly shore."

While still-hunting at Panther Pond one early morning during the 1912 deer hunting season, the year New York initiated its controversial Buck Law, Brandreth and her guide encountered a 10-pointer standing broadside and motionless as a statue in the misty sunrise with his head partially hidden behind a small spruce tree. She knelt down on the ground and placed the bead of her old Model 40-65 Winchester repeater on the buck's fore shoulder and pulled the trigger. When the smoke cleared, she saw the buck standing exactly in the same place.

"You didn't touch him," groaned Rube. "Shoot again!"

As the buck dashed off, she fired three more shots in rapid succession. At the last report the buck veered to the right and vanished into a vast array of alders.

The buck's trail, which they quickly found, led up through a steep slope of spruces. Halfway to the top, the trail sharply swung off at a right angle. Following the sharp turn in the trail, Rube stepped forward, shouldered his rifle and fired the final shot. Behind the roots of a fallen spruce lay the magnificent 10-pointer.

"Let's see where you hit him," he said to her.

"I held for his shoulder on those shots," she insisted.

When they turned the buck over, they "found a bullet hole in a place that makes even a tyro blush with shame," as Brandreth admitted.

"Held for the shoulder and shot the buck through the ham," the old guide remarked in a frowning and unsympathetic manner!

"The mist and the fog did me in," she quickly exclaimed.

Like many of us, she said that because human nature often provides us with a theory about how we should handle such a situation. That theory in Brandreth's own inimitable style goes like this: "The best thing to do if you make a fluke shot, when without doubt you should have made a good one, is to retire discreetly into the profoundities of silence, and blame the conditions—blame anything so long as it eases your conscience."

Brandreth also hunted in another fascinating and unique place called "Cathedral Meadow," an old beaver meadow consisting of 600 acres of swampland filled with lush aquatic food. Deer in this area attained a size definitely larger than the other animals within a radius of several miles. Not only were the bucks in this area larger in weight and antler mass, but they also offered a wider range of color variation. Bucks, especially bucks in the older age classes, in Cathedral Meadow displayed a distinct tendency to stick to the thickest part of the swamp and feed chiefly after hunting hours. This desolate place gave Brandreth and her camp mates a sense of utter detachment and afforded them a challenging prospect for still-hunting the whitetail.

At Cathedral Meadow, Brandreth and her friends constructed a small, picturesque log cabin. When covered with snow, its high-pitched roof made the cabin look like a miniature cathedral. Even when the deer season was closed, Brandreth and her hunting partners would snowshoe to Cathedral Meadow to cook venison tenderloins at the little camp half buried in snow drifts and enjoy the magnificent scenery of the rugged Adirondacks.

At this cherished deer camp, Brandreth would hold forth on shooting bucks in the magic area of the swamp. And a magic area it was. In an essay entitled "Bucks of Cathedral Meadow," published in the February 1938 issue of *Field & Stream*, she characterized the setting:

The still-hunter's pulse quickens at the sudden view of a buck. Oliver Kemp's *The Hunter*, circa 1930, clearly illustrates Brandreth's description of a white-tailed buck being a "shadow lurking in a shadow," and presents the essence of the solitary still-hunter.

"The skeleton figures of dead trees have toppled over, decayed and formed a rich seed bed for semi-aquatic plants. Black spruce, tamarack, balsam and clumps of alders have replaced the original stand of mixed timber. There are blueberry bushes and sweet-scented grasses. You walk on cushions of sphagnum and reindeer moss, conscious of dense aromatic shade or the delicious warmth of the sun. What was once a scene of devastation has become transfigured into one of exquisite beauty and enthrallment."

To the west of her camp a hardwood promontory extended into the meadow. Bucks traveled along well-worn runways on this hardwood promontory. These runways led from protective haunts to the timbered flats where the deer searched for acorns and beechnuts. Brandreth spent many days of her life still-hunting whitetails along this hardwood promontory. One November morning, just at daylight, Brandreth and her brother Curt left camp for a hunt on the promontory. Rain had fallen the night before. As they walked along in the drizzle, Curt suddenly stopped.

"I smell a buck," he whispered, as a strong musky odor of the rut greeted his nose.

As they stood there in the rain-drenched forest, they caught a glance for a fleeting moment of a magnificent rack set in motion. They heard a crash, a sharp snort and a brief glimpse of a white flag. The sudden realization that this buck had been quietly studying them as they walked along the old logging road seemed like a hard pill to swallow. Yet, Brandreth readily admitted that for every buck bagged at Cathedral Meadow, four evaded her:

"These swamp whitetails are seldom or never caught napping. They are wilder than any deer I have ever hunted. Suspicious, skulking, constantly testing the wind, they venture out from the dense sanctuary of the meadow only when conditions seem to preclude danger. If they see you first, the game is up. They never wait. Curiosity does not appear to be one of their failings; and, of course, this adds greatly to the sport and fascination of the chase."

Brandreth believed that whitetails exercise a highly developed telepathic instinct: they will stand motionless for a great length of time, if they feel that they are not being seen, regardless of how close you are to them. "This creature seems to know when you do not see it and it discovers instantly when you do. When the animal sees that you see it, it takes flight. Even when you look straight at it but do not see the animal, it seems perfectly aware of this fact and will not move. The instant you see it, it is gone!"

As she and Curt worked a level hardwood stretch of the promontory for several hours they only jumped one doe. Only two days remained of the open season and they both wanted one of those Cathedral Meadow

bucks. The rain gradually turned to sleet and the heavy, northwest wind made the prospects of success far from encouraging.

But as is so often the case in the game of still-hunting whitetails, the unexpected suddenly occurred. Through the driving sleet she saw a huge set of antlers; then the vague outline of the deer's body. She fired her 40-65 at the buck bedded not more than 60 yards ahead, but never cut a hair. With the wind in his face, the buck stood up, still looking in the opposite direction. As he began to move broadside, she fired a second shot. The buck jumped and disappeared over a rise of ground. Fifty yards ahead, she found the buck lying dead at the bottom of a deep depression.

"Well, there's a head worth workin' for," Curt remarked as he examined the 8-pointer.

Was it worth working for, this pioneer of the mythical minority of women who hunt deer asks? "Yes, that's the way I have always

The mythic minority begins to take charge by downing some quality bucks with their Winchesters in 1927.

felt about Cathedral Meadow bucks. They're worth working for. Moreover, of all places I have ever hunted, the promontory leading to this magic area of swamp holds the greatest charm."

Still-hunting white-tailed bucks in Cathedral Meadow in 1927 entailed a great deal of hard work, for after studying the deer population on the Brandreth Tract very intensely, deer researchers Townsend and Smith in their classic study, *The White-tailed Deer of the Adirondacks* (1933), concluded that the population only approximated five deer per square mile.

All deer hunters have their special places in deer country despite the number of deer per square mile. Cathedral Meadow in the heart of the Adirondacks captivated Paulina Brandreth and all who deer hunted with her at this sacred location.

Brandreth readily acknowledged that deer hunting success in any given year is largely due to luck. Throughout her life, she insisted that you grasp more opportunities than you make. In other words, the candid deer hunter will admit that the deer he works the hardest for are the very ones he never gets; that good luck is frequently of greater value in the chase of white-tailed bucks than a detailed, thoughtful, planned-out campaign.

"You may be the best kind of a hunter," she writes in *Trails of Enchantment*, "practiced, careful and an excellent shot, but if luck shuns you entirely, as it sometimes does, you will certainly fail where another less experienced will succeed. Luck may mean a number of things but primarily I should say it means a well-timed coordination of your own movements and those of the animal you are hunting."

Brandreth cites a memorable buck hunt with General Pershing, a frequent visitor at the Brandreth camp, as an illustration of being in the right place at the right time. The

night before the hunt, they retired to the "shop" to discuss strategy and select the territory to be hunted. They decided to start at the "flow," a body of water loggers used as a storage ground for pulpwood. From there they would still-hunt the old railroad track.

The morning of the hunt dawned clear, calm and cold. For breakfast they ate broiled venison and pancakes. From Brandreth Lake, they followed the trail to North Pond, which they crossed with a square-sterned, Adirondack guide-boat built by Reuben Cary. After landing at the mouth of the inlet, they took up the trail to the "flow," and arrived at the old railroad track. Several hours of still-hunting passed without a sign or sound of a white-tailed buck to give them much encouragement.

"But had we only known it," Brandreth tells us, "the gods of good luck were at that very moment preparing for us in their inscrutable way a most enlivening little drama."

The drama began to unfold as Ivan Stanton, an assistant to General Pershing, came across a very large buck track and a freshly rubbed sapling, still green in color. Ivan decided to take the track and Brandreth and the General cautiously still-hunted along both sides of the tracker. But it soon became impossible to continue to follow the track.

Several hundred yards beyond where Ivan lost the track, they topped a low hillock. While standing still and facing into the wind, they heard a loud crashing in the brush in front of them and the thud of bounding hooves. Shouldering his rifle, the General tried to get a shot at the buck with a splendid set of antlers but couldn't since the buck ran low to the ground through a tangle of brush and thick briar bushes. But as luck would have it, the buck suddenly landed on a little knoll, presenting a standing broadside shot. The General's Winchester echoed throughout the deer

General Pershing and the 10-point buck he killed while hunting with the Brandreth group.

woods as the 10-pointer landed and lodged itself against an old log.

All three hunters remained uncertain about what caused the buck to stir in the first place, since the hunters could have easily gone around the buck without seeing him, much less did they know why he stopped on the knoll and looked in the opposite direction. No one ever will know.

Brandreth, however, came to this conclusion with regard to the incident: "Luck in the hunting field is as variable as the winds of heaven. Some years it will be your constant companion, again it will pass you by, until you commence to feel as though you were haunted by malevolent spirits."

In *Trails of Enchantment*, she gives us another illustration of how the Red Gods smiled on her one cold, bright, October afternoon as she followed a tote road through a section of country traditionally associated with large antlers. The leaves that day were very crisp and noisy underfoot, as she hurriedly walked along in an attempt to reach a certain ridge. Approaching a shallow ravine, she experienced a dramatic shock:

"Out of the thicket of briars where he had been feeding was thrust the startled head of a gray-faced buck. I don't know which one of us was the most surprised, the deer or myself. I worked just about as fast as was possible, and as is often the case when there isn't time to get shaky or overexcited from waiting, the result was entirely satisfactory.

"Scrambling hastily across the ravine, I reached the top of the knoll ready to plant another bullet if the buck jumped. But he was dead with a shot through the neck, and when I saw how big he was, I dropped the rifle and did a war dance. Although carrying a moderate-sized pair of antlers with only nine points, the weight of this animal was far above the average, as I soon came to find out when I tried to hang him up. The following day he tipped the scales at 197 pounds dressed."

Paulina Brandreth remained literally fascinated with white-tailed deer antlers. Antlers painted by Major Allan Brooks (1869-1946), the great Canadian hunter, artist and naturalist, graced the dust jacket of her book. Photos of antlered bucks illustrated the text. She talked about the great variation in the color of antlers and their shape, spread and symmetry in an endless way; she dreamed about antlers. Thoughts of seeing antlers moving through the brush accompanied her on every hunt. She viewed antler collecting as one of the chief charms of hunting the white-tailed deer.

During the late 1930s, Brandreth traveled and hunted throughout the western states with her father. On that hunting trip, she contacted a serious fever from which she never fully recovered. She died on April 18, 1946 in Bethel, Connecticut, after a prolonged illness.

What prompted a woman like Paulina Brandreth to pursue white-tailed bucks in the Adirondacks with such vigor and relentless gusto? The same thing that prompts all deer hunters—men and women alike: a love of nature, a desire to study the magnificent whitetail in its natural habitat and to ultimately experience the charm and freedom of life in the wilderness.

Brandreth hunted whitetails to study them; she studied them to hunt them, as did such legendary hunter/naturalists as Audubon, Theodore Roosevelt and Aldo Leopold. *Trails of Echantment* stands as a masterpiece in that great tradition. As professor/hunter Mary Zeiss Stange says, "It is high-time we come home to the image of the hunter-woman within us all."

In her writings on white-tailed deer and deer hunting, Paulina Brandreth exhibits a visionary quality that one seldom sees in the field of outdoor literature and natural history. No one expresses the real meaning and significance of deer hunting more eloquently than does this prominent buck hunter, a giant amongst white-tailed deer hunters and deer enthusiasts:

"Hunting is a recreation and invigorating pastime that never should, through a super-civilized, over-artificialized state of living, be allowed to die out. In this age of neurotic haste it means rest and renewed health to the man whose brain and energies are being constantly overtaxed. It means stronger muscles, a more vigorous constitution, self-

An early edition (1930) of Paulina Brandreth's deer-hunting classic. Not wanting to be an outsider, Brandreth chose "Paul Brandreth" as her pen name.

reliance, hardihood. A real man does not care for sport that does not involve difficulty, discomfort and sometimes danger. The trouble with modern life is that physically it is terribly softening. We need something to counteract the effects of luxury and too easy living. Hunting does this because it takes a man to places where he has to depend on first principles, and where he comes in contact with obstacles that tend to build up and strengthen his natural abilities and manhood. It makes his eyesight keener, teaches him patience, and unfolds many natural laws and beauties and wonders that otherwise would remain to him unknown. We all need something of the primitive in us in order that we may have a rock bottom on which to stand."

Two Fast Bucks by Bob Kuhn.

"Deer stands have a magnetic attraction for any deer hunter.

He learns from his pals that many deer have been killed from

Patterson's Rock or the Twin-Oak Stand or Skunk Gully; he

swells mentally in anticipation as he approaches any of these

hallowed spots, knowing that when the drive comes through,

his chances of killing that whitetail buck are better than those

of the unfortunates who may be watching less favored areas.

Every deer club has these sacred spots, and sacred they are,

indeed. They have achieved reputations simply because deer

favor these places for moving from hideout to hideout."

–Larry Koller,
Shots at Whitetails, 1948

LARRY KOLLER

I n looking at Bob Kuhn's oil on canvas, *Jumping Buck*—this sacred spot in deer country—I know I have been there before. Maybe it was the Twin-Oak Stand or Patterson's Rock or Skunk Gully ...I am not sure. Bob Kuhn's classic white-tailed deer and deer hunting paintings and drawings frequently illustrated Larry Koller's writings and book dust jackets and greatly enhanced the text.

I never met Larry Koller (1912-1967), but I wish I had, for he wrote one of the greatest books of all time on white-tailed deer and deer hunting. The book provides a warehouse of detailed, practical information. When *Shots at Whitetails* first appeared in the fall of 1948, *The New Yorker* magazine reported "not one of the whitetail's pursuers could fail to learn something helpful from this detailed volume, which surveys a buck's career from fawn hood to the library wall."

As a die-hard buck hunter, who shot close to 100 white-tailed bucks in his short lifetime, Larry Koller maintained a profound passion for pursuing that elusive and mythic monster-buck that always succeeds in baffling the hunters. One such buck, "The Buck of Beech Ridge," haunted Koller's dreams and always seemed to do the impossible. This wise, old buck, which hung out in the heart of the

The Eden Falls Hunting and Fishing Club.

Inset: This photo of Larry Koller appeared on the dust jacket of the original printing of *Shots at Whitetails* in 1948.

Catskill Mountains, where Koller hunted, had a penchant for brush, thickets and swamps. He only entered open country under special circumstances: (1) when deer season was closed; (2) at night under the cover of darkness; (3) when starvation brought him to the farmer's wheat field; and (4) when he chased estrous does. This majestic, royal, 10-point buck eluded local hunters for years – unscathed except for a slight limp from a leg injury. Koller paid a great tribute to this phantom Buck of Beech Ridge in his book *The Treasury of Hunting* (1965):

"On a bright autumn Sunday, when the local hunters had organized a network of drivers and standers from which there could be no escape, the buck gimped through the village churchyard. It was said that if the proper window had been opened, the minister could have killed him from the pulpit.

"This buck had an immense capacity to withstand rifle fire; rifle fire meant no more than the shattering violence of a bolt of lightning during a thunderstorm. *Pow! Pow!* Went the rifles to no avail.

"Before the hunter made his move, the deer's powerful hindquarters were bunched for a leap. On his slim forelegs, he pivoted to one side and crashed from the brush in a single great bound. Within two seconds he was bouncing down the slope, dipping and ducking through the timber as bullets from the rifles of two hunters rained wood chips and shreds of bark on his sleek back. They fired again and again, until they could no longer see the white beacon of his tail flashing through the trees."

But the Buck of Beech Ridge did not live forever. His travels came to an end on one sharp, crisp November day in the Catskills. With terse prose, Koller describes what happened:

"He had escaped. He was on familiar ground. Once in the alder thickets he could hide safely, as he had done many time before when hunters prowled the ridges and shots thundered through the valley for days. He would never have achieved his size of antler spread if he had wandered around in the timber during daylight hours in those critical periods.

"But now as he neared his sanctuary, the strong scent of man wafted up to him on the rising warm air of morning and filled him with new alarm. He stiffened his forelegs and dug his hind feet into the soft earth, bringing himself to a slipping, slithering halt. The man smell was powerful. The hunter had to be nearby, and the buck knew instantly he must change course along the slope, must circle to right or left to locate this new source of danger. Again he bunched his powerful leg muscles, pivoted on the slim forelegs. It was as he made his turn that the bullet took him fair in the shoulder. His body crumpled down the slope. He rolled, kicking and jerking, until he came up against a coarse-barked oak tree, with one set of antler tips buried in the leaf-mold and the long span of dead-white belly hair turned upward, toward the pink haze of the November sunrise."

Lawrence Robert ("Larry") Koller was born on September 6, 1912, in Brooklyn, New York. He became an ardent outdoorsman by the age of six, when he moved to Middletown, New York, with his family. He shot his first white-tailed forkhorn with a 25-40. He began sports writing with a "Rod and Gun" column (later called "Sportsman's Notebook") for the Middletown *Times-Herald*.

His first job was with the largest sporting goods house in the Catskill area. In 1938, he opened his own sportsman's shop in Middletown, which he operated until the outbreak of World War II, when his special skills as a gunsmith and tool designer called him to the arms factories of Connecticut.

During his lifetime, he wrote dozens of books, became a taxidermist of wide reputation, a professional fly-tyer and an expert

Bob Kuhn's classic deer prints graced the writings of Larry Koller.

archer, who made his own equipment to bag deer. When he died of a heart attack at the age of 54 in 1967, *The New York Times* characterized him as "a famous outdoor writer who can shoot as well as he can write and write as well as he can shoot." When he died, he was working on a venison cookbook for Doubleday and a deer hunter's guide for Alfred A. Knopf.

He owned more than 100 guns and traveled extensively throughout the game areas of America, Canada and South America. His hobbies consisted of skeet, trap shooting and studying white-tailed deer. "For any man to gain the fullest success and enjoyment from hunting each year," Koller observes, "the whitetail must be made a hobby—a hobby of study which is as gratifying as the killing of the deer itself."

He read the writings of Francis Sell, Frank Edminster and Ernest Thompson Seton, and the great, blue-chip deer book of the era, Walter P. Taylor's *The Deer of North America* (1956). He greatly admired the deer prints of A. B. Frost and Bob Kuhn and used them to illustrate his work. He was twice nominated for the International Outdoorsman of the Year Award in 1964 and 1967.

In 1957, he founded *Guns & Hunting* as a quarterly after working for many years as a toolmaker, gunsmith, designer and freelance writer for men's magazines. *Guns & Hunting* eventually became a monthly publication.

In the winter of 1961, he started *The American Gun*, a beautiful, magnificent quarterly magazine about guns in history and sport. It appeared in a hardcover book format and from its pages we can clearly see that Koller pursued a passionate interest in the history and art of white-tailed deer hunting. I consider these three hardbound volumes to be a highlight in my 2000-volume plus library on white-tailed deer and deer hunting.

Larry Koller was what we would have to call "The Complete Deer Hunter." In the Foreword to *Shots at Whitetails*, Clay Seagears, former New York State Director of Conservation Education and founder of the *Conservationist* magazine, wrote that "there are exceedingly few persons today who can (1) consistently outsmart a particular white-tailed buck, (2) collect it with either a really good bow or rifle of his own manufacture, (3) properly dress and butcher the carcass, (4) concoct palatable dishes there from and (5) expertly mount the remains. Larry Koller can. Furthermore, he can write entertainingly of the whole operation. That last accomplishment just about puts Larry in a class by himself. It puts this book in a class by itself, too, for in our decidedly humble opinion it is the most practical and comprehensive work on the white-tailed deer and its by-products ever written. It should be standard for a long time to come."

For Larry Koller, every encounter with a whitetail provoked the same response: He was always *charmed* first by its sudden, ghostlike appearance and then absolutely *astounded* by its rapid and dramatic departure. Koller always hoped that the white-tailed deer would be the big game animal of the common man and always adorn the homes of the butcher, the baker and the candlestick maker.

In *Shots at Whitetails*, Koller talks at great length about the ultimate drama and excitement of hunting whitetails. "Much of the thrill and charm of deer hunting is influenced by our conscious knowledge of the whitetail's role in the romantic days of the Indian and buckskin-clad woodsman ...Of all our outdoor pursuits none is so wreathed by the aura of romance, none so connotative of our hidden pride in our American ancestry during its uphill climb for recognition." Koller read Frederick Jackson Turner's classic essay "The Significance of the Frontier in American History," which he frequently quoted, and knew well that the white-tailed deer served as the support system on which American pio-

Krause Publications Photo

The original 1948 Little, Brown & Co. edition (top left), the 1975 Alfred A. Knopf reprint (left) and the 2000 Krause Publications reprint in their Deer and Deer Hunting Classics Series (right). The first two editions featured the paintings and drawings of Bob Kuhn while the Krause 2000 edition features the painting *Play the Wind* by Michael Sieve on the cover and inside drawings by Ruth Pillath.

neers extended the western frontiers.

During Koller's early years as a deer hunter, the Catskill deer herd increased steadily. He saw the progression of larger and larger harvests over the years. In 1927, when deer kills were first tabulated, 613 adult bucks were taken from the four Catskill counties. Two decades later, when *Shots at Whitetails* appears, the harvest of bucks increased to 2595. Twenty year later, at the time of his death, a new record was established with 10,571 bucks.

Carl Oleberg argues in his *Guide to Deer Hunting in the Catskill Mountains* (1969) that the 1967 deer season, the year Koller died, was indeed a benchmark, "demonstrating the result of conditions favoring the deer and the deer hunter. It was the payoff for the previous four successive mild winters, three previous years of record beechnut and acorn crops and good tracking snow on the ground and clear visibility in the woods during the open season." Koller made the most of these ideal deer hunting conditions during the mid-1960s and read every report he could find on deer and deer hunting written by New York State's legendary deer biologist Bill Severinghaus, who popularized his detailed scientific reports for the deer hunters in the *New York State Conservationist*. This highly popular publication entertained an entire generation of deer hunters – Koller included.

Koller spent a great deal of time hunting deer in the Upper Neversink River Valley of Sullivan County with such renowned deer hunters as old Abe Wykoff of the Buck Mountain Hunting Club; Bert Sauer, an old-time deer hunter and charter member of Sullivan County's Iroquois Hunting Club; and Jim Deren of the Angler's Roost.

His most cherished spot, his sacred space in deer country, where he did most of his deer hunting and much of his writing, centered around the Eden Falls Hunting and Fishing Club, a campsite on the Neversink River south of Monticello, New York, that he helped to create in the late 1940s. Here he maintained his deer-hunting cabin at "Long Eddy" in the Neversink Gorge.

The Eden Falls Hunting and Fishing Club controlled about 3000 acres that Ab Wexler and his family owned and ran. Ernie Thiesing of Monticello, New York, belonged to the club and hunted with Koller. In the Third Edition of *Shots at Whitetails* (2000), he comments on Larry Koller, the deer hunter:

"He was a natural teacher and an unselfish hunter. Larry loved to teach you everything he knew about the woods, and explain how hunters should handle themselves in the woods. He never missed a deer season, and when he was here, he ran the drives. He knew these mountains very well and he knew where the deer would go. He would tell you where to sit and why you should sit there, and then he would go help on the drive. We could never get Larry to sit down. He always had to be one of the drivers."

The Club still exists as the Eden Falls Hunt & Fish Club Inc., located in the heart of the Neversink Gorge in 2003, and maintains a web page at *www.edenfalls.com*. It is surrounded by more than 7000 acres of wilderness with great white-tailed deer hunting opportunities with limited associate memberships available. In 1987, the Town of Forestburgh named an unnamed island "Koller Island" in honor of Koller's achievements as a deer hunter and avid conservationist.

Although Koller liked to hunt deer as part of the group at Eden Falls, like T. S. Van Dyke, he ultimately preferred to still-hunt the whitetail alone – one on one with the deer in the steep ridges and dense alder thickets of the Catskills on the far side of the Neversink and in the Adirondacks. He was well known for his incredible shooting skills. He maintained a great preference for making a neck shot, and discussed neck shots at great length in his writings. In fact, he might have been nick-named "Neck Shot" Koller, for many of his bucks went down on still-hunts after being hit in the famous "White Patch."

Koller preferred to still-hunt a ridge with a cross breeze "keeping on the downwind shoulder of the ridge as I move slowly along. Deer often keep constant watch along the very top of the ridge in both directions. They seem vaguely to expect a higher incidence of danger along the crest of a ridge. It is wise then to keep just far enough away from the top of the ridge to yet be able to see any movement upon it."

Koller often became obsessed with the pursuit of legendary bucks and dreamed about shooting them on his still-hunts. Two of his favorite white-tailed bucks haunted his imagination, both shot in Allegany County and in the same year, 1939: the typical Roosevelt Lucky buck, the state record, scoring 198-2/8 with 14 points and the non-typical Homer Boylan buck, the non-typical state record, scoring 244-2/8 with 26 points.

During the late 1930s, he frequently returned to a backwoods deer camp deep in the Adirondacks with a fellow Canadian guide named Gordon Grant. Here they packed in on foot to a 12x16 rustic log/tarpaper shack – the exact whereabouts Koller kept a secret as he also did with his favorite Adirondack trout fishing streams.

In late November of 1940, Koller made one of his annual pilgrimages to this sacred place to still-hunt bucks along big beech ridges and dine on venison liver and heart in camp. One overcast, cloudy morning he poked slowly along a deer trail where gray beeches had dropped showers of nuts on the leaves. As he worked slowly along the side of the ridge top, he suddenly encountered a massive windfall.

"To my right, only 30 yards off, a windfall lay in a tangle – big white oaks with trunks crisscrossed in confusion, the dead leaves, still clinging to the branches, making a high mound. I had gone a few yards past this windfall when I noticed fresh tracks – big ones – leading toward it. As always, I stopped to study them, glancing casually back at the windfall, wondering whether a buck lay in hiding?

Koller in deer camp during the late 1940s (fifth from left).

"And as I pondered this question for a few seconds, the buck decided that the jig was up. He bounced up and out of the screen of dead oak leaves, leaving his bed with a great crashing of branches and thumping of hoofs as he headed for the top of the ridge behind. Unluckily for him, he chose to exit in fairly open cover and I managed to ground him on about the fourth jump."

He downed the buck with a Winchester 30-30. While Koller shot most makes and models of deer hunting rifles, he argued that the time-tired Winchester 30-30 carbine remained the deer hunter's stand-by for still-hunting, and rightly so.

Another one of his most interesting still-hunts took place in this favorite deer cover in 1946. He received word of a huge buck with wide-spreading antlers that had been seen for several seasons in the area. For two years, he failed to gain any information as to where the buck fed and bedded, and even though he hunted the region those two years, the rumors and stories persisted. During the third year of pursuing this phantom buck, Gordon Grant led Koller to a little ravine where a tiny mountain brook tumbled down a mountainside into a valley below. Here Koller saw deep, widely splayed tracks of a very large deer, large rubs and dramatic scraped areas.

Several days later, he went back to do some more investigating. With snow on the ground, he once again found the big tracks following the little brook down the mountainside. He soon discovered tracks going back up the mountainside.

"I took the track and followed it to the mountaintop about a mile off. At this spot the mountaintop had a flat plateau for a crest; a plateau half a mile wide and every foot of this half-mile covered with the thickest sort of scrub oak, jack pine and laurel. Through all of this went the buck's track,

Sonic Boom by Bob Kuhn. Koller loved to pursue huge, 10-point, white-tailed bucks with wide spreading antlers.

heading for a swamp, which lay in the middle of this flat plateau. The swamp was a forbidding place, filled with tangled catbriers, piles of windfalls, thick heavy swamp huckleberry and crowed stands of pin oak.

"Just within the edges of the swamp I found beds – one for each day that the snow had been on the ground. One bed fairly steamed – I had jumped the buck in my snooping! I took the fresh track and followed him throughout the length of the swamp; leaving the swamp he had circled and gone off into the scrub-oak morass surrounding the whole place. But I was satisfied – I had located this buck's hangout."

Several days later, Koller found the buck's tracks going up the mountain. As he stood there gazing at the great depth and span of these big deer prints, he heard several shots on the mountaintop above him.

"With the sound of the shots I was off like a sprinter at the starting gun. I raced across the ravine, jumped the brook and planted my feet in the runway coming down the mountain.

"Hardly had I stopped for breath when, with a great clatter of rocks, the buck came crashing down the hillside directly toward me. Now I could see the huge rack of antlers flashing over the tops of the underbrush. His feet hit the opening through the brush at the foot of the slope, thirty yards away, and my bullet met his chest as it emerged from the curtain of undergrowth.

"Never did he falter in his stride. He made a mighty leap to my left, bounding over the brush. Fifty feet away stood a high stonewall; beyond, the ground sloped down to the valley. Frantically I threw the Krag bolt and as he left the ground in the last leap to clear the way and to safety, my front sight swung with him. As the report cracked out, there was a heavy jump; then all was still. I ran to the wall and looked over. There in a mass of bloody snow lay my buck, on his back, all four feet kicking. His wide-spread-

ing antler points were buried in the snow—preventing him from turning his head in the least. The white throat-patch gleamed in the morning sunlight, offering my favorite target, so I ended his struggles quickly with a shot through the neck."

This was Koller's largest buck, but not the heaviest. The main beams of his antlers measured 26 inches in length. The inside spread reached 24 inches. The whitetail, a 16-pointer, weighed 202 pounds dressed. He shot it with his favorite 30-40 Krag, which he customized from a standard military rifle. After Koller mounted the head, it hung for many years in the entryway of the Angler's Roost, owned by Koller's deer hunting partner Jim Deren, where many people admired it.

Although Koller liked to play the role of the hunt master of deer drives, he was first and foremost a die-hard still-hunter like Van Dyke. And like Van Dyke, he was a master of making quick decisions followed by suburb instinctive shooting. Although he enjoyed the Thanksgiving Day deer hunts with the group, after everyone left camp, he stayed on and still-hunted whitetails by himself. Ernie Thiesing of Monticello, New York, one of his deer hunting companions, puts it this way: "He really liked to be out there on his own. He enjoyed trying to get a deer by himself when no one else was around."

No one admired the white-tailed deer more than Larry Koller. "No one has greater admiration for these grand, graceful wilderness spirits than I myself ...How I envy them their carefree, peaceful existence; their perfect liberty to move when and where they please!"

Yet, he considered the whitetail to be one of the most paradoxical animals: "The one statement of fact that can be definitely and unequivocally made is that no one knows exactly what any one deer will do under any given set of conditions, not even the deer itself."

Larry Koller with a 16-pointer he shot in the Adirondacks.

Koller's *Shots at Whitetails* was one of the first books on deer and deer hunting I purchased and read in the early 1960s. More than 2000 volumes later, I would have to say it's still one of the best. Koller's favorite deer painting, Bob Kuhn's *Jumping Buck*, graced the frontispiece and dust jacket. Kuhn also provided 11 classic line drawings throughout the text.

Originally published in the fall of 1948, by Little, Brown and Company, *Shots at Whitetails* was reprinted in 1952 and 1958. In commenting on this edition, one reviewer noted, "Koller's friends say he shoots consistently the biggest bucks each year of any man who seeks them. A 'hunter's hunter,' his vast and intimate knowledge of the ways of the whitetail and his expert familiarity with rifles, loads, equipment and method combine to make this the most complete book ever written on the white-tailed deer alone."

On April 21, 1970, Alfred A. Knopf, Inc., one of America's leading book publishers, issued a new edition of the book in conjunction with the Outdoor Life Book Club and described it as "much more than a fine hunting book ...Koller has that special touch for the wild that other sportsmen value and admire ...Koller's interest in hunting, as with all of his acquired skills, was primarily that of a man interested in nature and in the ways of the wild. It is this that gives *Shots at Whitetails* a value beyond its eminent practicality and makes it a classic of wilderness lore." In September of 1975, Knopf reprinted it again as a Borzoi Book For Sportsmen. In August of 2000, Krause Publications reprinted it in a new edition as volume one of their *Deer & Deer Hunting Classics Series*.

In his review of the book in the January 2001 issue of *Deer & Deer Hunting*, historian James Casada categorized the book as the cornerstone of any deer hunter's library:

"From the first page to the last, *Shots at Whitetails* is full of wisdom, spiced with wit, and distinctly winsome in its overall appeal. This reprint is as intriguing today as the original was a half-century ago. It's a book to read and reread. No serious deer hunter should be without it."

For more than a half century, this favorite deer-hunting book introduced several generations of deer hunters to the white-tailed deer, making it an essential component of the North American deer-hunting culture. Indeed, my own generation, boys and girls, came of age in the deer woods reading this book. As early as 1950, Koller, like Archibald Rutledge, encouraged women to deer hunt and Lady Dianas graced the pages of his books. In looking at Remington's classic "Twelve After Four" deer camp ad, one can imagine *Shots at Whitetails* laying on any one of the hunter's bedside tables. Koller's ideas reigned supreme in my house on all matters related to deer and deer hunting.

In their standard anthology of outdoor writing, *America's Great Outdoors: The Story of the Eternal Romance between Man and Nature* (1976), the Outdoor Writers Association of America ranked Koller with Elmer Keith, Jack O'Connor and Warren Page and called Koller, "one of the finest outdoor writers of recent history." In his annotated bibliography, *American Hunting and Fishing Books* (1997), Morris Heller, a nationally-known outdoor book collector/ seller, noted, "the author did not leave a stone unturned in writing this one, his first book."

Throughout his life, Koller worked with well-known, mainstream American publishing houses: Random House, Inc.; Little, Brown & Company; The Bobbs-Merrill Company; Doubleday & Company, Inc.; Simon &

Schuster; Alfred A. Knopf, Inc.; and most recently Krause Publications.

Those who knew Larry Koller said this about him:

Lamar Underwood, friend and outdoor editor: "Larry Koller's death in 1967, stunned the world of outdoor publishing with a tremendous sense of loss. Koller was not only one of the most respected writers and editors in the field, he was also one of the most loved and appreciated – for his friendly easy style, his wit and sense of humor, and his companionship. A superb outdoorsman, dedicated to every phase of sport, he was also a gourmet cook, gunsmith and tackle maker."

Jack O'Connor, world-renowned big game hunter: "He was honest, forthright, fond of a

Jumping Buck by Bob Kuhn was Larry Koller's favorite deer painting.

drink and a humorous tale. As I read *Shots at Whitetails*, I realized it was the best book on deer hunting since Van Dyke's *The Still-Hunter*."

Robert Elman, friend and outdoor editor: "Larry Koller was about as tolerant of people as H. L. Mencken, but he loved his fellow sportsmen, he forgave them all their sins except callousness toward the game and wildlife in general, and he was an amateur naturalist of the first rank. I believe the primary reason for his anger about people other than cronies and sportsmen was that he expected the same level of conduct and performance from them. He never stopped hoping – even believing – that they would behave as straightforwardly as a whitetail deer, a Canada goose, or a raccoon. I believe he died disappointed, as I guess a great many of us will."

Ernest Schwiebert, friend and author of *Remembrances of Rivers Past* (1972): "The most persistent memories of the Neversink are those hours spent with Larry Koller on his hunting-camp water below Bridgeville. There were afternoons with sunlight slanting through the pines, following hen grouse and their broods along paths deep in fiddleback ferns. The last evening I took a big brown fishing the ledges above the Long Eddy, with cooking smells of a woodcock cassoulet drifting down to the river. Koller is dead now, and no longer fishes the river or stalks whitetails or walks up grouse on the ridges. His friends ended his funeral in that simple hunting camp above Long Eddy, and scattered his ashes into the river."

Bob Kuhn, one of America's finest wildlife artists: "Thinking of Larry Koller takes me back several lifetimes. I first met him in the

During Koller's day, the 4:12 AM Remington deer camp ad remained in print as an integral part of the red-plaid, deer-hunting culture in this country; it remains so to this very day.

Early Snow on Good Hill by Bob Kuhn. Kuhn called Larry Koller "...a true Renaissance man."

late 1940s, through another certified out-doorsman, Angus Cameron, an editor at Alfred A. Knopf Publishers. Larry, indistinguishable from your favorite bank teller, was a true Renaissance man. In the area of field sports he could do anything. He was a crack shot with both shotgun and rifle; a keen and skillful fly fisherman, a gunsmith and bow maker. A fine writer. Although he was on the small side and only somewhat round, a trencherman man of epic capacity.

"Larry was a great guy to be with. His seal of approval opened doors magically, as one who benefited thereby can attest. He left the scene much too soon, but on terms of his own choosing. A true believer in the Mark Twain dictum – 'If you can't make 70 by a comfortable road – don't go.'"

Larry Koller was truly a giant amongst deer hunters. His greatest contribution to the sport of American deer hunting lies in his request that every deer hunter should become an environmental part of nature:

"Lucky is the man who can take his deer hunting in large doses; who can get off into the woods for a full two weeks or a month in close association with his quarry and, in a sense, become a part of the country he plans to hunt. These hunters extract the keenest possible enjoyment from the sport and in time will prove to be the most adept woods-men and the best deerslayers. There is no substitute in hunting for a close association with the territory one hunts and the game living therein. The hunter-camper who has the interest and courage to pack his duffel into the deer country, set up his camp and stay until he bags his buck, is a most self-sufficient individual. He willingly divorces himself from the cloying taint of civilization, temporarily at least, and once in the woods unconsciously becomes an environmental part of the scene."

The celebrated artist Alfred Jonniaux's commissioned painting of Old Flintlock. It hangs in the House of Representatives in Columbia.

"In discussing deer hunting as a sport, it seems to me

that we must never lose sight of the fact that its interest

is due chiefly to the nature of the game pursued … I hope

to be a stag follower as long as I can see a sight. This feeling

I attribute to the character of the deer—that noble, elusive,

crafty, wonderful denizen of the wilds, the pursuit of which

is surely the master sport of the huntsman."

–Archibald Rutledge,
Days Off in Dixie, 1924

Chapter Twelve

"OLD FLINTLOCK"

Archibald Rutledge (1883-1973), known to his deer hunting partners as "Old Flintlock," ranked the white-tailed deer at the top of his hunting passion. He studied and observed whitetails all his life. He philosophized and wrote poetry about them. From his deer stand in a century-old live oak, he watched white-tailed bucks travel along moonlit trails; later he captured their mystic radiance in high-level prose. From his plantation records that date back to 1686, Flintlock learned that whitetails had been using the same trails and crossings through the woods of his home for more than three centuries.

Rutledge killed his first white-tailed buck in December of 1894 at the 2000-acre Hampton Plantation along the banks of the Santee River near the town of Mc-Clellanville, South Carolina. He was only 11 years old at the time, but this isn't surprising for someone who, when only 11 months old, swung on the antlers of a pet buck named "Ben." He began to hunt deer at the age of six, and at the tender age of 10, he guided President Cleveland. The 2000 acres that formed the Hampton Plantation would remain his favorite hunting haunt throughout his long and amazingly productive life. The Hampton Plantation is one of the most

The Hampton plantation was made famous when Clark Gable mounted his horse in front of it and rode off into *Gone With the Wind* fame.

Inset: Old Flintlock, a legendary Dixie deerslayer (1883-1973).

impressive homes in the South Carolina Low Country. Its halls have welcomed famous hunters, patriots, soldiers and politicians for three and a half centuries, including George Washington, Lafayette and Francis Marion. It stands today as a landmark in the Hampton Plantation State Park.

When Old Flintlock died at the age of 90, his deer-kill statistics reached a total of 299 white-tailed bucks. "If 299 bucks seem just too many for one man," Rutledge tells us, "I will remind the reader that South Carolina is a good deer state and that some of its zones have the longest season in the United States. A hunter is allowed five bucks a season and I have hunted for 78 years." Following are samples of some of Flintlock's more memorable buck hunts together with a brief look at an individual who certainly ranks well to the forefront of those who pursued the gallant animal and described their adventures in print.

Like the medieval knight, Old Flintlock subscribed to the principles of St. Hubert, Patron Saint of the Hunter.

Courtesy of Wegner's Photo Collection.

Like most white-tailed deer hunters, Flintlock acquired his keen interest in the sport from his father, Colonel Henry Rutledge II, who spoke of deer and deer hunting, as Flintlock puts it, "with a gravity that gauged his feeling." As they tramped the great pine barrens and cypress swamps around the Hampton Plantation, the Colonel, who killed more than 600 whitetails and attained a remarkable record of 30 double shots on deer (one with each barrel), would suddenly stop and point out to the young boy the very spot where several years earlier he had dropped a magnificent 10-point buck. On their numerous journeys through the deep pinelands, the Colonel taught the boy to recognize the track of a buck from that of a doe: "A buck walks heavily, is blunt-toed and wears a number ten shoe; a doe is a lady. She minces along in high-heeled slippers."

Yet, Flintlock himself believed that his great love of deer hunting was not only born in him, since the men of his family always hunted deer, but that a curious happening which occurred when he was only 11 months old deeply instilled in him a profound love of the animal and an intense interest in the hunting of them. The incident took place one day after his mother left him alone in his crib in a large room in the plantation house. Up the cypress steps of the front porch and through the front door came "Ben," a magnificent, full-antlered buck that the Colonel had raised on a bottle. Old Ben bent over the little boy and nuzzled him intently. Unafraid of the buck, the infant reached up his tiny hands and seized the wide, beaded antlers. The buck suddenly snorted and when Flintlock's mother entered the room, she saw her baby swinging on the rack of a white-tailed buck. "I have always felt sure," Rutledge writes in a story entitled "That Christmas Buck," "that the old stag (since he knew that his own hide was safe) passed me the mystic word concerning the rarest sport on earth. He put it across to me, all right!" Thus spiritually inspired from the cradle in the tradition of Saint Hubert, Patron Saint of Hunting, whom Rutledge adhered to throughout his life, he would spend his whole life doing his best to pass on the glad tidings to all deer hunters of the animal's miraculous powers.

As the young Archie grew up, he became accustomed to seeing portraits of famous sportsmen and the antlers of many a white-tailed buck hanging on the walls of the old plantations. While visiting one plantation with the Colonel, he saw a collection of more than 400 white-tailed racks. The antlers gazed down at the boy and deeply affected his lifelong interests. While eating dinners at the Hampton Plantation, the boy enthusiastically admired the rack of one great chestnut-colored buck that hung in the dining room; its massive antlers carried 12 points. Later in life Flintlock recalled his early fascination with antlers:

"A plantation home without its collection of stag horns is hardly to be found, and in passing I may say that some of the collections, dating back almost to the time of the Revolution, are of remarkable interest . . . In some families, there is a custom, rigorously adhered to, that no deer antlers must ever leave the place, so that the antlers of every buck killed find their way into the home's collection. Such a frieze in a dining room seems to fill the place with woodland memories and serves in its own way to recall the hunts, the hunters and the hunted of long ago."

During his school days, the young boy longed to climb into the crotches of live oaks at Hampton and watch whitetails. Reading tales about giant, legendary bucks and being wise in the ways of the woods and whitetails intrigued the boy more than formal lessons in the classroom.

In his early years, Archie listened to the black huntsmen tune up their hunting horns and he heard the joyous yowling of the staghounds as they responded to the mellow blasts. For a young boy on the Hampton Plantation, white-tailed deer hunting with these sounds on Christmas Day was as much a part of the season as a Christmas tree. By the age of nine, deer and deer hunting had become one of the most serious things in the life of Archibald Rutledge. Later in life, he would acknowledge that, "there is no grander sport in the whole world than riding to hounds after deer; and this is sport typical of a plantation Christmas. With my Colonel, throughout his long life, it was almost a religious rite, and it never failed to supply the most thrilling entertainment for visitors. Indeed, I do not know exactly what the rural South would be without deer hunting as a diversion."

Beginning in 1730, deer hunting became an essential, integral ingredient of life at the Hampton Plantation, especially at Christmastime. "For a period of twenty shining years," notes Irvine Rutledge, the youngest of Flintlock's boys and later a judge in Maryland, "there was 'The Hampton Hunt'." The Hampton Hunts began in 1923, when Flintlock's sons Mid, Arch and Irv were old enough to look down the barrel of a shotgun. They ended in 1943, when Mid was killed in a car accident and Arch and Irv went off to fight in World War II.

Yes, Flintlock taught his three boys to be deer hunters, believing if more fathers taught their sons to be hunters, many of the so-called father-son problems would be eliminated. Quite often ladies and "lollypop sentimentalists" who came to visit the Hampton Plantation would be somewhat dismayed to learn that Flintlock and his boys enjoyed deer hunting. In defense of the sport, Flintlock would take them to his living room and show them that famous picture of natu-

During the years 1923 to 1942, the Hampton deer hunters – Old Flintlock, Archibald Rutledge, Jr., Henry Middleton Rutledge, IV, and Irvine Hart Rutledge – eagerly chased the Black-horn Buck.

Courtesy of Judge Irvine H. Rutledge.

hunters."

During the time of the Hampton Hunts, Rutledge and his boys coined many nicknames: Arch, Jr. they called "Buckshot," and Irvine was "Gunpowder." Uncle Hamilton was known as "The Holder of the Bottle." They referred to Flintlock's beloved 12-gauge Parker shotgun with the 30-inch barrel as "Annie Oakley." In his lifelong correspondence with his deer hunting cronies, Flintlock signed his letters with the drawing of a flintlock.

Like Audubon, their deer stands acquired such names as the Crippled Oak Stand, the Shirttail Stand, the Six-Master Stand and the Seven Sisters. They christened the wild bucks of the woods they pursued with such names as Bushmaster, the Black-horn Buck, Old Clubfoot and the Gray Stag of Bowman's Bank. They called their deer-hounds Old Buck, Old Bugle, Driver, Blue Boy and Red Liquor. The immense and inviolate swamp where many of their bucks often escaped they called the Ocean, and their deer drives were the Long Corner, the Huckleberry Branch, Boggy Bay and the Turkey Roost Drive.

ralist John J. Audubon holding his shotgun of awesome proportions. "Teach the young how to shoot," Flintlock would tell his guests. "There is something inherently manly and homebred and truly American in that expression 'shooting straight.'"

Flintlock's eloquent defense of hunting culminated in his essay "Why I Taught My Boys to Be Hunters," a classic statement of hunting that stands with Roosevelt's hunting works, Leopold's "Wildlife in American Culture," and Ortega y Gasset's *Meditations on Hunting* (1972).

"Hunting is not incompatible with the deepest and most genuine love of nature. Audubon was a hunter; so was the famous Bachman; so were both John Muir and John Burroughs. It has always seemed to me that any man is a better man for being a hunter. This sport confers a certain constant alertness, and develops a certain ruggedness of character that, in these days of too much civilization, is refreshing; moreover, it allies us to the pioneer past. In a deep sense, this great land of ours was won for us by

The Black-horn Buck, the most elusive creature in North American white-tailed deer hunting lore, dwelled and swelled in the mind of this Dixie deerslayer for more than half a century. Old Flintlock pursued this master strategist of the wild in one guise or another throughout all 2000 acres of his famous Hampton Plantation along the banks of the Santee River, and beyond.

The size, shape and ebony coloration of

his antlers epitomized greatness, beauty and majesty. Flintlock searched for his sheds and when found, considered them as tangible evidence of his survivability, his invincibility; this legendary, phantom buck seemed "unkillable." Indeed, the Black-horn Buck had no intention of ever entering the high-paneled living or dining room at the Hampton Plantation with its walls adorned with the antlered heads of many kings of the South Carolina Low Country's white-tailed deer tribe. The collection contained 300 sets, some dating back more than 100 years.

Nor did Flintlock want the Black-horn Buck there either! For his demise would negate the incredible yarns spun over his dexterity and mythic dimensions. His death was inconceivable; it would destroy any substance for future deer hunting strategies. It would be a tragedy to lose this old, master protagonist, who so deeply stirred the emotions of Flintlock, his boys and the black deer hunters of the Hampton Plantation.

The Black-horn Buck had "to remain at large, unrestrained by property lines, and free to roam the minds of men who are themselves restrained," as Stuart Marks so aptly writes in *Southern Hunting in Black and White* (1991). This amazing creature remained beyond the grasp of the buck hunters of the Hampton Plantation and through time, the Black-horn Buck came to symbolize the ones that always get away; the ones we constantly learn the most from in terms of deer hunting strategies, as T. S. Van Dyke, whom Rutledge read with great relish, always insisted.

Archibald Rutledge, who "rolled over" more than 299 white-tailed bucks with his "Old Reliable" double-barrel Parker shotgun, first introduced us to the adventures of the Black-horn Buck in his book *Tom and I on the Old Plantation* (1919). While on a deer drive in 1896, young Archie and his brother Tom were driving a dense thicket of bull pines, scrub oaks, myrtles and gallberry bushes. Suddenly, Archie heard above the chiming chorus of their deer-hounds the melodious voice of Prince, Archie's lifelong black, deer-hunting partner, plead insistently, "Tis the old Black-horn Buck! Don't let him by!" Rutledge describes his first youthful encounter with this mythic buck of monumental proportions:

"He was indeed a magnificent creature, with tall symmetrical antlers . . . he was the only buck I had ever seen with ebony-colored antlers. I understood why Prince called him the Black-horn Buck. He came bounding along in his graceful, powerful way, every muscle of his shapely body subservient to his will. He was heading straight

Old Flintlock holding his beloved Parker 12-gauge double barrel, which he used "to roll" some of his 299 white-tailed bucks in 78 years of intensive deer hunting.

White Flag by Carl Rungius, circa 1899. The Black-horn Buck was pursued by Old Flintlock throughout all 2000 acres of the Hampton Plantation and beyond.

for my brother . . . But with winding him or seeing him, or doing both things at once, the great buck veered swiftly away from my brother and from within deadly rage of his old Westley-Richards muzzleloader, an English gun of wonderful carrying power."

At that very moment, young Archie again heard Prince's voice sound melodiously above the chiming chorus of the pack: "Tis the old Black-horn Buck! Don't miss him!" But that crafty denizen of the deer woods leaped clear of Tom's Westley-Richards and swiftly vanished into a dense copse of young yellow pines without a trace or shadow, leaving the two young deerslayers in speechless admiration, but happy nonetheless. Why? Les Blacklock in his book, *Meet My Psychiatrist* (1977), gives us the answer:

"I'm always glad to see a famous buck get away. His legendary size and antler measurements could probably never be matched by the real thing. Besides, once you've nailed him, the fun is over; the speculative record measurements have shrunk to realistic mediocrity. And next year's hunting season is not the exciting prospect it would have been had The Phantom Buck still been out there."

Several hundred miles to the north in the land of famed deerslayer Philip Tome, one of Flintlock's great deer hunting heroes, an event occurred in November of 1896 that greatly affected Flintlock's impressions of mythic bucks and the development of their legendary stories: Pennsylvania deer hunter Samuel Strohecker shot a 26-pointer with dark, ebony-stained antlers in the Appalachian Mountains of Centre County, Pennsylvania.

The Strohecker buck had roamed and ruled the mountainous terrain of High Valley in the Seven Brothers for almost a decade. Through the original pines, Sam Strohecker and his brother Will, a noted deer hunter of this time, pursued and downed notable bucks while still-hunting, but this elusive, ebony-stained treasure escaped their best efforts time and again, as did the Black-horn Buck. But on November 23, 1896, Sam finally downed the old monarch as he silently tried to back track from a secluded deer bed in deep snowy pines. To accomplish the feat, he used his discounted Winchester Model 1866 – the famous "Yellow Boy" – which held 13 rounds of 44 rimfire ammo and that Strohecker ordered in 1895 from Montgomery Ward for the bargain price of $12.83.

The Strohecker head instantly became the most magnificent antlered specimen of the white-tailed deer clan and the immediate object of early collector's desires. As one of

Courtesy of Wegner's Photo Collection.

Samuel Strohecker's 26-pointer with dark, ebony-stained antlers taken in November of 1896 in the High Valley of Centre County, Pennylvania, served as one of Flintlock's models for the Black-horn Buck.

America's premier whitetail antler collectors, Rutledge set out to locate the noble head and possibly purchase it for the distinguished Hampton Antler Collection.

After arriving on the slopes of the Pennsylvania Alleghenies in 1904 to begin a 33-year teaching assignment as Professor of English at Mercersburg Academy, he traveled to Centre County to see firsthand this mythic buck that famed naturalist Charles H. Eldon of Williamsport had mounted with world-class distinction for Strohecker. In 1905, he finally located and viewed the magnificent buck at the genial nimrod's cozy retreat in Rebersburg and obtained photos, measurements and nostalgic deer hunting tales concerning the behavior and lore of this white-tailed buck.

Measurement procedures in those days were somewhat crude, but Flintlock recorded the length of the rack to be 31 inches, 21 inches at its widest point and 16 inches from tip to tip. The circumference above the brow tine measured 5-1/2 inches. It carried 15 points on the right antler and 11 on the left with an estimated field-dressed body weight of 278 pounds. Its exquisite, ebony-stained antlers reminded Flintlock of a waterbuck or an ibex and made the buck distinctly identifiable – mesmerizing Rutledge's imagination.

Rutledge often referred to it in his writings and conversations with old backwoods buck hunters. His friend, Colonel Henry W. Shoemaker, an authority on Pennsylvania deer, characterized the beauty and the mental image of that buck: "The sweep of the antlers was graceful in the extreme, they were still not top-heavy, and the excess points on the right antler were not large and did not detract from the harmonious effect of the whole. The antlers were of a rich chestnut brown in color, ivory at the tips and very sharp. The beading was uniform, and the head singularly free from rudimentary points. The expression of the head was most strikingly lifelike."

Strohecker retained a modest evaluation of its worth by offering to sell it for 15 dollars, only a little more than the cost of his discounted Winchester. For whatever reasons, neither Rutledge nor anyone else immediately purchased the rack. It hung in Sam's backwoods, deer-hunting retreat until 1913, when he died. His widow then sold it to some stranger. Apparently, a hotel in Tyrone displayed it for some time, but the historic record for this artifact then ends. Thus even in death, the Strohecker buck escaped the mechanical restrictions of the record books and once again vanished into ultimate freedom.

In looking for a historic prototype for his classic stories on the Black-horn Buck, Rutledge located a magnificent array of unusual bucks all taken between 1896 and 1897 in Ernest Thompson Seton's *Game Animals* (1929), a book Flintlock read with great delight. Plate XLII of that book illustrates the amazing variety that emerged during this time. But Flintlock clearly chose the Strohecker Buck above all of these as "The Monarch of the Glen" to give dignity, respect and credibility, not only to the adventures of the famous Black-horn Buck, but to all phantom, white-tailed bucks both in the deer forest and the literary domain.

When the fall academic semesters ended at Mercersburg Academy, the professor of English headed for the Hampton Plantation on the Carolina coast to chase the Black-horn Buck during Christmas vacations. Rutledge never tired of describing these Christmas deer hunting adventures. One Christmas morning, the Hampton deerslayer remained convinced the Black-horn Buck had run his last race and would not escape death. Old Flintlock and his boys had the buck surrounded "in a small islet of bushes not bigger than a dinner-table in the wide sea of broom sedge in the pine lands."

On this occasion his "dreadful implacable

Courtesy of Wegner's Photo Collection.

Charles H. Eldon, famed naturalist, with the world-famous Strohecker buck, Old Flintlock's prototype for the phantom Black-horn Buck.

enemies" were closing in on him. Six standers—all expert shots—stood tall and ready downwind from the bedded monarch. Coming from behind, walking 50 feet apart were five drivers, several on horseback, led by five deerhounds all giving tongue. When the foremost deerhound, "Old Hickory," approached within 50 yards of that wary veteran, he did not rocket from his bed; he just stood up. He was not going to be driven; he would rather charge the drivers. As Rutledge recalls, "memory and instinct told him that to be driven meant to run the chance of being killed . . . This buck was a strategist of sage experience, a veteran in the art of tactics." The obvious course of action was to

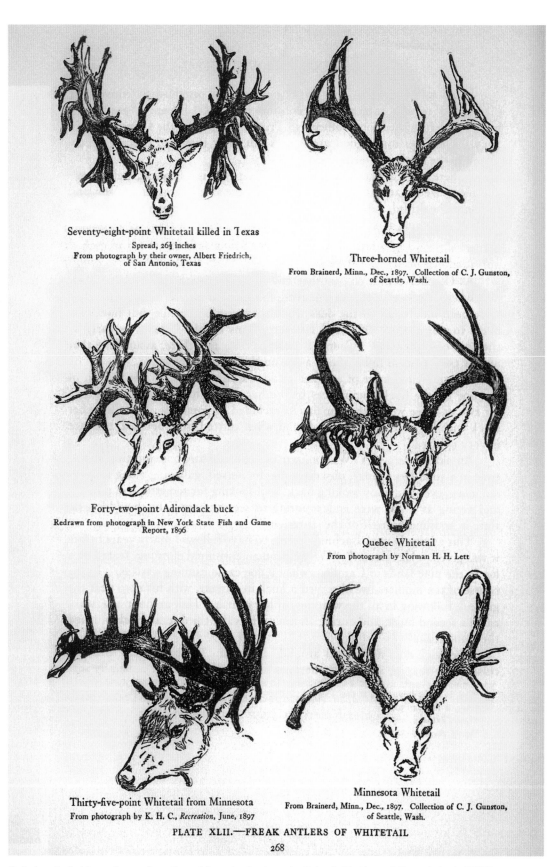

Seventy-eight-point Whitetail killed in Texas

Spread, 26½ inches

From photograph by their owner, Albert Friedrich,
of San Antonio, Texas

Three-horned Whitetail

From Brainerd, Minn., Dec., 1897. Collection of C. J. Gunston,
of Seattle, Wash.

Forty-two-point Adirondack buck

Redrawn from photograph in New York State Fish and Game
Report, 1896

Quebec Whitetail

From photograph by Norman H. H. Lett

Thirty-five-point Whitetail from Minnesota

From photograph by K. H. C., *Recreation*, June, 1897

Minnesota Whitetail

From Brainerd, Minn., Dec., 1897. Collection of C. J. Gunston,
of Seattle, Wash.

PLATE XLII.—FREAK ANTLERS OF WHITETAIL

268

Rutledge studied the antler configurations of these bucks drawn by Seton in his *Lives of Game Animals* (1929).

flee the oncoming, shouting drivers and clamoring hounds and run upwind using his nose to detect the danger of the standers waiting ahead.

"But the Black-horn Buck had learned that the apparently safe and easy way out is usually the path of peril, designedly prepared by his foes. For a moment, standing in his bed, he winded the gentle dry pineland air. He surveyed his crowding foes. Then he did the thing least expected of him under such circumstances, and probably for that very reason safest. He ran straight back toward the drivers . . . Men, dogs, and horses tried to turn the heroic fugitive. But he had set his heart to gaining the deep fastness of a wild river-swamp; and he never changed his direction, never altered his stride. He won his safety by as bold and gallant a maneuver as the greenwood ever saw. There was about it a superb uncertainty—wayward, sagacious, splendid."

Once again, the Black-horn Buck reigned supreme as he foiled Flintlock's dreams. The fame of this stag increased in an amazing way among the plantation workers and hunters. They attributed his uncanny ability to escape from deer hunters and hounds to superstition and magical powers, and ultimately to a supernatural presence. To what one Hampton deerslayer called "an ancient wildwood magic." This wariest of bucks reportedly waded across ponds before bedding to eliminate all telltale scent. He was known as a habitual, safe-guarding "maneuverer." "This deer could make himself very small," Rutledge insisted. "I did not know a better skulker." Many of the hunters shot at him but still he lived. The fame of the Black-horn Buck and his great crown of ebony antlers deeply stirred the entire foundations of the Hampton Plantation.

As one of the 20th century's greatest students of white-tailed deer behavior, Rutledge most admired his graceful movements and his tactics of motion. "Full into sight he now burst, running wildly, yet for all his speed with a continence of flight – planned and purposeful. With a woodland fugitive the great end is not alone to escape, but in doing so to avoid possible enemies in front as well as certain foes behind. His mighty yet graceful bulk, the ponderous grace of his movements, the heavy yet patrician elegance that such a primeval creature always possesses – all these impressed me . . . There was something superbly regal about his whole make-up, a gallant superiority that marked him as king of the wildwoods."

Indeed, this gallant, old fellow genuinely distinguished himself as an unconventional individual in the deer woods and in the mind of Archibald Rutledge. "There are distinct individuals in nature," Rutledge tells us, "creatures whose unconventional behavior is proof of their high intelligence. Most of them are superb solitaires. Now and then we encounter complete originals. So informal and arbitrary in their deep sagacity that the mere novelty of them is refreshing. And the Black-horn Buck is of this type."

In his classic, literary portrait of the Black-horn Buck, Flintlock acknowledges that, "it is now many years since I first became acquainted with the Black-horn Buck. Still he roams my plantation woods and in the summer helps himself to my peas and corn. Still my Black workers fear him; and still I am privileged to love and admire him, for he has taught me that the natural world can develop a great personality. And whenever a hunting season passes without proving disastrous to him, I rejoice that his magnificent ebony crown is not drying out at some taxidermists, but is thrusting aside dewy pine boughs in the moonlight or, deep in a fragrant bed of ferns and sweet-bay, is affording the shy moonbeams something really mystic on which to sparkle."

Archibald Rutledge was a die-hard buck hunter, a man motivated by a single-minded purpose: to study the white-tailed buck in its most intimate dimensions. His deep devotion, obsession and mystical attachment for this animal and his remarkable literary skill won for him The John Burroughs Medal for the best writing in America in 1932. Following his death in 1973, *The New York Times* reported that after spending more than a half century in the deer woods in pursuit of whitetails, Flintlock still managed to find time to write 80 books. After receiving 20 honorary degrees and more than 30 gold medals, he came in second in the Pulitzer Contest in poetry to Robert Frost. When William Faulkner, another diehard buck hunter from the South, received the Nobel Prize for literature in 1949, the judges told Rutledge he had lost by only one vote.

His sporting savvy and persistent pursuit of the Black-horn Buck made the glories of white-tailed buck hunting come alive. Chasing the Black-horn Buck became a kind of religion, a religious rite; for Old Flintlock lived in close communion with bucks in the wild haunts they preferred. With his spiritual infinity for the animal, his vast knowledge of deer behavior and lore and his spiritual consecration of venison loin, he *became* the white-tailed buck.

In a picture of Archibald Rutledge taken when he was 89, several months before his death, we see the bed-ridden buck hunter grasping with powerful hands a magnificent set of white-tailed deer antlers, his finest. In looking at the photo, a fellow hunter George Bird Evans noted in *Men Who Shot* (1983), "What a man, his face hollowed by years but with eyes burning with a fire like the life that flowed in the eyes of the Black-horn Buck."

Old Flintlock and his Dixie deerslayers loved to reminisce about the splendid, grandiose strategy and the "shadowy subterfuge," as Rutledge called it, of this famous 12-point buck. In Flintlock's many years of deer hunting, this buck stood out as having no equal. On numerous occasions Flintlock thought he had this buck helplessly cornered, only to learn that no one ever corners a world-class, white-tailed buck, not even Archibald Rutledge. While Rutledge studied the forest around the Hampton Plantation for a half-century, he admitted that this buck knew the terrain far better and more intimately than he. In his heart, Flintlock was often on the side of this master tactician. Of this buck, Flintlock once remarked, "When you get in antlers craggy massiveness, a twenty-three-inch

Rutledge greatly admired the world-class Caesar Buck seen in this photo as illustrated by Ernest Thompson Seton.

Courtesy of Wegner's Photo Collection.

spread and twelve points – Man, what more do you want?"

The wide-branching horns of the Black-horn Buck, the imagery, mythology and historic reality of this legendary, phantom buck haunted Flintlock's dreams throughout his life and inspired him to sketch this noble beast on his countless letter correspondence. The regal buck eventually inspired the professor of English to compose the following poem, *Hunter's Choice*, as a final tribute to the Black-horn Buck and to all phantom bucks in white-tailed deer country:

> *O it's not the bull moose of New Brunswick,*
> *Or Wyoming's wapiti tall,*
> *Or Canada's caribou tall,*
> *Or the Kodiak bear*
> *That I see and I hear*
> *When I vision the forest of fall:*
>
> *It's the buck with the wide-branching horns!*
> *My stratagems wary he scorns,*
> *My artifice wily he scorns.*
> *He is haunting my dreams*
> *Of the mountains and streams.*
> *My evenings, my nights, and my morns,*
> *The buck with the wide-branching horns!*
>
> *When red is the reedland at sunrise,*
> *And mallard and teal are in flight,*
> *And gray goose and black-duck in flight,*
> *Many men of good breed*
> *Find the sport that they need,*
> *But mine is a different delight:*
>
> *It's the buck with the wide-branching horns!*
> *His beauty the wildwood adorns,*
> *His wonder the wildwood adorns.*
> *He is haunting my dreams*
> *Of the mountains and streams,*
> *My evenings, my nights and my morns,*
> *The buck with the wide-branching horns!*

As he wrote these lines, the Poet Laureate of South Carolina stared at Ernest Thompson Seton's classic drawing of the famous buck shot in Maine in 1911 by Henry A. Caesar. This world-class whitetail reigned supreme for many years as the non-typical world record (228-1/8) and Flintlock saw this 27-pointer in many ways as a model for his literary creation of the Black-horn Buck, the buck with the wide-branching horns.

The Christmas Day deer hunt reigned supreme in the litany of the Hampton Hunt. It was a religious rite, an exhilarating affair in and of itself, never to be matched in the history of American white-tailed deer hunting "Not to have a stag hanging up on Christmas Eve," Rutledge once admitted, "is to confess a certain degree of enfeebled manhood – almost a social disgrace." According to an old English custom, instead of going to church on Christmas morning, Flintlock and his boys went deer hunting. In an article titled "A Christmas Hunt," Flintlock makes the argument for adhering to this custom:

"Quaintly, and very humanly, the chief business on Christmas Day on an old southern plantation is not going to church. While the women naturally think religion should come first, they do not greatly demur when their husbands, brothers and lovers like the attractively boyish barbarians men always really are, decide to take to the woods."

Buckskin, buckshot, horses, clamoring hounds, echoing horns, blaring shotguns, antlers and white tails flashing in the breeze gave the whole business an aura of religiosity and the appearance of a minor military campaign. Old Flintlock loved the hustle, bustle and hullabaloo of the whole affair. "To ride up deer in the open woods," Flintlock confessed in *An American Hunter* (1937), "and to shoot them from horseback, sometimes when both the deer and the horse are running at full speed, is to prove that deer hunting has not completely degenerated."

In the great tradition of Audubon, Herbert,

Elliott and Caton, Old Flintlock and his Dixie deerslayers took deer hunting seriously. If you have any doubts in this regard, consider the telling expressions Rutledge used in his writings. Bucks were not shot, killed or harvested; they were "rolled." In a letter to his son Irvine, then a senior in college, Flintlock used the expression "to roll one" to mean bringing down a buck:

"Forget life's triumphs and defeats,
Forget you Coleridge and your Keats;
Forget whatever you have saw –
Old Mercersburg and Old Nassau.
Forget your girl, but don't forget
Old Flintlock's going to roll one yet.
And if you think one is too few,
Old Flintlock's going to roll you two
He's going upon a killing spree –
Old Flintlock's going to roll you three!"

Flintlock received this reply from his son:

"When red leaves fall in October days,
Tis then I change my peaceful ways.

To shoot and kill I'm all Hell bent
By heredity and environment.

To peace and love I'm fully blinded –
I'm full-capacity killer minded."

These Dixie deer hunting comrades loved antlers on the wall but they also shot venison for the pot. When Old Flintlock shot, the boys and their black companions joyously cried, "Put on the pot!" These legendary Hampton Hunts remind us of the deer hunting campaigns and expeditions of Philip Tome and Meshach Browning. Following in the tradition of these giants among deer hunters, Flintlock takes his place in the picturesque gallery of American deer hunters.

Christmas deer hunts at the Hampton Plantation ended at the barn, where the quarry was hung, skinned and butchered by flickering lanterns and red-flaring lightwood torches. After the deerhounds received their portions, a hunting horn sounded and all the participants of the Hampton Hunt received their share of the venison. "With me deer hunting is a kind of religion," Flintlock writes in his essay "Blue's Buck," "and I have worshipped at this shrine ever since a grown oak was an acorn."

Flintlock did not know of any other sport that would whet the appetite more keenly than the sport of deer hunting. And no American writer ever more keenly expressed the ultimate excitement of a Christmas Day deer hunt in the South than Rutledge in this autobiographical excerpt from his book, *My Colonel and His Lady* (1937):

"As we ride our mounts down the sandy road, we are on the lookout for deer tracks; and these are seen crossing and re-crossing the damp road. The hunters who have charge of the pack have to use all their powers of elocution to persuade the hounds not to make a break after certain hot trails. The horses seem to know and to enjoy this sport as well as the men and the dogs do. No horse can be started more quickly or stopped more abruptly than one trained to hunt in the woods.

"We start a stag in the Crippled Oak Drive, and for miles we race him, now straight through the glimmering pinelands, sun-dappled and still, now through the eerie fringes of the Ocean, an inviolate sanctuary, made so by the riotous tangle of greenery; now he heads for the river, and we race down the broad road to cut him off . . . There is a stretch of three miles, perfectly straight and level, broad, and lying a little high. Down this we course. But the crafty buck doubles and heads northward for the sparkleberry thickets of the plantation. I race forward to a certain stand, and just as I get there, he almost jumps over me! The dogs are far behind; and the stag gives the appearance of enjoying the race. Away he sails, his stiffly erect snowy tail flashing high above the bushes. I love to watch running hounds when they do not observe me. They always run with more native zest and sagacity when they are going it alone.

"A rather common dog, of highly doubtful lineage, is in the lead. The aristocrats come last. I am always amused over the manner in which full-blooded hounds perform the rite of trailing. This business is a religion with them. They do not bark, or do anything else so banal and bourgeois; they make deep-chested music, often pausing in the heat of a great race to throw their heads heavenward and vent toward the sky perfect music. Their running is never pell-mell. A good hound is a curious combination of the powers of genius: he is Sherlock Holmes in that he works out infallibly the mazy trail; he is Lord Chesterfield in that he does all things in a manner becoming a gentleman; and he is a grand opera star, full of amazing music. I get a never-failing thrill out of listening to hounds and out of watching them at close hand. To me it appears that the music they make depends much upon their environment for its timbre. And as they course over hills and dip into hollows, as they ramble through bosky water-courses or trail down roads, as the leafy canopies over them deepen or thin, their chorus hushes and swells, affording all the notes with many a winding bout that the best melody offers.

"Our stalwart buck makes almost a complete circle, outwits us, enters the mysterious depths of the Ocean, and is lost. But perhaps – at any rate, on Christmas Day – for us to lose his life is better than for him to have lost it. Yet his escape by no means ends our sport."

Their Christmas Day deer hunt would end in the dining room with antlered bucks from previous campaigns looking down from above on the candlelight dinner with its wild rice, brown sweet potatoes, roasted rice-fed mallards and venison tenderloins fattened on acorns. At twilight, the boys would form a great semicircle before the fireplace to watch the giant Yule log and to "rehunt" the chases of that day. The presence of several of their deerhounds lying on the rug before the fireplace added substance and reality to their tales. As the deer came out of their coverts again to roam the darkness of the plantation's woods and as the cold moon of December cast its silvery glamour over the Hampton Plantation, the echoes of the laughter and merriment of the Hampton deer hunters faded into the shadow of the past.

As the master of the Hampton Hunts, Flintlock remained an incurable optimist who always believed, like Paulina Brandreth, in the possibility of last chances. In his splendid essay "A Buck in the Rain," he wrote that "men who know deer nature best know that the element of chance is perhaps about as great in the pursuit of this superb game animal as it is in the following of any other game in the world."

Old Flintlock steadfastly maintained that each deer hunt should make sporting history, not create mystery with hunters giving faulty, elaborate reasons why missing that buck seemed altogether reasonable. No, Rutledge didn't care much for refined dissertations on how the buck successfully escaped into the eternal, inviolate sanctuary. Instead, he wanted to see the Old Boy fall to the forest floor with his last race run as if he had been struck by lightning. Then and then only could the hunter get that special thrill out of the possibility of wrenching success from failure at the last minute of the game. As a pragmatist, Flintlock wanted the buck on the meat pole, not a masterpiece in the way of a Great Excuse. In this regard, a primordial element of blood lust drove him until his dying day.

The object of the game for the Rutledge

Old Flintlock's first love: chasing the Black-horn Buck through the low country of South Carolina as shown here in the illustrations from Paul Bransom in Rutledge's *Hunter's Choice*.

boys was to stick with the deer hunt until the black dark sky set in on the very last day of the season. Old Flintlock rightly believed that many deer hunters go home defeated because they stop too soon.

"So often has the very last chance afforded me the best luck that I have become almost superstitious about this business of last chances . . . Faith, superstition, persistence – call it what you will; but I know that the luck of the last chance has often taken the empty cup of bitterness and disappointment and brimmed it with the wine of achievement. I can recall killing no fewer than 16 bucks on last chances . . . the actual shooting of them is usually a thing of the moment; the

only question is whether you have patience to wait for the moment. Often, the last moment is the moment."

Such was the case with "Old Clubfoot," a mysterious buck, crippled, wiser than most buck hunters, gallant and seemingly immortal. Not even Joel Mayrant, a prominent buck hunter of the pinelands, could shoot this 300-pounder with the 4-inch track. Rutledge and his boys hunted this particular buck for three years. They also managed to collect a set of his shed, freak antlers the year before the last chance came.

Most hunters could easily recognize Old Clubfoot because of his antlers. The bases of the beams were heavily encrusted with ivory

and brown beading. His antlers were unique and atypical: the right antler, heavily palmated, pitched forward, while the left antler towered over the right and leaned curiously toward the rear. This buck ran with an unusual rocking gait due to an old injury. During his lifetime, this wise and seasoned strategist of the deer woods waved a mocking farewell to many a buck hunter, including Archibald Rutledge.

His downfall came one morning when Rutledge had to leave Hampton early to return to the Mercersburg Academy in the mountains of Pennsylvania, where he taught English. Believing in last chances, Flintlock and his boys arose early that morning and left for the big wooded pasture east of the house. They were dressed in their traveling clothes to get in one last hunt. The morning broke clear, warm and still. Traveling to the wooded pasture, Flintlock wondered to himself why a reasonable man would leave the South in midwinter and travel northward into the blizzards of Pennsylvania to teach English at a boy's academy. While leaning against a pine tree and enjoying the sunshine, Flintlock suddenly saw a superb buck take flight.

"From the moment I first saw him I knew not only that he was a deer of remarkable size and beauty, but also that he was an ancient acquaintance of mine. Identification was made immediately possible by his freak antlers."

After an abrupt takeoff, Old Clubfoot stopped in an old logging road about 130 yards away – clearly out of range for Flintlock's "Annie Oakley." The buck next made a splendid leap away from the startled hunter. The whole affair seemed over; the last chance was gone. Watching Old Clubfoot's rapid departure, Flintlock seemed ready to take, as he admits, "a long pull from the flask of saint's delight and call the business off." But as Flintlock always told his boys, you can often count on the unexpected to happen. Suddenly, and most unexpectedly, Old Clubfoot made a sharp slant to the right and came running toward the hunter full bore.

"Out of the corner of my left eye I saw the stag coming like a Barnegat breaker. He was going to give me a fair chance. I started breathing hard, as you may well believe. I steadied myself as best I could, and as the splendid old fugitive sailed by broadside I let him have the choke barrel. I saw him flinch – a sure sign that he had been struck. But he went on without apparent effort, and a myrtle thicket swallowed him, horns and all.

"Within half a mile, stretched beneath one of the pines under which I doubt not, he had often roamed, lay the rugged old veteran, his last race over. He had been struck by nine buckshot."

This victory in the last moments of the deer season inspired the triumphant return to the plantation. Old Clubfoot's strange rack looked down at Flintlock from the walls of his den for many years as a fine reminder of the possibilities of last chances; that the great chance does in fact come to the faithful, that the buck hunter's insane faith often results in the greatest reward.

Like most serious students of white-tailed deer behavior, Rutledge knew that no one really knows white-tailed deer unless he studies them after dark, especially under a full moon. So Flintlock built himself a large platform, 16 feet up in the forks of an oak tree, overlooking a heavily used deer crossing. In this deer stand in the oak, Flintlock spent countless hours studying and watching the secret lives of white-tailed deer under moonlight. He did this during October, November and December and quickly learned of the great difficulty involved in watching whitetails in the moonlight, for they are sometimes visible and then vanish as quickly as you see them. In his book *Home By The River* (1941), he describes the excitement of discerning the shadowy outlines of two white-tailed bucks under the moonlight:

"I have a long wait, but who will not wait amid deepening peace and increasing loveliness? At last they come: two fairy shapes, silent, elusive, beautiful. The mild night air is drifting from them to me, so that they do not detect my presence. Here are two great silvery stags with silver horns, moving with unpostured grace through a silvery world. They pause, as if posing for an urgent picture. Nearer they come, and I notice that at certain angles in the moonlight they are almost invisible; at others they are vividly visible. Past me they glide like spirits of the wilderness, having all the meaning connoted by the night, by stillness and by the unwearied charm of nature. Into the silver silences they vanish."

While George Shiras III, a friend and a contemporary of Flintlock's and the founder of deer photography, captured the magnificent radiance of white-tailed deer in the moonlight in his award-winning, nighttime photos, Flintlock immortalized the animal in the moonlight in his great nature essay "My Friend the Deer," first published in *The New Country Life* in May of 1918:

"No other creature of the forest seems more a shape of the moonlight than does the deer. It is apparently possible for the largest

This photo of a white-tailed buck in the moonlight by Rutledge friend and contemporary George Shiras III won extraordinary honors at the Paris (1900) and St. Louis (1904) exhibitions.

buck to move through the dense bushes and over beds of dry twigs with no perceptible sound. A movement rather than a sound off to my left had attracted my attention; another glance showed me the glint of horns. A full grown stag was in the act of jumping a pile of fallen logs. He literally floated over the obstruction, ghostlike, uncanny. I noticed that he jumped with his tail down – a thing he would not do if he were startled. Behind him were two does. They negotiated the barrier still more lithely than the buck had done . . . All three of them were feeding; their heads down at the same moment. One always seemed to be on watch, and this one was usually the buck.

For a few seconds at a time his proud head would be bowed among the bushes; then it would be lifted with a jerk, and for minutes he would stand champing restlessly his mouthful of leaves, grass, and tender twigs. Often he would hold his head at peculiar angles – often thrust forward – as if drinking in all the scents of the dewy night woods. After a while, moving in silence and in concert, the shadowy creatures came up on the space of white sand that stretched away in front of me. Now they paused, spectral in the moonlight, now moved about with indescribably lithe grace, never losing, even amid the secure delight of such a time and place, their air of superb readiness, of elfin caution, suppressed but instantly available. The steps they took seemed to me extraordinarily long; and it was difficult to keep one of the creatures in sight all the while. They would appear and reappear; and their color and the distinctness of their outlines depended on the angle at which they were seen. Broadside, they look almost black; head-on they were hardly visible. At no time could I distinguish their legs. When they moved off into the pine thicket, whither I knew they had gone to eat mushrooms, they vanished without sound, apparently without exerted motion, and I was left alone in the moonlight."

Flintlock killed many white-tailed bucks in his long life, but his most thrilling deer hunt occurred in December of 1942, when he decided to drive

This photo of Old Flintlock with a 13-pointer with 14-inch tines appeared in the July 1971 issue of *Outdoor Life*. The article, entitled *My Most Memorable Deer Hunt*, documents how Rutledge downed this 278-pound white-tailed buck in December of 1942.

Wambaw Corner, a famous hangout for bucks. While sitting on a pine stump at a deer stand called Dogwood Hill, Flintlock had a premonition that something unique would happen on this drive, and it did. As the drivers neared the end, he suddenly heard twigs breaking and the sound of deer hooves. Then he saw tall tines rising and falling before him. A buck of gigantic proportions came running straight for him and abruptly stopped, almost wedging itself between two pines 55 yards in front of the startled hunter. At the blast of Flintlock's Parker, the buck reared straight up and then fell backward. Four buckshot struck the deer.

Flintlock stood in awe when he came up on the dead buck lying at the foot of a huge cypress. The buck carried 13 symmetrical tines—seven on one side and six on the other. Some of the tines reached 18 inches in length with a basal circumference of five inches. The antlers exhibited a beautiful chestnut color, with heavy beading and a 25-inch inside spread. The buck weighed 278 pounds; Flintlock never shot a better one. He called the buck "Flora's Buck," since his daughter-in-law, Flora, had missed the same buck on the same drive two weeks earlier.

Who of Rutledge's readers will ever forget the strategic and dramatic tactics of the Jasper Hill Buck that charged straight into four guns, 11 deerhounds and four drivers mounted on horses? At first glance it looked as if the buck were hunting the hunters. Flintlock de-scribes the wild scenario for us in his essay, "That Hunt at Jasper Hill," published in his blue-chip deer book *Those Were The Days* (1954):

"The buck, seeing the hounds but apparently not aware of us. Lowered his head and charged straight through the whole pack of waiting dogs. And they were so amazed that they dodged, skulked and ran. We, too, made way. Here then, was the singular spectacle of a stag scattering dogs and men before him.

"In a moment the stag had passed by, entering a pine thicket beyond the road. As he was vanishing, four guns blared out, giving him a special salute of honor of eight barrels, speeding after his broad white tail about a hundred and fifty buckshot. I saw the tops of several little pines jump up. But so did the deer. As far as I could see, he was heading for the tangled wilds of Jasper Hill, and for freedom."

One-half mile from where the four gunners poured two barrels of buckshot apiece at the old boy, the Hampton Hunters found the great Jasper Hill Buck stretched out on the forest floor with only two buckshot out of the 150 fired at him, but dead nonetheless. While deer hunters might forget the name of the church in which they were married, they never forget the most-minute details of the shooting of each and every buck.

Flintlock's curious and never-failing fascination with antlers lasted throughout his life. Becoming one of the first antler collectors in this country, his collection consisted of more than 300 sets, most taken from his own plantation, some dating back almost 100 years. One 26-pointer sported a 28-inch spread. When he heard of an unusual rack in his area, he would travel miles to see it. He traveled all over the country, visiting museums of natural history to view famous bucks. He not only collected sheds, but also studied in detail the Boone and Crockett record books of his time as well as Roland Ward's *Records of Big Game*. In short, he liked to "tamper with kingly crowns," as he put it in his inim-

One of Rutledge's many blue-chip deer books published by The Dietz Press in 1954.

itable way. One wonders what Old Flintlock would think of the current antler mania in this country, of the thousands of trophy bucks that decorate the deer classics of our time. (He would probably be both thrilled and appalled; thrilled by the massive heads, appalled by the crass commercialization.)

For buck hunters interested in shooting bucks of record-book stature, Flintlock offers short and simple advice:

"Always be willing to go the second mile and to do the hard thing; don't quit and take the backtrack to camp. Punish yourself a little; use more strength from your body and more patience from your mind and more cool-headed determination from your brain than you have ever used before. You are playing a hard man's game against no mean antagonist; and you need all you have to

Courtesy of Wegner's Photo Collection.

The artwork of Lynn Bogue Hunt, one of the sporting artists who brought Old Flintlock's stories to life, will help to ensure the deer hunting tales of Rutledge will live forever.

play it right. The greatest deer hunters have always been second milers; men of tireless energy and infinite patience; men who would follow a trail all day, and who would, when the game was close, do the serpent act over a rocky hillside for the distance, however great, that would bring them within shooting range." In short, when it came to deer hunting, Rutledge believed in the full-scale application of what Theodore Roosevelt called the strenuous life.

During his lifetime, and unlike most deer hunters, Flintlock observed thousands of deer in the wild; he once estimated the number at about 7000. But like most deer hunters, he never got over the amazing appearance of them. There was always something new, special and dramatic about the appearance of each one of them. After 78 years of hunting and watching deer, he came to view the life of the whitetail as one long, strategic maneuver. "Successfully stalking one of these heavy-shod, burly-horned, seasoned old strategists," Flintlock writes in "Stalking Your Buck," "is a woodland victory of the first order . . . No other creature so large lives so silently, so secretively and so self-effacingly."

His countless articles and books on white-tailed deer and deer hunting stand as precious possessions and vast warehouses of natural lore that time will never diminish in appeal. As long as the American deer hunter stalks the old, noble buck in the forests of fall, the deer and deer hunting tales of Old Flintlock based on the famous Hampton Hunts, illustrated with the sporting art of Lynn Bogue Hunt, Charles Livingston Bull and Paul Bransom and highlighted with the great deer photos of George Shiras III, will live forever. We will always remember Archibald Rutledge as the most eloquent chronicler of American white-tailed deer hunting, as a master huntsman-narrator, as the deer hunter's buck hunter – the storyteller of buck hunting tales par excellence. I have met many incurable buck hunters in my life, but none with the flair and religious enthusiasm of Archibald Rutledge; he lived and breathed deer and deer hunting. Deer hunting for Flintlock was like going to Heaven.

White-tailed deer, whom Rutledge fondly referred to as "the masterminds of the wildwoods," also owe Flintlock a considerable debt, for no one better expresses the real meaning and the ultimate value of this animal for American cultural history. Every deer he saw left him with a sense of awe; in the presence of every white-tailed buck, Flintlock perceived America in prehistoric times, and he captured that view best of all in his poem "The Stag." His lines stand as a singular tribute to the animal he loved, revered and immortalized:

> Today in the wild pinelands a stag I saw,
> A noble buck in the lone pinelands today.
> I was walking upwind.
> At the end of a swampy draw,
> Bounding from his bed of ferns, he fled away.
> It was not for long I saw him, but long enough
> To see his lithe and powerful grace, to mark
> His craggy antlers,
> beaded and brown and rough,
> And his flag that glimmered white
> through the forest dark.
>
> It was more than a deer
> I saw in the wildwood green
> And the presence of him
> filled me with awe; for I
> In that shaggy, proud, primeval stag had seen
> America under a prehistoric sky;
> A tawny sleeping empire, boundless, blest,
> Before Columbus dreamed there was a West.

REFERENCES

Chapter 1

A. F. Tait: Artist in the Adirondacks: An Exhibition of Paintings and Other Works. New York: The Adirondack Museum, 1974.

Altherr, Thomas L. "Wasty Ways: Natty Bumppo's Ecological Consciousness in James Fenimore Cooper's Leatherstocking Novels."" *Cynegeticus: A Publication Devoted to the Interdisciplinary Study of Hunting.* 1 (3): 2-11

Bergman, Charles, *Orion's Legacy: A Cultural History of Man as Hunter.* New York: Dutton, 1996.

Byron-Curtiss, A. L. *The Life and Adventures of Nat Foster, Trapper and Hunter of the Adirondacks.* New York: Thomas J. Griffiths, 1897.

Cadbury, Warder H. and Henry F. Marsh. *Arthur Fitzwilliam Tait: Artist in the Adirondacks.* New Jersey: Associated University Presses, 1986.

Cartmill, Matt. *A View to a Death in the Morning: Hunting and Nature Through History.* Massachusetts: Harvard University Press, 1993.

Cooper, James Fenimore. *The Deerslayer; or the First Warpath: A Tale.* Philadelphia: Lea & Blanchard, 1841.

_____. *The Pioneers; or the Sources of the Susquehanna.* London: John Murray, 1823.

_____. *The Prairie: A Tale.* Philadelphia: Carey, Lea & Carey, 1827.

Cooper, Susan Fenimore. *Rural Hours.* New York: Syracuse University Press, 1968.

Darrow, Robert W. "Deer Hunting--Then and Now." *New York State Conservationist.* August/September, 1955. 10(1): 19-22.

Franz, Eleanor. "Hunting the Hunter: Nat Foster Today." *New York Folklore Quarterly.* December 1964. Pages 270-275.

Herman, Daniel Justin. *Hunting and the American Imagination.* Washington, D. C: Smithsonian Institution Press, 2001.

Hoffman, C. F. *Wild Scenes in the Forest and Prairie.* London: Richard Bentley, 1839.

King, Roy and Burke Davis. *The World of Currier & Ives.* New York: Bonanza Books, 1987.

Lawrence, D. H. "Fenimore Cooper's Leatherstocking Novels." In *Studies in Classic American Literature.* New York: Penguin Books, 1961. Pages 52-69.

New York Times. "Town Marks Grave of Natty Bumppo. July 4, 1937. Section II, page 3.

Powell, Earl A. *Thomas Cole.* New York: Harry N. Abrams, Inc., 1990.

Roth, Richard Patrick. The *Adirondack Guide (1820-1919): Hewing Out an American Occupation.* Ph. D. Dissertation, 1990. Syracuse University.

Severinghaus, C. W. and C. P. Brown. "History of the White-Tailed Deer in New York." *New York Fish and Game Journal.* July, 1956. 3(2): 129-167.

Simms, Jeptha R. *Trappers of New York: or, A Biography of Nicholas Stoner and Nathaniel Foster.* New York: J. Munsell, 1871.

Slotkin, Richard. *Regeneration Through Violence: The Mythology of the American Frontier, 1600-1860.* Connecticut: Wesleyan University Press, 1973.

Swann, Charles. "Guns Mean Democracy: The Pioneers and the Game Laws." In Robert Clark (ed), *James Fenimore Cooper: New Critical Essays.* New Jersey: Barnes & Noble Books, 1985. pp. 96-120.

Taylor, Alan. *William Cooper's Town.* New York: Vintage Books, 1995.

Terrie, Philip G. *Wildlife and Wilderness: A History of Adirondack Mammals.* New York: Purple Mountain Press, 1993.

Wegner, Robert. *Wegner's Bibliography on Deer & Deer Hunting.* Wisconsin: St. Hubert's Press, 1992.

_____. "Whitetail Folklore: Natty Bumppo and His Clan." *Deer & Deer Hunting.* 23(1): 109-115. September, 1999.

Chapter 2

American Turf Register and Sporting Magazine. Baltimore, 1829-1844.

Arthur, Stanley Clisby. *Audubon: An Intimate Life of the American Woodsman.* New Orleans, Harmanson Publisher, 1937.

Audubon, John James. "Deer Hunting." *Audubon and His Journals.* Edited by Maria R. Audubon. Volume 2. New York: Peter Smith, 1972. pp. 466-473.

_____. "Cervus Virginianus." *Audubon Game Animals: From the Quadrupeds of North America.* New Jersey: Hammond Incorporated, 1968. pp. 146-149.

_____. *John James Audubon: Writings and Drawings.* Edited by Christoph Irmscher. New York: The Library of America, 1999.

_____, and Dr. John Bachman. *The Quadrupeds of North America.* New York: Studio Productions, 1951.

Chancellor, John. *Audubon: A Biography.* New York: The Viking Press, 1978.

"Death of the Buck." *Spirit of the Times.* August 15, 1840. 10(24): 277.

Dormon, James H. *Audubon: A Retrospective.* Louisiana: University of Southwestern Louisiana, 1990.

Durant, Mary and Michael Harwood. *On the Road with John James Audubon.* New York: Dodd, Mead & Company, 1980.

Ford, Alice. *John James Audubon: A Biography.* New York: Abbeville Press, 1988.

Harris, Edward. *Up the Missouri with Audubon.* Oklahoma: University of Oklahoma Press, 1951.

Herman, Daniel Justin. *Hunting and the American Imagination.* Washington D. C.: Smithsonian Institution Press, 2001.

Lindsey, Alton A. et al. *The Bicentennial of John James Audubon.* Indiana: Indiana University Press, 1985.

Peirce, Bradford K. *Life in the Woods; or, The Adventures of Audubon.* New York, 1863.

Ramsay, David. "Historian Ramsay on Deer-Hunting in South Carolina." In Willard Thorp, *A Southern Reader.* New York: Alfred A. Knopf, 1955. pp. 227-229.

Reid, Captain Mayne. "Deer Hunt in a Dug-Out." *The Hunters' Feast; or, Conversations Around the Camp-Fire.* London: Thomas Hodgson, 1855. pp. 195-211.

Ringwood. "Deer Hunting." *American Turf Register and Sporting Magazine.* December, 1829. 1(4): 194-197.

Sage, Jno H. "Description of Audubon." *Auk.* Volume 34. April, 1917. pp. 239-240.

Spirit of the Times. New York, 1831-1861.

Stewart, Gail. (ed.) *The Cabinet of Natural History and American Rural Sports with Illustrations.* Boston: Barre, 1973.

Streshinsky, Shirley. *Audubon: Life and Art in the American Wilderness.* New York: Villard Books, 1993.

Wegner, Robert. *Wegner's Bibliography on Deer & Deer Hunting.* Wisconsin: St. Hubert's Press, 1992.

_____. "Audubon: America's First Pioneer of Deer Hunting." *Deer & Deer Hunting.* 21(6): 50-56. March, 1998.

Chapter 3

A Gentleman of Arkansas. "Fire Hunting for Deer." In Peter Hawker, *Instructions to Young Sportsmen In All That Relates to Guns and Shooting.* Philadelphia: Lea and Blanchard, 1846. pp. 362-365.

Allen, Desmond Walls. (ed.) *Turnbo's Tales of the Ozarks: Deer Hunting Stories.* Arkansas: Privately printed, 1989.

Atkinson. J. H. "Friedrich Gerstaecker in Arkansas." *Pulaski County Historical Society Review.* 17(2): 29-32.

Bukey, Evan Burr. "Friedrich Gerstaecker and Arkansas." *Arkansas Historical Quarterly.* 31(1): 1-14. Spring, 1972.

Cartwright, Mike, et. al. "A History of Arkansas' Deer Herd." *The White-Tailed Deer in Arkansas.* Arkansas: Arkansas Game & Fish Commission, 1987. pp. 6-8.

Donaldson, David, et. al., *Arkansas' Deer Herd.* Arkansas: Arkansas Game and Fish Commission, 1951.

Evans, Clarence. "Friedrich Gerstaecker, Social Chronicler of the Arkansas Frontier." *Arkansas Historical Quarterly.* 6(1948): 440-449.

Garzmann, Manfred R., et. al., *Gerstaecker - Verzeichnis.* Braunschweig: Friedrich-Gerstaecker-Gesellschaft, 1986.

Gerstaecker, Friedrich. *The Arkansas Backwoods. Tales and Sketches.* Missouri: University of Missouri Press, 1991.

_____. *Wild Sport in the Far West: The Narrative of a German Wanderer Beyond the Mississippi, 1837-1843.* North Carolina: Duke University, 1968.

_____. *Wild Sports in the Far West. (Review). New Englander and Yale Review.* 17(66): 570. May 1859.

_____. *Wild Sports in the Far West. (Review). Library Journal.* 93(October 15, 1968): 3777.

_____. *Wild Sports in the Far West. (Review). Southwestern Historical Quarterly.* 72(1969): 567-568.

_____. *Western Lands and Western Waters.* London: S. O. Beeton, 1864.

_____. *Streif- und Jagdzuege durch die Vereinigten Staaten Nord-Amerikas.* Leipzig: Arnold, 1844.

_____, "Gerstaecker's Arkansas." VHS, 20 min., 1987. Arkansas Humanities Council.

Hoffman, Charles Fenno. *Wild Scenes in the Forest and Prairie.* London: Richard Bentley, 1839.

Keefe, James F. and Lynn Morrow. (eds.) "Drinking Honey Out of a Deer's Leg." *The White River Chronicles of S. C. Turnbo: Man and Wildlife on the Ozark Frontier.* Arkansas: The University of Arkansas Press, 1994.

Kolb, Alfred. "Friedrich Gerstaecker and the American Dream." *Modern Language Studies.* 5(1975): 103-108.

_____. "Friedrich Gerstaecker and the American Frontier." Ph. D. Dissertation. Syracuse University, 1967.

_____. "Gerstaecker's America." *Thoth.* Winter, 1965. pp. 1-21.

Moore, Waddy William. *"In the Arkansas Backwoods: Tales and Sketches by Friedrich Gerstaecker." (Review.) Arkansas Historical Quarterly.* 51(2): 186-189. Summer,1992.

Murdoch, Alex. *"In the Arkansas Backwoods: Tales and Sketches by Friedrich Gerstaecker." (Review.) German History: Journal of the German History Society.* 12(2): 263-264. 1994.

Nolan, Charles Fenton Mercer. "Deer Hunting in Arkansas: My First Fire Hunt." *Spirit of the Times.* September 6, 1845. p. 321.

Norman, Rex Allen. *The 1837 Sketchbook of the Western Fur Trade.* Texas: Scurlock, 1996.

Steeves, Harrison R. "The First of the Westerns." *Southwest Review.* Winter, 1968. pp. 74-84.

Sutton, Keith. (ed.) *Arkansas Wildlife: A History.* Arkansas: The University of Arkansas Press, 1998.

_____. "The Age of Discovery and Settlement." *Arkansas Game & Fish.* May/June 1986. pp. 1-12.

Tyler, Ron (ed.). *Alfred Jacob Miller: Artist on the Oregon Trail.* Texas: Amon Carter Museum, 1982.

Wegner, Robert. *Wegner's Bibliography on Deer & Deer Hunting.* Wisconsin: St. Hubert's Press, 1992.

_____. "Friedrich *(Miller)* Gerstaecker: A Legendary Ozark Deerslayer." *Deer & Deer Hunting.* 24(7): 54-59. March, 2001.

Williams, Harry Lee. "Market Hunters in Early Arkansas." *Arkansas Game and Fish.* Fall, 1968. pp. 8-10.

Worley, Ted R. "An Early Arkansas Sportsman: C. F. M. Noland." *Arkansas Historical Quarterly.* Spring, 1952. pp. 25-2239.

Young, Kenn R. (ed.) *Arkansas' Biggest Bucks of All Time.* Arkansas: Privately printed, 1997.

_____, and Dan Doughty. *Monster Whitetails of Arkansas.* Arkansas: Privtely printed, 1994.

Chapter 4

Beck, Harold Thomas. "Cornplanter's Wager." *The Mountain Laurel Review.* 1998. www.mlrmag.com.

Bronner, Simon J. *Popularizing Pennsylvania: Henry W. Shoemaker and the Progressive Uses of Folklore and History.* Pennsylvania: Pennsylvania State University Press, 1996.

Cooper, James Fenimore. *The Deerslayer.* Philadelphia: Lea & Blanchard, 1841.

Forbes, Stanley E. et. al. *The White-Tailed Deer In Pennsylvania.* Pennsylvania: The Pennsylvania Game Commission, 1971.

Frederick, Paul. "Philip Tome - Legendary Hunter." www.allegheny-online.com.

Kosack, Joe. *The Pennsylvania Game Commission, 1895-1995: 100 Years of Wildlife Conservation.* Pennsylvania: The Pennsylvania Game Commission, 1995.

Kraybill, Spencer L. *Pennsylvania's Pine Creek Valley.* Maryland: Gateway Press, Inc., 1991.

Longfellow, Henry W. *The Song of Hiawatha.* Boston: Ticknor and Fields, 1855.

Neal, Don. "The Allegheny Elk Hunter." *Pennsylvania Game News.* February 1959. pp. 22-27.

Pennsylvania Atlas & Gazetteer. Maine: DeLorme, 2001.

Perkins, Mr. George A. "The Deer Hunt of 1818." *Early Times on the Susquehanna.* Pennsylvania: The Herald Company of Binghamton, 1870. pp. 181-185.

Russell, Helen H. "Philip Tome, 1782-1885, Was Pioneer, Hunter, Author, Man of Many Skills." *The Express,* Lock Haven, Pennsylvania, Saturday, February 6, 1965. pp. 13-14.

_____. "Philip Tome Had Indians' Trust as Their Agent and Interpreter." *The Express,* Lock Haven, Pennsylvania, Saturday, February 16, 1965. pp. 15-17.

Sajna, Mike. *Buck Fever: The Deer Hunting Tradition in Pennsylvania.* Pennsylvania: Univeristy of Pittsburgh Press, 1990.

Shoemaker, Henry W. *Pennsylvania Deer and Their Horns.* Pennsylvania: The Faust Printing Company, 1915.

Tome, Philip. *Pioneer Life or, Thirty Years A Hunter.* Buffalo, 1854. (First Edition.)

_____. *Pioneer Life or, Thirty Years A Hunter.* Harrisburg: Aurand, 1928.

_____. *Pioneer Life or, Thirty Years A Hunter.* New York: Arno Press Inc., 1971.

_____. *Pioneer Life or, Thirty Years A Hunter.* Salem: Ayer, 1989.

_____. *Pioneer Life or, Thirty Years A Hunter.* Baltimore: Gateway Press Inc., 1991. (Reprint of the 1928 Edition wth an index by the Lycoming County Genealogical Society.)

Van Dyne, Ed. "The Mighty Nimrod Of Pine Creek." *Pennsylvania Game News.* 32(7): 22-25. July, 1961.

Wegner, Robert. *Wegner's Bibliography on Deer & Deer Hunting.* Wisconsin: St. Hubert's Press, 1992.

_____. *Legendary Deer Camps.* Wisconsin: Krause Publications, 2001.

_____. "A Pioneer Deerslayer." *Deer & Deer Hunting.* 10(5): 8-14. June, 1987.

Chapter 5

"A Hunting Song." *Spirit of the Times.* 15(12): 133. May 17, 1845.

Beverley-Giddings, A. R. "Editor's Foreword." *Frank Forester On Upland Shooting.* New York: William Morrow and Company, 1951. pp. 7-13.

Buntline, Ned. "Anecdote of Frank Forester." In Fred E. Pond, *Life and Adventures of "Ned Buntline."* New York: The Cadmus Book Shop, 1919. pp. 4-8.

"Forester School of Bathos." *Forest and Stream.* December 18, 1897.

Gellert. "Frank Forester: In Memoriam." *Forest and Stream.* May 23, 1878.

"Henry Wiliam Herbert." *The Spirit of the Times.* 91(11): 258-259. April 22, 1876.

Herbert, Henry William. *The Complete Manual for Young Sportsmen.* New York: Stringer & Townsend, 1857.

_____. *The Deer Stalkers.* Philadelphia: T. B. Peterson & Brothers, 1843.

_____. "Deer Hunting." *Frank Forester's Field Sports of the United States and British Provinces of North America.* New York: Stringer & Townsend, 1849. pp. 239-252.

_____. "The Death of the Stag." In *Life and Writings of Frank Forester* edited by David W. Judd. New York: Orange Judd Company, 1882. pp. 192-203.

_____. "The American Deer." *American Game In Its Season.* New York: Charles Scribner, 1853. pp. 221-234.

_____. "The Death of the Red Deer." *Godey's Lady's Book.* 35(6): 61-63. August, 1847.

_____. "Deer and Deer Hunting." *Graham's Magazine.* Volume 39. August, 1851. pp. 120-123.

_____. "The Outlying Stag." *The Warwick Woodlands.* New York: Stringer & Townsend, 1851. pp. 144-155.

_____. "Long Jakes, The Prairie Man." In *Life and Writings of Frank Forester* edited by David W. Judd. Volume 2. New York: Orange Judd Company, 1882. pp. 204-217.

Herman, Daniel Justin. "Disciples of Sport Hunting." *Hunting and the American Imagination.* Washington D. C.: Smithsonian Institution Press, 2001. pp. 173-187.

Hunt, William S. "The Most Unhappy One --A Study of Frank Forester's Life." *Proceedings of the New Jersey Historical Society.* 13(1): 1-17. January, 1928.

_____. *Frank Forester: A Tragedy in Exile.* New Jersey: Carteret Book Club, 1933.

Johns, Elizabeth. *American Genre Painting: The Politics of Everyday Life.* Connecticut: Yale University Press, 1991.

Mander, Mary S. "Henry William Herbert." In Sam G. Riley (ed.) *American Magazine Journalists, 1741-1850.* Michigan: A Bruccoli Clark Layman Book, 1988. pp. 175-183.

McLellan, Isaac. "A Poem by Frank Forester." *Forest and Stream.* September, 1878.

Meats, Stephen. "Henry William Herbert ("Frank Forester")." In *Antebellum Writers in New York and the South* edited by Joel Myerson. Michigan: A Bruccoli Clark Book, 1979. pp. 150-159.

_____. "Addenda to Van Winkle: Henry William Herbert (Frank Forester). *Papers of the Bibliographical Society of America.* 67(First Quarter, 1973): 69-73.

_____. "The Letters of Henry William Herbert, 'Frank Forester,' 1815-1858." Ph. D. Dissertation. University of South Carolina, 1972.

Reiger, John F. *American Sportsmen and the Origins of Conservation.* Oregon: Oregon State University Press, 2001. Third Edtion, Revised and Expanded.

Severinghaus, C. W. and C. P. Brown. "History of the White-tailed Deer in New York." *New York Fish and Game Journal.* 3(2): 129-166. July, 1956.

Sheldon, Charles. "Popularity of Frank Forester's Writings." *Forest and Stream.* April, 1916. pp, 912-913.

Street, Alfred Billings. "Deer Shooting." *The Poems of Alfred B. Street.* New York: Clark & Austin, 1845. pp. 241-243.

Tyler, Ron. et. al. *American Frontier Life.* N.Y.: Cross River Press, 1987.

Van Winkle, William Mitchell. (ed.) *Henry William Herbert (Frank Forester): A Bibliography of His Writing, 1832-1858.* New York: Burt Franklin, 1971.

Wegner, Robert. *Wegner's Bibliography on Deer & Deer Hunting.* Wisconsin: St. Hubert's Press, 1992.

_____. "Frank Forester: A Hunter and Naturalist." *Deer & Deer Hunting.* 21(8): 85-92. August, 1998.

Weidner, Ruth Irwin. "Images of the Hunt in Nineteenth Century America and Their Sources in British and European Art." Ph.D. Dissertation. University of Delaware, 1988.

White, Luke Jr. *Henry William Herbert & The American Publishing Scene, 1831-1858.* New Jersey: The Carteret Book Club, 1943.

Wildwood, Will. "Tribute to Frank Forester." *Forest and Stream.* June 6, 1878.

W. W. W. "Reminiscence of Frank Forester." *Forest and Stream.* October 3, 1878.

Chapter 6

Brown, Jacob. *Brown's Miscellaneous Writings.* Maryland: J. J. Miller, 1896.

Browning, Meshach. *Forty-Four Years of the Life of a Hunter.* Philadelphia: J. B. Lippincott & Company, 1859.

_____. *Forty-Four Years of the Life of a Hunter.* Philadelphia: J. B. Lippincott & Company, 1928.

_____. *Forty-Four Years of the Life of a Hunter.* Maryland: Appalachian Background Inc., 1982.

_____. *Forty-Four Years of the Life of a Hunter.* Maryland: Gateway Press Inc., 1993.

Browning, R. Getty. *Browning's "Foreword:" Background Notes About Meshach Browning . . .* Maryland: Appalachian Background Inc., 1989.

Dean, David M. "Meshach Browning: Living off the Land on Maryland's Western Frontier." In *Maryland: Unity in Diversity* edited by A. Franklin Parks and John B. Wiseman. Iowa: Kendall/Hunt Publishing Company, 1990. pp. 135-142.

_____. "Meshach Browning: Bear Hunter of Allegany County, 1781-1859." *Maryland Historical Magazine.* 91(1): 73-83. Spring, 1996.

Dentry, Ed. "The Hearty Life of Meshach Browning." *The News American.* December 12, 1982. p. 5D.

Eyrie. "Meshach Browning/The Origin of Deer Park." *Baltimore Sun.* September 6, 1900.

"Forty-Four Years of the Life of a Hunter." (Review). *The Outdoorsman.* 1(2): 3. January/February, 1983.

_____. (Review). *Baltimore Sun.* January 4, 1983.

_____. (Review). *Herald Mail.* January 9, 1983.

_____. (Review). *Pennsylvania Game News.* November, 1993.

_____. (Review). *The Evening Sun.* December 2, 1982.

_____. (Review). *Gray's Sporting Journal.* Spring, 1986. p. 135.

Glades Star, The. Publication of the Garrett County Historical Society.

Hoye, Charles E. *Garrett County History of the Browning and McMullen Families.* Maryland: Appalachian Background Inc., 1987. Reprint from the *Mountain Democrat,* 1935.

"Is Meshach Browning's Story True?" www.pennswoods.net.

Laycock, George. "Point the Small End Foremost." *The Hunters and the Hunted.* New York: Outdoor Life Books, 1990. pp. 40-51

Meshach Browning: His Ancestors and Descendants in America. Maryland: Appalachian Background, Inc., 1898.

"Powder Horn and Shot Pouch of Meshach Browning are Discovered." *The Republican.* September 28, 1988.

Sajna. Mike. "Life of a Hunter." *Pennsylvania Game News.* 65(6): 28-32. June, 1994

————. "Deer-Hunting Anecdotes Dot Landscape of Colonial Life." *Pittsburgh Tribune Review.* Sunday, May 22, 1994. p. 7.

Schlosnagle, Stephen. *Garrett County: A History of Maryland's Tableland.* Virginia: McClain Printing Company, 1978.

Wegner, Robert. *Deer & Deer Hunting: Book 2.* Pennsylvania: Stackpole Books, 1987.

————. *Wegner's Bibliography on Deer & Deer Hunting.* Wisconsin: St. Hubert's Press, 1992.

————. "Meshach Browning and his Famous Buck Fight." *Deer & Deer Hunting.* 23(3): 123-130. October, 1999.

Weidner, Ruth I. "Images of the Hunt in Nineteenth-Century America and their Sources in British and European Art." P.h. D. Dissertation. University of Delaware, 1988.

Chapter 7

Anderson, Charles R. "Thoreau Takes a Pot Shot at *Carolina Sports.*" *The Georgia Review.* XXI(3): 289-299. Fall, 1968.

"*Carolina Sports, by Land and Water.*" (Review). *North American Review.* Volume 63. October, 1846. pp. 316-334.

Ekirch, Arthur A. Jr. *Man and Nature in America.* New York, Columbia, 1963.

Elliott & Gonzales Family Papers, #1009. Southern Historical Collection. The Library of the University Press of North Carolina at Chapel Hill. (35 reviews of *Carolina Sports by Land & Water.*)

Elliott, William. *Carolina Sports by Land & Water.* New York: Arno Press, 1967.

————. *Carolina Sports by Land and Water.* South Carolina: The University of South Carolina, 1994.

————. "Preservation of Deer." *The Charleston Mercury.* May 27, 1856.

Evert, A., and George L. Duyckinck. "William Elliott." *Cyclopaedia of American Literature.* New York: Charles Scribner, 1856. Volume 2. pp. 101-103.

Gohdes, Clarance. (ed.) *Hunting in the Old South.* Baton Rouge: Louisiana State University, 1967.

Gonzales, Ambrose Elliott. Unpublished letter to James Henry Rice, February 3, 1922, quoted in James Henry Rice, *The Aftermath of Glory* (South Carolina, 1934).

"H." "Deer Hunting." *American Turf Register and Sporting Magazine.* October, 1830, 2 (2): 86

Herman, Daniel Justin. *Hunting and the American Imagination.* Washington D. C.: Smithsonian Institution Press, 2001.

Hubbell, Jay B. "William Elliott." *The South in American Literature, 1607-1900.* Duke university Press, 1954. pp. 564-568.

Hundley, Daniel R. *Social Relations in our Southern States.* New York: Henry B. Price, 1860.

Jones, Lewis Pinckney. "William Elliott, South Carolina Nonconformist." Ph. D. Dissertation. University of North Carolina, 1952.

Kibler, James E. Jr. "Not-So-Intellectual Imperialism." *Mississippi Quarterly.* 48 (Spring, 1995): 337-342. Review of William Elliott's *Carolina Sports* with a new introduction by Theodore Rosengarten.

————. "William Elliott III." In *Dictionary of Literary Biography.* Volume 3. Michigan: Gale Research Company, 1979. pp. 111-118.

Laurie, Pete. "The Vision of William Elliott." *South Carolina Wildlife.* September/October, 1985. pp. 41-45.

Marks, Stuart A. "William Elliottt's Hunting Narratives." *Southern Hunting in Black and White: Nature, History, and Ritual in a Carolina Community.* New Jersey: Princeton University Press, 1991. pp. 18-23

Parkman, Francis. "The Chase." *The Oregon Trail.* New York: Times Mirror, 1950.

Proctor, Nicholas W. *Bathed in Blood: Hunting and Mastery in the Old South.* Virginia: University Press of Virginia, 2002.

Rice, James Henry, Jr. *The Aftermath of Glory.* South Carolina: Walker, Evans and Cogswell,1934.

Rivers, Jacob F. III. "William Elliott's *Carolina Sports by Land and Water.*" *Cultural Values in the Southern Sporting Narrative.* South Carolina: University of South Carolina Press, 2002. pp. 1-29.

Rubin, Louis D. Jr. *William Elliott Shoots a Bear: Essays on the Southern Literary Imagination.* Louisiana: Louisiana State University Press, 1975.

Scafidel, Beverly. "William Elliott, Planter and Politician: New Evidence from the Charleston Newspapers, 1831-1856." In *South Carolina Journals and Journalists,* edited by James B. Meriwether. South Carolina, 1974. pp. 109-119.

Simms, William Gilmore. "Carolina Sports." (Review). *The Southern Quarterly Review.* Volume XII. July, 1847. pp. 67-90.

Skardon, B. N. "William Elliott: Planter-Writer of Ante-Bellum South Carolina." Masters Thesis, University of Georgia, 1964.

Thomson, C. W. "A Hunting Carol." *The Cabinet of Natural History,* 1830.

Thorp, Willard. (ed.) "Historian Ramsey on Deer Hunting in South Carolina." In *A Southern Reader* (New York: Alfred A. Knopf, 1955). pp. 227-229

Wauchope, George A. "William Elliott" in *Library of Southern Literature* edited by E. A. Alderman & J. C. Harris (Atlanta, Georgia, 1907, Volume 4, pp. 1569-1571.)

Wegner, Robert. *Wegner's Bibliography on Deer & Deer Hunting.* Wisconsin: St. Hubert's Press, 1992.

————. "Chee-Ha Deer Shooting with William 'Venator' Elliott." *Deer & Deer Hunting.* 23(5): 35-42. December, 1999.

"William Elliott." (Obituary). *Charleston Mercury.* February 4, 1863.

Chapter 8

"*Antelope and Deer of America* by J. D. Caton." (Review.) *The Atlantic Monthly.* 61(265): 401-403. March, 1878.

"*Antelope and Deer of America.*" (Review.) *American Naturalist.* June, 1877. pp. 354-358.

"*Antelope and Deer of America.*" (Review.) *Forest and Stream.* Febrauary 14, 1884.

"*Antelope and Deer of America.*" (Review of original edition.) *Forest and Stream.* October 18, 1877.

Beardsley, Levi. *Reminiscences.* New York: Charles Vinten, 1852. 575 pages.

Calhoun, John. *Prairie Whitetails.* Illinois: Department of Conservation, n. d. 49 pages.

Caton, John Dean. *The Antelope and Deer of America.* New York, 1877. 426 pages.

————. and W. B. Leffingwell. "The Ethics of Field Sports." In *Big Game of North America* edited by G. O. Shields. London, 1890. Pages 567-581.

————. "Unpublished Autobiography." Caton Manuscript. Library of Congress. Washington D. C. N. D. 597 pages.

————. Caton Papers. M. S. 62-4603. Library of Congress. Washington, D. C.

————. "Distinguishing Marks of Mule and Blacktail Deer." *The American Sportsman.* April, 4, 1874. p. 5.

————. "Deformed Antlers." *The American Sportsman.* July 4, 1874. p. 210.

————, "Wounds from Deer's Antlers." *Rod & Gun.* April 10, 1875. p. 22.

————, "A Wild Turkey Hunt." *The American Sportsman.* 1875. Volume 15. pp. 210--212.

————, "A New California Deer." *American Naturalist.* 1876. Volume 10. pp. 465-468.

"Death of Judge Caton." *Forest and Stream.* August 10, 1895.

Fergus, Robert. *Biographical Sketch of John Dean Caton.* Chicago: Fergus Printing Company, 1882. 48 pp.

Flanagan, John T. "Hunting in Early Illinois." *Illinois Historical Journal* 72(1): 2-12. February, 1979.

Follansbee, Mitchell Davis. "John Dean Caton, 1812-1895." In William D. Lewis (ed.). *Great American Lawyers.* Voume VI. Philadelphia, 1909. pp. 309-343.

"John D. Caton." *Album of Genealogy and Biography, Cook County, Illinois with Portraits.* 3rd Editon. Chicago: Calumet Book & Engraving Company, 1895. pp. 115-118.

"Judge Caton Is Dead, Pioneer Citizen and Eminent Jurist Passes Away." *The Chicago Tribune.* July 31, 1895.

Low, Jr., James *Floating and Driving for Deer, or The Adventures of a Night and Day in the Adirondacks.* Geneva: Printing Offices of The Continental Herald and Swiss Times, 1873. 62 pages.

Pietsch, Lysle R. "White-Tailed Deer Populations in Illinois." Natural History Survey Division. *Biological Notes No. 34.* June, 1954. 22 pages.

Pratt, Harry Edward. Typescript Biography of John Dean Caton. Chicago Historical Society, n. d. 150 pp.

Townley, Wayne C. *Two Judges of Ottawa.* Illinois, Bloomingdale, 1948. 43 pp. (Photo copy from Reddick Library.)

Walmsley, Timothy D. (ed.) *Records of Illinois Trophy Whitetail Deer.* Illinois: Privately printed, 1994. 196 pages.

Wegner, Robert. *Wegner's Bibliography on Deer & Deer Hunting.* Wisconsin: St. Hubert's Press, 1992. 323 pages.

_____. "Judge Caton: Deer Hunter, Naturalist." *Deer & Deer Hunting.* 9(5): 10-21. May/June, 1986.

Chapter 9

Peterson, Larry Len. *Philip R. Goodwin: America's Sporting & Wildlife Artist.* Idaho: The Coeur d'Alene Art Auction, 2001.

Tyler, Ron, et. al. *American Frontier Life: Early Western Painting and Prints.* New York: Abbeville Press, In., 1987.

Van Dyke, Dix. *Daggett: Life in a Mojave Frontier Town.* Edited by Peter Wild. Maryland: The Johns Hopkins University Press, 1997.

Van Dyke, John C. *The Autobiography of John C. Van Dyke: A Personal Narrative of American Life, 1861-1931.* Edited by Peter Wild. Utah: University of Utah Press, 1993.

_____. *The Raritan: Notes on a River and a Family.* New Jersey: Privately printed, 1915.

Van Dyke, Theodore Strong. *South California: Its Valleys, Hills and Streams; Its Animals, Birds and Fishes; Its Gardens, Farms and Climate.* New York: Fords, Howard & Hulbert, 1886.

_____. *Flirtation Camp: or, The Rifle, Rod and Gun in California.* New York: Fords, Howard & Hulbert, 1881.

_____. *The Still-Hunter.* New York: The MacMillan Company, 1923.

_____. *The Still-Hunter.* Introduction by Robert Wegner. Michigan: Gunnerman Press, 1987.

_____. *The Still-Hunter.* Foreword by Robert Wegner. South Carolina: The Premier Press, 1988.

_____. *The Still-Hunter.* Edited with a Foreword by Robert Wegner. Maryland: Gateway Press Inc., 1995.

_____. "The Philosophy of the Field Sports." *Forest and Stream.* May 15, 1879. pp. 290-291.

_____. "The Philosophy of the Field Sports." *Forest and Stream.* August 21, 1879. pp. 570-571.

_____. "Deer Hunting in Southern California." *Land of Sunshine.* 1(7): 2-3. December, 1894.

_____. "Hunting the Virginia Deer." *Outing.* October, 1902. pp. 20-30.

_____. "Deer Hunting in Southern California Twenty Years Ago." *The American Field.* Volume 54. September 8, 1900. p. 184.

_____. "The Skulking Deer." *The American Field.* Volume 54. July 14, 1900. p. 22.

_____. "The Ambitious Deer Hunter." *Collier's Outdoor America,* November 2, 1912. p. 36.

_____. "The Tracking of Deer." *Collier's Outdoor America.* October 16, 1909. p. 20.

_____. "The Deer and the Elk of the Pacific Coast." In *The Deer Family.* By Theodore Roosevelt, T. S. Van Dyke, D. G. Elliot and A. J. Stone. New York: Grosset, 1902. pp. 165-256.

_____. "A Hunt Around the Vineyards." *Forest and Stream.* July 30, 1885. pp. 5-6.

_____. "Temecula Canyon." *Outing.* September, 1893. pp. 432-435.

Wegner, Robert. "T. S. Van Dyke: A Famous American Deer Hunter." *Deer & Deer Hunting.* 3(6): 22-28. July/August, 1980.

_____. "The Still-Hunter." *Deer & Deer Hunting, Book 1.* Pennsylvania: Stackpole Books, 1984. pp. 36-47.

Wild, Peter. *Theodore Strong Van Dyke.* Idaho: Boise State University, 1995.

_____. "A Writer in a Wild Frontier Town: The Contribution of Theodore Strong Van Dyke." *South Dakota Review.* 32(3): 51-64. Fall, 1994.

Chapter 10

Abbott, Henry. *The Birch Bark Books of Henry Abbott.* New York: Harbor Hill Books, 1980.

Aber, Ted and Stella King. *The History of Hamilton County.* New York: Great Wilderness Books, 1965.

Adamski, John. "Franklin Brandreth." *Adirondack Life.* 31(5): 84-95. August, 2000.

Brandreth, Franklin B. Unpublished letters to the author. 2/1/89, 1/25/90.

Brandreth, Paul. *Trails of Enchantment.* New York: G. Howard Watt, 1930.

_____. *Trails of Enchantment.* Introduction by Robert Wegner. Pennsylvania: Stackpole Books, 2003.

_____. "Bucks of Cathedral Meadow." *Field & Stream.* Volume 42. February, 1938. pp. 30-31, 64-65.

Brumley, Charles. *Guides of the Adirondacks: A History.* New York: North Country Books, Inc., 1994.

Conner, Fox B. Unpublished letter to the author. 1/26/90.

Donaldson, Alfred L. *A History of the Adirondacks.* New York: Century, 1921. Two volumes.

Gilborn, Craig. "Brandreth Park." *Adirondack Camps, Homes Away From Home, 1850-1950.* New York: The Adirondack Museum/Syracuse University Press, 2000. pp. 120-125.

Kaiser, Harvey H. *Great Camps of the Adirondacks.* Boston: David R. Godine. 1982.

"Paulina Brandreth." (Obituary). *The New York Times.* April 21, 1946. p. 46.

Plum, Dorothy A. *Adirondack Bibliography.* New York: Adirondack Mountain Club, Inc., 1958.

_____. *Adirondack Bibliography Supplement, 1956-1965.* New York: The Adirondack Museum, 1973.

Roth, Richard D. "The Adirondack Guide (1820-1919): Hewing Out an American Occupation." Ph.D. Dissertation. Syracuse University, 1990.

Schaefer, Paul. *Adirondack Cabin Country.* New York: Syracuse University Press, 1993.

Stange, Mary Zeiss. "The Woman Who Hunts: Some Implications, Mythological and Social of Jean Auel's Earth Children Novels." *Cynegeticus.* 10(4): 2-7. October 1986.

_____. *Woman The Hunter.* Boston: Beacon Press, 1997.

_____, & Carol K. Oyster. *Gun Women: Firearms and Feminism in Contemporary America.* New York: New York Univrsity Press, 2000.

Terrie, Philip G. *Wildlife and Wilderness: A History of Adirondack Mammals.* New York: Purple Mountain Press, 1993.

_____. *Forever Wild: A Cultural History of Wilderness in the Adirondacks.* New York: Syracuse University Press, 1994.

Townsend, M. T. and W. W. Smith. *The White-tailed Deer of the Adirondacks.* New York: Bulletin of the Roosevelt Wild Life Experiment Station, 1933.

Wegner, Robert. "A Woman Buck Hunter." *Deer & Deer Hunting: Book 3.* Pennsylvania: Stackpole Books, 1990. pp. 26-37.

_____. *Wegner's Bibliography on Deer & Deer Hunting.* Wisconsin: St. Hubert's Press, 1992.

_____. *Legendary Deer Camps.* Wisconsin: Krause publications, 2001.

Woods, Lynn. "First Estate." *Adirondack Life.* 33(6): 36-45. October, 2002.

Chapter 11

Bashline, L. James and Dan Saults. *American's Great Outdoors: The Story of the Eternal Romance between Man and Nature.* Chicago: J.G. Ferguson Publishing Company, 1976.

Biscotti, M. L. *"Shots at Whitetails." A Bibliography of American Sporting Books, 1926-1985.* New Jersey: Meadow Run Press, 1997. pp. 243-244.

Bob Kuhn: Painting the Wild. Wyoming: National Museum of Wildlife Art, 2002.

Casada, Jim. *"Shots at Whitetails* is Back, and Better than Ever." *Deer & Deer Hunting.* 25(6): 79. January, 2002.

Dam, Brian. (ed.) *Whitetail Record Book of New York State.* New York: New York State Big Buck Club, 1997.

Elman, Robert. Unpublished letter to Robert Wegner. August 17, 1988. 2 pp.

Ethridge, James & Barbara Kopala. (eds.) "Larry Koller." *Contemporary Authors.* Michigan: Gale Research Company, 1967. pp. 547-548.

Heller, Morris. *"Shots at Whitetails." American Hunting and Fishing Books: An Annotated Bibliography of Books and Booklets on American Hunting and Fishing, 1800-1970.* Volume 1. New Mexico: Nimrod and Piscator Press, 1997. pp. 51-52.

Koller, Larry. *Shots at Whitetails.* New York: Alfred A. Knopf, 1975.

_____. *Shots at Whitetails.* Wisconsin: Krause Publications, 2000.

_____. "Whitetail Deer." *The Treasury of Hunting.* New York: Odyssey Press, 1965. pp. 40-48.

_____. "The Best Way to Hunt Deer." *Argosy.* September, 1953.

_____. "Getting Your Venison." *The Complete Book of Hunting.* New York: Maco, 1954. pp. 22-32.

_____. "Whitetails." *Larry Koller's Hunting Annual.* New York: Random House, 1957. pp. 26-33.

_____. "Whitetails." *The New Hunting Annual.* New York: The Bobbs-Merrill Company, Inc., 1955. pp. 4-23.

_____. (ed.) *The American Gun.* New York: Madison Books, 1(1-3): 1961.

_____. *The Fireside Book of Guns.* New York: Simon and Schuster, 1959.

"Larry Koller." Publicity Department Little Brown & Company. April, 1950.

"Larry Koller, 54, Outdoors Writer." *The New York Times.* August 19, 1967.

Oleberg, Carl. *Guide to Deer Hunting in the Catskill Mountains.* New York: Outdoor Publications, 1969.

Schwiebert, Ernest. *Remembrances of Rivers Past.* New York: Macmillan, 1972.

Severinghaus, C. W. and C. P. Brown. "History of the White-tailed Deer in New York." *New York Fish and Game Journal.* 3(2): 129-167. 1956.

"Shots at Whitetails." (Review). *Texas Game and Fish.* 7(1):34. December, 1948.

"Shots at Whitetails." (Review). *The New Yorker.* 24: 151. November 13, 1948.

Underwood, Lamar. (ed.) "Woodcraft and Whitetails" by Larry Koller. In *The Deer Book.* New Jersey: Amwell Press, 1980. pp. 106-130.

_____. "Still-Hunting the Whitetail," by Larry Koller. In *The Deer Book.* New Jersey: Amwell Press, 1980. pp. 131-171.

Wegner, Robert. "Larry Koller: The Legend Behind *Shots at Whitetails.*" *Deer & Deer Hunting.* 21(4): 106-115. November, 1997.

Chapter 12

Anonymous. "Memories of Archibald Rutledge." *Sandlapper.* November, 1973. pp. 57-58.

"Archibald Rutledge Biography Page." *www.abebooks.com.*

Blacklock, Les. "The Phantom Buck." *Meet My Psychiatrist.* Minnesota: Voyageur Press, 1977. pp. 65-66.

Campbell, Bob. "The Nature of Will Alston." *South Carolina Wildlife.* May/June, 1974. pp. 15-17.

Casada, James (ed.) *Tales of Whitetails: Archibald Rutledge's Great Deer-Hunting Stories.* South Carolina: University of South Carolina Press, 1992.

"Day-Book of a Naturalist Who Likes to Be in Dixie." Review of Archibald Rutledge, *Days Off in Dixie. (1924). The New York Times Book Review.* June 15, 1924. p. 11.

Evans, George Bird. "Archibald Rutledge, 1883-1973." *Men Who Shot.* Old Hemlock, 1983. pp. 164-169.

Lewis, Carolyn Baker. "The World Around Hampton: Post-Bellum Life on a South Carolina Plantation." *Agricultural History: A Publication of the Agricultural History Society.* 58(3): 456-476. July, 1984.

Marks, Stuart A. *Southern Hunting in Black and White: Nature, History, and Ritual in a Carolina Community.* New Jersey: Princeton University Press, 1991.

Mead, Frank S. "Meet Archibald Rutledge." In *Beauty in the Heart* by Archibald Rutledge. New Jersey: F. H. Revell Company, 1953. pp. 9-20.

Owens, Loulie Latimer. "Guide to the Archibald Hamilton Rutledge Papers, 1860-1970." Manuscript on file at the South Carolinian Library, University of South Carolina, Columbia, 1974.

Ravenel, Virginia. "South Carolina's Poet Laureate." *Sandlapper.* October, 1968. pp. 47-51.

Rivers III, Jacob F. *Cultural Values in the Southern Sporting Narrative.* South Carolina: University of South Carolina, 2002.

Rutledge, Archibald. "Hunter's Choice." *Deep River: The Complete Poems of Archibald Rutledge.* South Carolina: The R. L. Bryan Company, 1960.

_____. "The Black-horn Buck." *Tom and I on the Old Plantation.* New York: Frederick A. Stokes, 1918. pp. 194-202.

_____. "The Black-horn Buck." *Wildlife in the South.* New York: Frederick A. Stokes, 1935. pp. 79-82.

_____. "The Black-horn Buck." *Santee Paradise.* Indianapolis: Bobbs, Merrill, 1956.

_____. "The Black-horn Buck." *Fireworks in the Peafield Corner.* Edited by Judge Irvine H. Rutledge. New Jersey: The Amwell Press, 1986. pp. 349-357.

_____. "The Black-horn Buck of Hampton." Unpublished manuscript. South Caroliniana Library. University of South Carolina.

_____. *Tom and I on the Plantation.* New York: Stokes, 1918.

_____. "Meshach Browning." *Those Were The Days.* Virginia: The Dietz Press, 1955. pp. 14-27.

_____. *Old Plantation Days.* New York: Frederick A. Stokes, 1907.

_____. *An American Hunter.* New York: Frederick A. Stokes, 1937.

_____. *Hunter's Choice.* New York: A. S. Barnes and Company, 1946.

_____. *My Colonel and His Lady.* Indianapolis: Bobbs Merrill, 1937.

_____. *Home by the River.* Indianapolis: Bobbs Merrill, 1941.

_____. "Meshach Browning: Wilderness Hunter." (2-part article in *Sports Afield*.) Incomplete citation. Rutledge Papers. South Caroliniana Library. University of South Carolina, Columbia.

Rutledge, Frederick. *Fair Fields of Memory.* North Carolina: Privately printed, 1958.

Rutledge, Irvine H. *We Called Him Flintlock: A Picture Story of Archibald Rutledge.* South Carolina: The R. L Bryan Company, 1974.

_____. Unpublished letters to the author. July 13, 1987. January 7, 1990.

Seton, Ernest Thompson. *Lives of Game Animals.* New York: Doubleday, 1929.

Shoemaker, Henry W. *Pennsylvania Deer and Their Horns.* Pennsylvania: The Faust Company, 1915.

Wegner, Robert. "Flintlock: A Dixie Deerslayer." *Deer & Deer Hunting: Book 3.* Pennsylvania: Stackpole Books, 1990. pp. 13-25.

_____. "Flintlock: A Dixie Deerslayer." *Deer & Deer Hunting.* 13(6): 28-44. June, 1990.

Wheeler, Mary Bray and Genon Hickerson Neblett. *Hidden Glory: The Life and Times of Hampton Plantation, Legend of the South Santee.* Tennessee: Rutledge Hill Press, 1983.

Woodell, Harold. "Archibald Rutledge." In *Southern Writers: A Biographical Dictionary,* edited by Robert Bain, *et. al.* Louisiana: Louisiana State University, 1979. pp. 391-392.

Yates, Nancy. "My Christmas Memories of Rutledge." *The State.* Columbia, South Carolina. January, 1974. p. 87.

Young, Benton. "The Squire of Hampton." *South Carolina Wildlife.* October 1983. pp. 16-21.

INDEX